Worlds of Women

Susan M. Socolow, Samuel Candler Dobbs Professor of Latin American History, Emory University
Series Editor

The insights offered by women's studies scholarship are invaluable for exploring society, and issues of gender have therefore become a central concern in the social sciences and humanities. The Worlds of Women series addresses in detail the unique experiences of women from the vantage points of such diverse fields as history, political science, literature, law, religion, and gender theory, among others. Historical and contemporary perspectives are given, often with a cross-cultural emphasis. A selected bibliography and, when appropriate, a list of video material relating to the subject matter are included in each volume. Taken together, the series serves as a varied library of resources for the scholar as well as for the lay reader.

American Women in a World at War

American Women in a World at War

Contemporary Accounts from World War II

Edited by
Judy Barrett Litoff and David C. Smith

Worlds of Women

Number 1

A Scholarly Resources Inc. Imprint
Wilmington, Delaware

Scholarly Resources Inc.
104 Greenhill Avenue
Wilmington, DE 19805-1897

Library of Congress Cataloging-in-Publication Data

American women in a world at war : contemporary accounts from
  World War II / Judy Barrett Litoff, David C. Smith, editors.
      p.   cm. — (Worlds of women ; no. 1)
    Includes bibliographical references.
    ISBN 0-8420-2570-7 (alk. paper). — ISBN 0-8420-2571-5
(pbk. : alk. paper)
      1. World War, 1939–1945—Women—United States.
2. Women—United States—History—20th century. 3. World
War, 1939–1945—United States. I. Litoff, Judy Barrett.
II. Smith, David C. (David Clayton), 1929–   . III. Series.
D810.W7A543   1996
940.53'15042—dc20   96-8148
                                                        CIP

⊗ The paper used in this publication meets the minimum requirements of the American National Standard for permanence of paper
for printed library materials, Z39.48, 1984.

Acknowledgments

Without the perspicacious editorial prodding of Richard Hopper, this book would not have been written. In an era when civility has all but disappeared, he exemplifies what it means to be "a scholar and a gentleman."

Although research and writing are, in many ways, lonely endeavors, it is also true that the publication of a historical work always depends on the help of others. At Bryant College, we would like to thank the staff of the Hodgson Memorial Library. Special kudos are due Colleen Anderson and Gretchen McLaughlin for the courteous and creative way that they went about solving our numerous research requests. Tracy Banasieski spent many hours during her junior and senior years at Bryant working on this project. We especially appreciate her ability to accept our foibles. Conny Sawyer, more than any other individual, is responsible for our completing this book in a timely fashion. She miraculously created the time for us to get the job done. The institutional support of Bryant continues to be exemplary. Course reductions, travel funds, and summer research stipends make the opportunity for producing scholarly works much easier. We also wish to thank the staff of the Fogler Library of the University of Maine, especially Frank Wihbey and Dawn Lacadie, for their help in meeting difficult research challenges.

Nadja and Alyssa have grown up learning about women and World War II. Their abiding support, both personal and professional, has been invaluable. Sylvia, Clayton, Kit, Jamie, and Joshua remain cheerfully tolerant of Dave's "fixation" on World War II and the members of that generation. To each of you, we offer our love and thanks.

_J.B.L._
_D.C.S._

About the Editors

Judy Barrett Litoff, professor of history at Bryant College, and David C. Smith, Bird and Bird Professor of History Emeritus at the University of Maine, have researched and written about women and World War II for the past decade. Their books include *We're in This War, Too: World War II Letters from American Women in Uniform* (1994); *Dear Boys: World War II Letters from a Woman Back Home* (1991); *Since You Went Away: World War II Letters from American Women on the Home Front* (1991); and *Miss You: The World War II Letters of Barbara Wooddall Taylor and Charles E. Taylor* (1990). They have collected thirty thousand wartime letters written by American women and are preparing a seventy-reel microfilm edition, *The World War II Letters of American Women*, to be published by Scholarly Resources.

Contents

Introduction

Our interest in the contemporary writings of American women from World War II dates back to the early 1980s when we launched a nationwide search for women's wartime letters. That search resulted in the collection of thirty thousand letters and the publication of four books based on women's wartime correspondence.[1]

During the course of our search for the "missing letters," we also began to locate books and articles written by women during the war years. We were astounded by the number of works that we located, as well as by the breadth and depth of the material contained in this treasure trove. Almost every aspect of life for wartime women is explored in these long-forgotten publications. Indeed, this wealth of material represents the *weltanschauung* of the World War II generation. One of our objectives in producing this book is to reconstruct the worldview of the 1940s for modern readers. To a large extent, this volume represents a "retrieval and salvage" operation.

The commemoration of the fiftieth anniversary of World War II produced an avalanche of historical and literary works about that conflict. They included biographies of military and political leaders, battle accounts, unit histories, and memoirs of soldiers, sailors, and marines. As important as these works are, however, nearly all of them focus on military, strategic, and political issues of primary importance to men.[2] Prize-winning books, such as Gerhard Weinberg's *A World at Arms: A Global History of World War II*, give short shrift to the participation of women in the war effort. Even works devoted to the personal meaning of the war, such as *World War II, Personal Accounts: Pearl Harbor to V-J Day*, produced by the National Archives and the Lyndon Baines Johnson Library, concentrate mainly on men in battle.[3] As recently as April 1995, a *New York Times Book Review* essay on World War II memoirs, "So Many Men, So Many Wars: 50 Years of Remembering World War II," reported on only three works by women—none of them from the United States.[4]

One of the central themes to emerge from the contemporary writings of American women during World War II is that "woman-power is part of this war. . . . It is [woman's] war as no war has ever been."[5] Most scholars would agree with this statement. Indeed, it has become a truism to state that a total war, such as World War II, spares no one. Yet historians are rarely able to venture beyond the most superficial analysis of the meaning of total war. How the cataclysmic events of the conflict that raged from 1939–1945 affected the lives of American women has yet to be fully incorporated into our collective understanding. Moreover, women's active participation in the war effort is still not accepted as part of the World War II canon.

The contemporary accounts selected for this volume provide rich materials on gender, class, and race during World War II. They include selections from "classic" studies on the wartime experiences of women, as well as a number of important, but lesser-known, works. While most of these accounts enjoyed wide readership during the war years, the wartime paper shortage limited their print runs. All of the selections are now out of print or difficult to locate. Most of them cannot even be found on the shelves of the nation's largest libraries.

Modern readers may be surprised and jarred by the fact that the well-educated authors of the selections included here often referred to women as "girls." However, these authors did not use the term in a pejorative sense. One of the best examples of this seeming anomaly is found in *Arms and the Girl* by Gulielma Fell Alsop and Mary F. McBride—a work that repeatedly extols the importance of "womanpower." Simply put, the linguistic standards of the 1990s do not apply to the 1940s.

Part I, "Preparing for War," uses writings from the early 1940s to show how women rose to the challenges of a world at war. In the opening selection, well-known journalist Margaret Culkin Banning provides a succinct analysis of the role to be played by American women in winning the war when she states that "aggressive defense in this total war against the democracies not only can use women's help but it needs all they can give." The selections chosen for this section build upon Banning's theme. They also illustrate the high ideals shared by women from diverse walks of life as they confronted the wartime emergency.

World War II provided American women with the unprecedented opportunity to become official members of the military services.

The selections in Part II, "In the Military," focus on the experiences of the 350,000 "pioneers" who joined the women's branches of the Army, Navy, Coast Guard, and Marine Corps. They describe the extraordinary transformations that occurred in the lives of civilian women as they became soldiers, sailors, and marines.

American women did not officially engage in combat during World War II, but overseas assignments often brought them close to the front lines of battle. The selections in Part III, "At 'Far-Flung' Fronts," include dramatic accounts of the courage of Army and Navy nurses, the important achievements of Red Cross workers and United Service Organizations (USO) entertainers, and the dangerous life of war correspondents.

Part IV, "On the Home Front," demonstrates that significant changes also occurred in the lives of women at home. War brides and war wives regularly encountered challenging situations as they adjusted to their new status. Included in Part IV is a war bride's account of hunting for a room in a crowded military town and a government pamphlet that offers advice on how to ease the difficulties of traveling with a baby in wartime. The crucial importance of good letter-writing habits is the topic of the third selection. Part IV concludes with a discussion of the many and varied volunteer activities of African-American women on the home front.

Perhaps the best-known American heroine of World War II is "Rosie the Riveter." This sobriquet has become a generic term used to describe all women war workers in the United States during the period. In Part V, "War Jobs," the first selection provides a general overview of the types of employment available to women during the war. It emphasizes that "the manpower of the war cannot prevail without the womanpower of the war behind it." The second selection focuses on the specific contributions of African-American working women to the war effort. Part V concludes with excerpts from the wartime diary of a woman welder as well as information about the important work of the largely forgotten Women's Land Army, an agency of the U.S. Department of Agriculture.

Part VI, "Preparing for the Postwar World," suggests that from the earliest days of the war American women were deeply concerned about the world that would emerge from the conflict. An excerpt from a study conducted by the Women's Bureau emphasizes the importance of safeguarding the gains obtained by women war workers. Part VI also includes information about the campaign of American women to be included as equal partners with men on postwar planning councils. It concludes with a powerful discussion of women's stake in the postwar world.

These twenty-five contemporary accounts from World War II constitute incontrovertible evidence that women played an active and resourceful part in the war effort. They further demonstrate that World War II was "everybody's war." The transformations that occurred in the lives of these women were immense. Taken together, the selections in this book confirm that World War II served as a major watershed in the lives of American women. Despite some initial setbacks in the immediate aftermath of the war, the changes wrought by World War II were not forgotten. They provided the foundation for the emergence of the modern feminist movement a generation later.

Life would never be the same for the women of World War II. With fortitude and ingenuity, they had surmounted the challenges posed by total war. As the women of the wartime generation are quick to acknowledge: "We knew that if we could overcome the trials and tribulations of the war years, we could do anything."

Notes

1. On the extent of the search, see Judy Barrett and David C. Smith, "Introduction: The Case of the Missing Letters," *We're in This War, Too: World War II Letters from American Women in Uniform* (New York: Oxford University Press, 1994), 3–9. The other World War II letter books that we have produced are *Since You Went Away: World War II Letters from American Women on the Home Front* (New York: Oxford University Press, 1991; paperback ed., Lawrence: University Press of Kansas, 1995); *Dear Boys: World War II Letters from a Woman Back Home* (Jackson: University Press of Mississippi, 1991); and *Miss You: The World War II Letters of Barbara Wooddall Taylor and Charles E. Taylor* (Athens: University of Georgia Press, 1990).

2. See, for example, the six-part series on selected books and articles about World War II published in *World War II Studies Association Newsletter* (Spring 1991–Fall 1993): 45–50. A follow-up article on books published since 1992 appeared in *World War II Studies Association Newsletter* 53 (Spring 1995): 15–55.

3. Gerhard L. Weinberg, *A World at Arms: A Global History of World War II* (New York: Cambridge University Press, 1994). Gary A. Yarrington, ed., *World War II, Personal Accounts: Pearl Harbor to V-J Day* (Austin, TX: The Lyndon Baines Johnson Foundation, 1992).

4. Samuel Hynes, "So Many Men, So Many Wars: 50 Years of Remembering World War II," *New York Times Book Review* (April 30, 1995): 12, 14–17.

5. Gulielma Fell Alsop and Mary F. McBride, *Arms and the Girl: A Guide to Personal Adjustment in War Work and War Marriage* (New York: Vanguard Press, 1943), 5.

I Preparing for War

The Nazi invasion of Poland on September 3, 1939, left little doubt in the minds of most Americans that the peace structure established at the end of World War I had failed. Although no one could predict when the United States would formally enter the conflict, only the most staunch isolationists believed that the nation could avoid entrance into the war that was then raging. The "Phoney War" during the winter of 1939 provided a brief reprieve for disquieted Americans, but the Blitzkrieg of the spring of 1940, followed by the Battle of Britain, brought the reality of war even closer to home. Beginning in December 1939, American women launched the Bundles for Britain campaign to send food, clothing, and medical supplies to their beleaguered sisters across the Atlantic. They also volunteered as nurses in British hospitals.

With the establishment of the National Defense Advisory Commission in May 1940, official mobilization for war began. Passage of the Selective Service Act in September 1940, the first peacetime draft in the history of the nation, virtually assured that the United States would be brought into the conflict. And, as young men departed for military service, their mothers, sisters, wives, and sweethearts braced themselves for the inevitable.

Over the course of the next twelve months, a steady stream of events pushed the nation closer to war. Congress passed the Lend Lease Act, which provided crucial aid to the Allies, in March 1941; during the latter part of May the Office of Civilian Defense was created; and, on May 27, President Roosevelt declared a "state of national emergency." In August 1941, Roosevelt and Prime Minister Winston Churchill met at Argentia, Newfoundland, and issued the Atlantic Charter, proclaiming that the war was being fought "to ensure life, liberty, independence and religious freedom, and to preserve the rights of man and justice." By the time of the December 7, 1941, Japanese attack on Pearl Harbor, American citizens had anticipated the nation's entry into World War II for many months. Together, American women and men emphatically supported the call to arms.

1   Women for Defense

Margaret Culkin Banning

In a writing career that spanned half a century, Margaret Culkin Banning produced more than forty books and four hundred articles, many of which focused on the changing lives and work of women. Banning's 1942 book, Women for Defense, *offered an early guide for American women as they faced the challenges posed by the entrance of the United States into World War II. In June 1942, shortly after the publication of* Women for Defense, *Banning flew to England to observe how English women's lives, both civilian and military, were being dramatically altered by the war. She describes those changes in* Letters from England: Summer 1942 *(1943). Together, these two books underscore the crucial responsibilities and activities faced by wartime women. This passage from* Women for Defense *illustrates Banning's belief that "total war takes all the energy and brains it can get and it does not spare women from effort or danger."*

WOMEN BY THEMSELVES CANNOT WIN this war. But quite certainly it cannot be won without them. For aggressive defense in this total war against the democracies not only can use women's help but it needs all they can give. In this Second World War women will be used physically as never before, for production of war material, for substitute labor in factories and on farms as manpower is drained by the armed forces, and for guard and emergency duty of all kinds in threatened areas, and for management of evacuations, if it comes to that. They will be tired and grimy before we are through with what we anticipate. They will be hurt. They often will be in danger.

They will have to serve in increasing numbers as nurses and as nurses' aides. They must make, pack, and distribute Red Cross supplies in numbers which have not yet been estimated but which are already astronomical. They must work with men in the research laboratories of the nation and even in the machine shops. And all that experience in the organization of communities which women

From Margaret Culkin Banning, *Women for Defense* (New York: Duel, Sloan and Pearce, 1942), ix–xii, 228–38. Reprinted by permission of Brandt & Brandt Literary Agents, Inc.

have been building up in peacetime will now be put to fullest use. Total war takes all the energy and brains it can get and it does not spare women from effort or danger.

We have begun as other warring countries have begun by increasing the numbers of women in industry, by harnessing volunteer ability and energy to the tasks for which they are suited. . . .

Nothing can or will stop this procedure now, and women must be ready for it. They must be intelligently ready; not only waiting to be told what to do but understanding why their services and brains are required. Many women have already thought this through. But there are thirty-seven million adult women in this country, and though most of them are deeply patriotic there are many among them who are bewildered, shaken, even frightened, who don't know which way to turn. They will do anything necessary. But they will

Posters of the U.S. Office of War Information displayed at Lansburgh's Department Store, calling for women to enroll as student nurses in the Army and Navy, Washington, DC, May 1943. *Courtesy Library of Congress*

do it better if they have a comprehension of their own essential place in world events, and they will be heartened and sustained if they realize that their help is vital.

Total war is something this country has never yet experienced. Now we are to find out, along with the rest of the world, that total war recognizes no limitations of battlefields, but that the whole area of the enemy's life is its battlefield. Far more than wars in the past, it uses two new arms which involve civilians, women along with the men. One of these arms is production on an unparalleled scale, production of everything from food to ammunition, which may be necessary to the prosecution of war. This production must be carried out with a scope which men alone cannot compass if they are to fight in the armed forces as well. Great responsibilities fall consequently on women, to produce and to conserve. Without this aid from women in both production and consumption, a country at war cannot develop to its full strength.

Women in the United States have controlled the pocketbooks of the nation for a long time. They have done most of the buying. They have been free to organize their households with almost complete authority. They have earned a great deal of money. So the necessary control of consumption falls with peculiar force on the shoulders of American women. If they have been allowed to spend in peacetime they must accept the responsibility for what is spent in wartime, with all the inevitable adjustments and sacrifices that will be entailed.

The second new arm of warfare in which women are inextricably involved is morale. The morale of armies in the field has always been vital to victory. Civilian morale did not matter so much in the past. Now it is increasingly important, both because of the coverage of modern war and because communication between the [armed] services and civilian population is highly developed, so that the spirit and mood of one affect the other. By indifference, by unsuitable desires, by complaint, even by the lack of realization that every mood and habit is important, women can sabotage civilian morale and have a serious effect on the morale of the armed forces.

Women can be told categorically what they must do. This is happening already. But the discipline which will be imposed on the American people will be in consonance with our way of life if it goes along with willing self-discipline. In that mood the best morale takes root and grows. . . .

Courtesy National Archives

When the Japanese bombed Pearl Harbor the plans for defending the country had been made and many of the leaders chosen. Now all the women of the country have been committed by the president and the Congress to its defense. . . .

The women of this country can do much for national unity if they will. The beauty and comfort of it, as revealed when war came upon us, must be sustained. In the preservation of this unity women can be continually active, mending rents and breaches if they appear. . . .

Women properly belong in democracy's greatest battle and in the total war over its determination to survive. Because it is total war, with new civilian fronts, because victory is dependent on health and ability to produce, and on character, they can be basically useful. The effort must be made to draw all women—every one—into definite fields of active usefulness, where differences of education and advantage and income bracket would disappear. If the women of the nation so come together, the men would come with them, for though we often separate "women's activities" for administrative reasons, in every activity a woman's life relates back to the men around her. If women could be united in support of a few very practical defense efforts, it might result in that merger which the country needs.

There are on the face of it few meeting grounds for all American women. They should not be exaggerated. We should accept realistically and be proud of the great variety of ability and divergence of ambition which are characteristic of women of the United States. Employed and nonemployed women do not follow an identical plan of life. They never will. But their lives often dovetail. A woman employed before marriage may give up her job. A widow may take one. So the ability and opportunity to earn her living must be regarded as an integral part of the American woman's pattern.

The woman of leisure is disappearing all over the world. In Russia, Germany, France, she is gone. In North America she is on her way out. In South America she is beginning to be questioned and to question herself. In a woman's life there will be periods, and perhaps long ones, of deliberate nonemployment outside the home. But whatever the outcome of this war, the world of the future will need the full efforts of women in all countries. Whether they will be properly rewarded for those efforts depends on whether the democracies win or not.

For that reason this occasion of war is a time to break down, insofar as it can be done, the artificial and dangerous barrier which exists between women who work for a living and those who do not. Their interests are common in this struggle, and they should never again become separate. Differences of income in the United States have been responsible for much of this separation between groups of women, and the income situation has deeply eroded democracy in the United States as well as in other countries. But now, in our dark hours, we think little of money and much of other values, such values as can last through war and extend into future peace. . . .

The thing we must prove is that women are not so greedy or so dependent on possessions as some of their critics declare; to prove that they strengthen instead of soften the men of this country. They have their big chance now to show an identity of interest with men, a merging of ambition. They can demonstrate by economy, by quiet sacrifice, even by gaiety, that the things they want most will not burden men but relieve them, and that it is essential for happiness that men and women go along together mentally.

It has not always been easy to find common denominators in wants or interests among the women in this country any more than it has been easy to find the norm among American women. But suddenly the war defines the common interests. Women first of all want safety, for themselves and others. They will fight for it. Women are all interested in health, so in nutrition. Women are all consumers, and their skills turn naturally to the wartime adjustment of income, personal wants, and national need.

Women want happiness, usually a happiness identified with human relations. They want security for the future, for that establishes the basis of happiness and peace. . . .

National consumption, national nutrition, and national morale are arms of total war. If women ignore these problems of nutrition and of consumption they inevitably sabotage the country's defense. Even more subtly, by evasion or lack of conviction, they can wreck the country's morale. All the fine speeches in the world will not support the morale of the United States if the spirit and philosophy of the American woman is tainted with pessimism or despair.

There is no reason why each woman in the United States cannot actively interest herself from the day war was declared in the fundamental facts of nutrition. If she is a housewife, she can do this by scientific attention to the meals which are served in her own home, and she will have every supporting advice and direction from the best governmental sources to help her. But even if she has no home, if she is a girl who lives in a rooming house and eats habitually at the drugstore and the cafeteria, she can inform herself sufficiently on nutrition so as to choose and order meals which will keep up her own health, and she can spread the information she gathers on nutrition among her acquaintances. The teacher who is cooperating in the serving of school lunches, the public health nurse, the minister's wife, the clubwoman, and the society woman, all can come together in this common effort for a better-fed, healthier, and stronger citizenry.

There is no reason why these women should not be informed as to the far-reaching aspects of the food program of the United States. It is no secret that it is the plan and hope of those who have made a close survey of the possible food resources of the United States to have enough food produced in the next year for three purposes: to give everyone in the United States a decent maintenance diet; to have sufficient food to feed England and other countries who may demand and deserve our sympathy, during the balance of the war; and to have a sufficient supply of food so that at the peace conferences which will ultimately come, the United States will be in a position to back up its arguments and requests and principles with the strength of food resources. The vast implications of this program should interest every woman and every man in the United States. But in the conservation of food every individual woman can have an important and effective part.

Defense means business when the government calls upon every individual, as has already been done. Many instructions on the matters of nutrition and consumption will come from the government to each woman, who by her cooperation will establish a personal relation to her government. We need that in this country. It has been a lesson to the youth of the United States that the government has a claim on their time and their lives. They have learned· it. And so must women learn that the government will issue to them, personally and directly, definite instructions which must be followed.

There is in so simple and necessary a contact no suggestion of totalitarianism, no abrogation of our way of life. The instruction is coming from those to whom we have yielded direction, with explanation of necessity, with warning of shortage, with interpretation. It will come from the highest authority.

But . . . a universal program for women in wartime cannot be completely a matter of instruction or direction. Though the way may be pointed, the individual must proceed by herself.

This country needed faith until war came. It was by way of becoming skeptic. For this there were many causes, but among them was the attitude of the women. The women lacked faith, and many of them leaned toward despair. Almost without awareness. The morale in some army camps reflected this. It has not been camp conditions alone which sometimes have been unsatisfactory, but there was too often no heartening influence outside of them.

Men's happiness depends on women, even more than does their pleasure. It is an hour when it is necessary to remember that. The morale in England, in Russia, and certainly here, depends on the women of the country.

This is not work which a government can dictate or follow up. It is personal work for each woman, in addition to what else and to all else she does, going along with it, unremittingly, constantly. Teaching or typing, acting as hostess in a nightclub or filling powder bags, she can still make maintenance of faith and cheerfulness part of her daily routine.

And if she does not? It is hard to threaten the consequences for it is so obvious that the worst threats might come true. If she does not, there will be a chance of defeat, and, after the defeat of the democracies, there will be little place for a woman who wants to develop her abilities, her intellect, and her individual life. Women would be ruled; a few idolized, a few influential, many wasted and spoiled, most drudges of sex and of industry. It is not a pretty picture. And though there may be a few women among us who are willing to gamble on getting something out of such a system personally, they must not be allowed to try it or to spread such a pernicious hope.

The defense which the women of the United States put up for their country must extend into the subsequent peace. We are defending a system, not a boundary alone. There must be no postwar economic collapse to make the world doubt democracy. There must be no moral collapse, no super-jazz era to make other democracies, particularly those in Latin America, fear the effect of our example.

Looking back, we see that the peace societies of the past failed, and that very probably that failure was due to the fact that they were negations of war, not instruments of a lasting peace. The new peace societies of the world will have more to do than cry down the horrors of war. They must conceive and back up an organic peace, must create a working democracy which all men will trust and credit.

This is man's job and woman's job, as exacting as their work in war. There is no end in sight, no conclusion of the task even with armistice, and we are wise not to delude ourselves in that respect. But the rewards should keep women's heads high. . . .

What will . . . [women] ask in return? First, I hope they will insist that if they have done well and shown staying power and ability, they suffer no more in the period of readjustment than do men. They should not be penalized or discriminated against as women. But, more than that, they should, if they do their full share, enter the postwar economy with the right to a seat at the council tables, and the right to a stronger voice in national and world conferences. Wherever women have vitally contributed to strengthen their democracy in time of war, in China, in England, in Czechoslovakia, we must be sure that they will be allowed to continue to contribute in peacetime.

American women wish to defend their country in the present emergency and also permanently against war. So do women everywhere. . . .

Our present defense looks to the future for inspiration and sustenance. There are few sane men in the world who want war to continue as part of the historical pattern.

There are no women.

2   Women in the War

Elizabeth Gurley Flynn

Elizabeth Gurley Flynn, "The Rebel Girl," devoted her life to left-wing causes. During the 1940s she played an active role in the American Communist Party. Following the Nazi invasion of the Soviet Union in June 1941, American Communists expressed strong support for the war against fascism and totalitarianism. In his introduction to Flynn's 1942 pamphlet, Women in the War, *American Communist Party leader William Z. Foster highlighted the wide-ranging contributions of women to the "struggle against Hitlerism":*

> *As in no other war in history women of all the United Nations are taking an active part in the struggle against Hitlerism. This is because they are awake to the degrading fate that would befall them, as part of their peoples' enslavement were the Nazi barbarians to win the war. There is no*

From Elizabeth Gurley Flynn, *Women in the War* (New York: Workers Library Publishers, 1942), 5–27.

*sphere of the war in which women are not playing a vital
and increasing role. In production, in civilian defense, in the
sale of war bonds and even on the battlefield itself they are
to be found giving their all. The coming forward of women
to such great activity is one of the democratic achievements
of the war. When Hitlerism is finally crushed the victory will
be very largely due to the courage, endurance, skill and clear-
headedness of anti-Hitler women.*

*Recognizing that "war creates extraordinary demands for
labor," Flynn emphasized in* Women in the War *that "work is
the right of all, regardless of sex, color, creed, or language."
She called for the use of Lanham Act funds to provide for the
expansion of federally funded child-care facilities and con-
cluded by admonishing the labor movement to include women
as full and equal members.*

P ICTURE A SUNNY SUNDAY MORNING in Detroit, Michigan.
A congregation is coming out of a Catholic church, after Mass.
A shadow falls across their path. The helpless people are driven
into the churchyard and sorted out like animals in the stockyard.
The young girls and women are packed into trucks and carried away.
This happened in Warsaw, Poland. Two hundred and seventy thousand Polish women, torn from their families by Nazi storm troop-
ers, are in brothels or working at forced labor in Nazi-ridden lands.
Picture 500 Jewish children in New York City rounded up, taken
to the dog pound, and put to death by poison gas. This happened at
the hands of the Nazis in Warsaw, Poland, to starving little ones.
Picture "breeding stations" in California, where pure young girls
are forced to become pregnant to perpetuate "racial supremacy"
and are told, "The Fuhrer is the child's father!" This happens to
young German girls. In all human history there has been nothing so
vile and revolting as this Nazi innovation to reproduce Aryan storm-
trooper stock.
Suppose these were our children, our daughters? It is equally
horrible and terrifying anywhere. We cannot live complacently in a
world where homes are destroyed, children starved, women raped,
religion violently suppressed, democracy stamped out, minority
groups exterminated, human dignity degraded. There can be no
peace or happiness for all people until Nazi-Fascism is destroyed.
Our security, honor, self-respect, humanity, demand that we win

this just war. There can be no compromise with savagery and slavery.

We American women, like the Chinese, British, and Soviet women, will work till we drop and fight till we die to defend our beautiful country and our democratic liberties from the brutish ideology of the Nazis. We are not called upon to engage in actual military action. But in mortal crisis, as the heroic Soviet girl, Liudmila Pavlichenko, became a crack sniper; as Ma-Lu, the young Chinese girl, led a Japanese regiment to death over a mined bridge; as the strong Basque women hurled the fascists into the sea; as the Czech, Dutch, and French women patriots carry on guerrilla warfare to resist the Nazi masters, so will we take arms, if necessary, in the spirit of our Molly Pitcher and Harriet Tubman.

Today it is more useful and just as heroic to *make arms* for our fighting forces and our brave allies. Our main tasks are on the home front. Eighteen people are required at work to keep one fighter on the field, at sea, or in the air. Women's work is manifold today. It includes industry, civilian defense, politics, the labor unions, and as trained auxiliaries to the armed forces. General H. H. Kitchener said in the last war: "If the women of either side should stop their war work, that side would lose." This is even more evident today. The women of the nation are essential to winning the war. They are the reservoir of labor. In ever-increasing numbers women will be called out of the kitchen onto the assembly line. It is a matter of patriotism, necessity, and arithmetic. Women are cheerfully answering the call.

Our armed forces are expected to reach ten million in 1943. They are drawn mainly out of production. Their needs take precedence. They must be fed, clothed, shod, trained, transported, given tanks, guns, airplanes, bullets, bombs, Jeeps, ships, parachutes, and myriad other essentials. Civilian needs must also be adequately met to keep our home-front forces healthy and efficient. It is estimated that fifty-eight million workers will be required in 1943. War Chief [Paul V.] McNutt announces that eighteen million must be women or five million more than are employed today. *One out of six able-bodied women, over eighteen years old, will be in war jobs within the next year.*

In England over five million women have entered industry and auxiliary war service. Over 50,000 are employed on the railroads. Thirty million women are on the home front behind the dauntless Soviet battle lines—in agriculture and industry, including coal mines, steel plants, and on ships. We women will not lag behind our Allied sisters in working while our men fight. Soviet women today inspire the women of the whole world by their work and bravery.

War creates extraordinary demands for labor. The Axis powers meet them by lashing slave labor to work. In free countries women proudly volunteer to do their share in defense of freedom. Over a million and a half women are registered with the U.S. Employment Service, ready for war work. If conscription becomes necessary, as in England, American women will accept it as gallantly as have the men in our people's army. Local registration has been completed in Seattle, Detroit, Akron, Connecticut. In Oregon, 99,000 women volunteered for the fruit harvest; 116,532 women of Detroit signed as willing to take war jobs. The [War] Manpower Commission announces that 80,000 will be needed in Detroit, 50,000 in Seattle, 12,000 in Syracuse, and 40,000 in Buffalo, N.Y., in the near future. . . .

All women who want war jobs should register with the U.S. Employment Service. Do not be disheartened if you are not called immediately. All who volunteer for our armed forces are not called at once. One's turn will come more quickly if qualifications and experience are on record. State what you want to do and apply for training. Prepare for a job while you wait for it. We must grasp new opportunities firmly and demand to be made able to meet the requirements.

Prejudices break down in a national crisis. Women and the Negro people must be given the right to show their mettle as workers. Work is not *man's* versus women's, any more than it is white's versus Negro's, or *native-born's* versus foreign-born's, or Christian's versus Jew's. Such a characterization as "male, white, Christian, native born" is typically Nazi, repugnant to American concepts of democracy. Women's role in industry, like that of the Negro people, is not of a temporary nature. War emergency accelerates the entry of women into industry. But there were ten million women employed in 1930, two and a half million more than in 1920. Many more will remain in industry after this war than were there before, especially in new industries.

To refer to this normal process as "taking men's jobs" is historically incorrect. Women in the homes once did the spinning, weaving, sewing, cooking, and baking; made butter, cheese, soap, candles, and home-brew; [and did] the laundry, cleaning, preserving, and personal service work. During the last century power-operated machinery took over "women's work," so called since time immemorial. Most of it is now outside the home. Women followed their jobs into factories and shops. Great national industries such as textile, needle trades, hotels, packinghouses, breweries, dairies, [and] laundries, employ thousands of men at tasks once left entirely to women. Men sew, bake, spin, and weave today. Women weld and rivet. Work is the right of all, regardless of sex, color, creed, or language. A lack of clarity on this creates discord in families and shops, indifference in unions, and insecurity among women workers, just as discrimination causes the deepest resentment among Negro workers.

The Negro people and women must have permanent access to all jobs and professions. This is democracy. To deny it is to disrupt national unity and cripple production in a critical war period. Victory is at stake.

Women, white and Negro, will not sit at home with folded hands. They want to "do something" to help their fighting sons, brothers, husbands, fathers. Pearl Harbor widows set a heroic example when they went to work as a group in a California aircraft plant. Old and young, married and single, mothers, yes, and grandmothers—are busy at all kinds of jobs today. They test tanks and machine guns at Army proving grounds; ferry airplanes from factories to fields; run stores, farms, hotels, gas stations. They work in banks, copper smelters, Army warehouses, canneries, grinding diamonds for tools, as mechanics in the Navy yards, on bombers and tanks, at wood turning, in aluminum plants, on shells, at ship building, parachute rigging, servicing and repairing planes, as guards for plants, assembling carburetor parts, at air-traffic control, as streetcar conductors, in the electrical industries as assemblers, welders, inspectors; loading detonators, making guns and bullets; building Jeeps, making glass for planes. These are just a few random samples of the *Victory girls at work*.

Paul McNutt, head of the War Manpower Commission, said last May: "Women have shown that they can do or learn to do almost any kind of work." A survey of twenty-one key war industries proves that 80 percent of the jobs can be done by women.

Any job, except some very heavy types of physical labor, can be undertaken by women. With mechanical assistance most of these can be handled, too. "Can Women Do the Job?" is being answered by demonstrations from Brooklyn to Seattle. A "Consolidated" engineer in California told a reporter recently: "There are more than one hundred and one thousand separate and distinct parts in one of our bombers, not counting rivets, and most of them are so light in weight that women can assemble and test them as easily as men. Better in most cases."

Ten months ago when the first women went to work at "Consolidated," the foremen growled, "The factory is no place for a woman!" Today the industrial relations director of North American Aviation says, "Women do approximately 50 percent of the work required to construct a modern airplane."

Women are proving best adapted to jobs requiring patience and alertness, keen eyesight, and finger and hand dexterity. They use blueprints, micrometers, gauges, and other precision tools expertly. Because they are anxious to learn they are easy to teach. The labor turnover has decreased, accidents diminished, and damage to tools and materials is less. Employers and male fellow workers agree that the women, if they are treated merely as "new workers" without prejudice or favor, and are given proper guarantees for health, safety, and sanitation, are able to carry on efficiently.

A lively interest in the mobilization of women is sweeping the country. It is not only a recognition of their importance but a campaign to stimulate larger numbers to enter plants. The "soldierettes" of the home front are interviewed, featured on the fashion pages of newspapers and magazines in their snappy uniforms, are the heroines of movies. The glamour girl of today, the woman in the news, is the working woman. Every day brings a thrilling account of a new, difficult, or delicate job mastered by a woman; every such accomplishment lays low some ancient superstition about women. They are not afraid of heat, electricity, noise, lights, gas, smells, high, dark, or dangerous places. They do not worry about their appearance. "Feminine vanity" does not balk at dirty faces, greasy hands, hair plastered down under a protective cap, severely tailored uniforms, shoes conditioned for safety, and a lunch box instead of a fancy purse. Our women measure up to the stern requirements of modern industry. Why not? Their maternal ancestors were immigrants to New England and the Atlantic Coast and pioneers in covered wagons to mid-America and the far West. Our country wasn't built the soft way. Women worked hard on farms and in households. They carried on in every war while their men were on the battlefields. Privation, sacrifice, work, are in the blood of American women, whose ancestors cleared the wilderness, built railroads and cities, tamed rivers, dug mines, made homes in log cabins, and taught their children by candlelight.

Employers are accepting women in new and strange jobs as a necessity, some gracefully—some in "die-hard" desperation. New industries, such as Pacific Coast Aircraft, are giving women the greatest opportunities. There, skillful feminine fingers are carrying out President [Franklin D.] Roosevelt's assignment for 60,000 planes in 1942 and 125,000 in 1943. Pacific aviators gratefully dub them "angels with dirty faces" who "keep us flying." In reply to a

Information is given to young women interested in joining the Women's Army Auxiliary Corps by Lieutenant Harriet West and Lieutenant Mildred Osby, Washington, DC, November 1942. *Courtesy Library of Congress*

questionnaire sent out by *Modern Industry* to 1,000 plant executives, 74 percent reported present or contemplated employment of women. It is encouraging, too, to hear that their experience condemns "all women" departments. Men and women working side by side is more satisfactory, once men overcome their fear of women as rivals. A preference for young married mothers, whose menfolk are already employed or are in the armed forces, indicates a discrimination against older women which must not be tolerated. They foresee the need of improvements in the plants to accommodate women.

I wonder if a questionnaire sent to 1,000 labor leaders would indicate a similar alertness to women workers' needs and problems? Frankly, I doubt it. Recent trade-union conventions have either not discussed the requirements of these millions of new women workers or disposed of them with the customary general resolutions, a hangover of their past bad practices. A pat on the back does not suffice today, brother trade unionists. Intelligent understanding and prompt action are needed.

A scrapping of past prejudices, underestimation, and antagonism to women workers is imperative. The needs which these 1,000 employers list should have been a *must* long ago, especially of unions of war-production industries, where women are flocking into the plants. These requirements are special lockers, washrooms, rest and recreation rooms; first-aid equipment, medical and sanitary supplies; stools, chairs, benches, and tables; special material-handling equipment; safety shoes, goggles, and work uniforms; lifts, platforms, ladders; increased feeding facilities; special transportation for night shifts and child-care facilities. Employers may recognize the need of all this. But their replies do not indicate a too-great readiness to furnish them. Labor will have to insist upon them, as union demands, in many places. The Women's Bureau of the Department of Labor (Mary Anderson, director) is publishing an excellent series of pamphlets and bulletins on the standards required for women in war industries. I recommend a careful study of them by special committees in every union. . . .

These are the minimum needs which labor unions should press for women workers. The success of the unions in organizing the twelve million women, who are as yet unorganized in our country, depends upon the promptness and firmness with which they take up such demands as basic union issues. In addition and equally important are adequate training; housing facilities—especially in boomtowns of mushroom growth; equal pay for equal work; protection against all forms of discrimination, especially as practiced so generally against Negro women. *Proper child care is the crying need of many women workers.*

The employers will undoubtedly make all necessary mechanical shop changes, to expedite production. Anti-union employers will even take advantage of the occasion to play Santa Claus to the ladies. Let us not forget that many of the women workers are very young, without shop experience. Many come from areas, especially South and mid-West as well as from farm regions, where there is indifference and prejudice, if not active downright opposition to trade unions. To gain the confidence and sympathetic support of these new workers, and to organize them as a dependable, permanent part of the labor movement, unions must demonstrate an understanding of their needs [as well as the] ability to settle grievances quickly and to secure just demands. The labor movement must include women as full and equal members, encouraging them to active participation in its affairs, electing them as shop stewards, chairmen of locals, to executive boards, to grievance and other committees, as delegates to central bodies and to conventions. . . .

When women delegates at auto, steel, and other conventions insist that women's problems are today the concern of the whole labor movement, they are absolutely right. *There are over twelve million unorganized women workers in America today. This figure nearly equals the total membership of all existing trade unions put together.* In other words, organized labor could double its strength and influence by organizing all the women workers now outside its ranks.

Why are these millions of working women unorganized? Is it because American women are averse to belonging to organizations? Far from it. There are actually twelve million women in various organizations in this country—political, cultural, patriotic, religious, educational, farm, consumers—and why not? Women's clubs are peculiar to America. They indicate a high level of progress and intelligence. Margaret C. Banning, in her book *Women for Defense*, remarks: "You have to be very poor or very stubborn not to belong to something if you are an American woman." The General Federation of Women's Clubs totals about two million. They are not a solid bloc, but they are serious, sincere, and honest. Many are already discussing, as a part of national defense, the very issues to which labor should be giving its earnest attention. Up to recently the Y.W.C.A. had more working girls attached to its industrial section than were in trade unions. It is evident that American women are organizable. Let the labor unions launch a campaign with the vigor and enthusiasm with which the C.I.O. [Congress of Industrial Organizations] was started—with women organizers, special literature, posters, conferences, meetings—and results would follow immediately. Discuss shop issues, the needs of national war production, the history and value of labor unions, the particular interests of the women workers, and have top-ranking leaders of American labor take part in this campaign, and the women will gladly enlist in organized labor. The militant struggles of women to organize the textile and needle trades unions demonstrate this. Sixty percent of the 150,000 in the Amalgamated Clothing Workers and 75 percent of the International Ladies' Garment Workers' 200,000 members are women.

If women workers remain unorganized, the labor unions will have themselves to blame. The dire results of neglect will most directly affect the women. It will lower their standards, deprive them of strength to defend themselves, and weaken their morale as workers in a war period—and after. It will make them ready prey for anti-union schemes such as company unionism. In addition to the disastrous effects upon the women workers, labor unions must face the reality that the security of already established standards, the guarantee of hard-fought gains, the very existence of some unions depend upon enlisting these new workers. As the labor composition changes, it must either be absorbed in the union or the union is thereby weakened. Several million male trade unionists are away in our armed forces. More will follow. Not only the jobs they vacate but the unions they built will depend upon the women they leave behind them. . . .

The right of all women and the Negro people, men and women alike, to work at all occupations and to be full-fledged labor union members is a basic principle of democracy. Recently a dramatic struggle occurred between 22 women welders in San Francisco and the International Boilermakers and Welders Union (A.F. of L. [American Federation of Labor]). The union, which traditionally barred women members and Negroes, refused women clearance to work at the Marin Ship Yards at Sausalito. The women demonstrated angrily before the union headquarters. A national referendum voted to welcome women to union membership, 400 locals out of 600 voting favorably, and the women returned to work triumphantly.

All trade unions should overhaul their constitutions to avoid similar disagreeable incidents. In 1920, the Women's Bureau of the Department of Labor made a study of unions which barred women from membership. There were ten. The Blacksmiths Union replied: "If there ever was a job that is a man's job, it is this work!" But circumstances alter cases, as the California women made clear.

It is likewise a disgrace that some A.F. of L. and independent unions adhere stubbornly to their bars against Negroes as members. This automatically excludes them from occupations where a closed shop or union contract exists. Or they are denied equal status, discouraged from joining, or "Jim Crowed" into separate locals, deprived of the right to hold office or to be delegates to conventions. Jurisdictional rights are invoked by the offending unions to resist efforts of the A.F. of L. Council to remedy the situation—just as Southern states invoke "state's rights" to resist abolition of poll-tax restrictions on voting and national antilynching legislation. The C.I.O. has taken a strong position opposing all forms of discrimination against Negro workers. It encourages Negro membership on an equal basis and has many Negro organizers and officials. C.I.O. contracts in iron and steel, maritime and mining industries, among others, have eliminated wage differentials between Negroes and whites on similar jobs. The result is that the C.I.O. has a large Negro membership, and Negroes have proven themselves efficient workers, loyal and intelligent members, and capable leaders.

Eternal vigilance is the price of democracy. The best resolutions and declarations of principle must be put in practice or they are empty words, "full of sound and fury—signifying nothing." The doubly shameful and un-American discrimination against Negro women, as Negroes and as women, is widespread. It demands the most emphatic protest and action by women's organizations, by trade unions, and by government agencies. Despicable and widespread discrimination still prevails in spite of President Roosevelt's Order No. 8802, which specifically bars discrimination against Negroes in plants working on war orders. I heard in Lancaster, Pennsylvania, of Negro high-school graduates applying for work at the Armstrong linoleum factory, now converted to war purposes. They were told: "We don't need any domestics or porters here!" Negro girls of Oakland, Cal., fruitlessly apply for war jobs and are told: "No help wanted.". . .

"Jim Crow" is a provocative agent of Hitler and Hirohito—whispering to people whose patience and long-suffering quietude is nearing the breaking point, "You see—this is a 'white man's war'!" Lynchings, poll tax, frameups, enforced unemployment through discrimination, segregation, insults are not good food for democracy. Race hatred cuts at the deepest roots of real Americanism, endangering our country. Our government and our unions must take a firm, uncompromising stand against "Jim Crow." Let us white women follow the admirable example set by the Ford Women's Auxiliary in fighting for the rights of our Negro sisters to work at all jobs and professions for equal pay. Every gate and door must open for them. Help them cast aside the apron and cap of domestic service and put on the coveralls of the shop!

The best resolution on child-care centers passed thus far by any labor convention was adopted unanimously by the Auto Workers' Convention. Unfortunately there was no discussion. It often happens that splendid resolutions meet the unhappy fate of being buried away in archives and are not read by the membership of the unions which fathered them. I hope the Auto Workers Union is aware of the importance of making this a live issue. It is the key to organizing millions of women. We must not be deterred by reactionary opposition. "Breaking up the home!" say some old fogies, as did their forerunners about kindergartens and public schools. "Mothers with children should not work," cry others, as if they never heard of thousands upon thousands who work in peacetime and for whom there should have been child-care provisions made long ago. The most stupid recommendation I have heard yet is that mothers should work nights so they can take care of their homes and children in the daytime. I suppose they can sleep at odd times like horses or elephants—standing up! . . .

Child care is a major political issue in our country today. The unions who sponsor it and the congressmen who fight for further appropriations will win the ardent support of women. Funds can be secured under the Lanham Act. Six million dollars of W.P.A. [Works Progress Administration] funds are already allocated for this purpose. More must be made available.

There are thirty child-care committees in various places. The first wartime Child-Care Project was approved by the president and opened up in New Haven, Conn., in August. It is for preschool, kindergarten, and school-age children, and is open from 6:30 A.M. to 6:30 P.M. Hundreds more are needed. Juvenile delinquency is on the increase to an alarming degree in our country. Proper care, feeding, and supervision of children will help to overcome it. Every industrial community should apply for government child-care projects. Let Uncle Sam mind the children while Mother works to win the war. Indifference and neglect of their children may reap a whirlwind of resentful feeling among working mothers against the government, unions, and the war.

Housing is another major need of workers in war production centers. The Manpower Commission could far more readily move labor forces around the country if this problem were adequately met. New workers coming into cities like Oakland, San Diego, Buffalo, and Bridgeport are worn out by the search for a place to stay. Many cannot bring their families for lack of accommodations, and their cost of living is doubled.

Women are even more sensitive to bad housing conditions than men are because they carry the burden of domestic duty after a day's work. Homes are working places to them. Let a woman worker come home to a modern, comfortable government project house with all facilities for a quick bath, a dinner already prepared in the Frigidaire or partly cooked in an electric stove—and the world looks different to her. Workers who live in these houses are happy. The only trouble is, there are too few of them, just samples to satisfy the lucky few and aggravate the disappointed many.

To summarize—the vital needs of American women workers to help win the war are as follows:

1. Equal opportunity to work for all women (Negro and white) at all occupations.

2. Adequate training for jobs, under government and union supervision.

3. Equal pay for equal work.

4. Safe and sanitary shop conditions.

5. Equal membership, protection by and participation in labor unions.

6. Child-care centers, with federal funds and supervision.

7. Adequate modern housing. . . .

The voice of women must be heard in the highest councils of the trade union movement and the government. Let us overcome our past shortcomings now in the white heat of a war for human liberation. There should be more than 6 women out of 531 in Congress. England has 13 women members in a Parliament of 615. The Supreme Soviet has 50 percent women, from all regions and occupations. Labor, as the vanguard of all progressive forces in our country, can blaze a trail, set an example. Have confidence in our women of the labor unions. Encourage them to speak up, elect them to positions of responsibility. They are inexperienced. They'll make mistakes. So did you, brother, when you first started out. But they'll make worse mistakes if you suppress them. And you'll be making the biggest one of all. Elect a proportionate number of women delegates to all bodies, including conventions, as there is a percentage of women in the industry. They are new but don't forget they are adults, they are equals.

These are their rights. American women will not tolerate second-class citizenship in trade unions. The A.F. of L. and C.I.O. conventions will be closely scrutinized by the women workers of America. "Unionism as usual" will not suffice. We need new, modern, streamlined unionism. There are deep disappointment and dangerous doubt because there were not a goodly number of women delegates, because women in industry were not a major item on the order of business, because plans were not mapped out for high-powered organization campaigns among women, and because a national conference of labor organizations was not projected at once. There are thirteen million women in industry today—there will be eighteen million tomorrow. They await your call, eagerly. Do you want them, brothers, to work, to fight, to win with you? Speak up and act now. Victory is at stake!

3   The Negro Woman in National Defense

Annabel Sawyer

In response to a call issued by Alpha Kappa Alpha Sorority and the National Council of Negro Women, representatives from forty-three national African-American women's organizations

From Annabel Sawyer, "The Negro Woman in National Defense," *Aframerican Woman's Journal* (Summer and Fall 1941): 2–5; Series 13, Box 2, Folder 8, Records of the National Council of Negro Women. Reprinted by permission of the Bethune Museum and Archives, Washington, DC.

*met in Washington, DC, June 28–30, 1941, to discuss "ways
and means of improving the social, economic, and political status of the Negro woman through her participation in the program of national defense." The conference, held just three days
after President Roosevelt issued Executive Order #8802 banning discrimination in defense industries and government facilities, shared many of the aspirations and ideals of A. Philip
Randolph's March on Washington movement.*

*The report of the conference, written by Annabel Sawyer, a
prominent member of Alpha Kappa Alpha, appeared in the*
Aframerican Woman's Journal, *the official publication of the
National Council of Negro Women. It demonstrates unequivo-
cally that African-American women, even in the face of "mounting discriminatory practices," strongly supported the U.S.
defense program.*

M OTIVATED BY MOUNTING DISCRIMINATORY PRACTICES against
women generally, and Negro women specifically, the Washington committee for the Negro Woman in National Defense was
organized. This committee was called by Miss Norma E. Boyd,
National Chairman of the Non-Partisan Council on Public Affairs
of Alpha Kappa Alpha Sorority, and Mrs. Mary McLeod Bethune,
President of the National Council of Negro Women. Because they
were aware of the tragedy that has overtaken minorities in other
countries of the world, it seemed highly expedient to these women
to issue a nationwide call to all Negro women's organizations to
send their delegates to assemble in Washington for a conference on
ways and means of improving the social, economic, and political
status of the Negro woman through her participation in the program of national defense. In view of the struggle in which the world
is now engaged for maintenance of the democratic ideal and the
tremendous stake Negro women must have in its outcome, the nationwide call was issued. Women from forty-three national organizations responded in convention at Howard University, June 28 to
30, 1941, and studied defense planning and the Negro woman's
relationship thereto.

As stated in the call the aims of the conference were:

1. To discover ways and means through which Negro women
   should aid in the protection of America from external dan-
   gers and set up precedents by means of which true democracy may be maintained within.

2. To provide for the integration of Negro workers according to their training and skill in all phases of the national defense program.

3. To seek the placement of qualified Negroes on policymaking committees and boards so that racial problems may receive due consideration in the light of diverse needs.

4. To secure health provisions for all Americans: good food, adequate hospital facilities, and sanitary living conditions that will permit vigorous physical development, basic to any efficient performance.

The conference in session revealed many inadequacies in our approach to national defense recognizing at the same time some comprehensive attempts to appropriate the resources of the nation in the present emergency.

The following problems were considered in the three-day session:

Training, Employment, and Organized Labor

The problem of training and employment in defense is a tremendous one. We have a shortage of apprentices which the N.Y.A. [National Youth Administration], the W.P.A. [Works Progress Administration], and industrial Plant Training and Apprenticeship programs are attempting to correct.

In the whole training and apprenticeship field very few trades are followed by women apprentices. Apprenticeship opportunities are being investigated so that some plan may be devised for the inclusion of women. Opportunities for apprenticeships of any kind are limited, especially for Negroes where no ratio has yet been established.

There are three classifications of job opportunities for women in national defense: (1) unskilled—airplane, munitions, and arsenal plants where women will be taken on as workers to do a certain kind of machine work; (2) skilled—where a knowledge of power machine operation will be required; (3) clerical and stenographic— in government and private defense plants.

Negroes have been benefited by union membership, but Negro women have been reluctant to join unions or encourage their men to belong to them. Union affiliation is highly desirable because of the alertness of labor organizations as to social, economic, and po-

litical problems. The exclusion of domestic and agricultural workers from Social Security is detrimental to the moral, physical, and
economic welfare of the nation. Organized labor may help in the
solution of this problem.

Health, Housing, Recreation, and Consumer Needs

The Negro is not the major health problem of America but in-
herits every health problem known to the nation as a whole. These
problems are not necessarily peculiar to the Negro, but are intensi-
fied in his experience by lack of facilities, social conditions, low
economic status, poor knowledge of community and personal hygiene, and maternal care. The major health menaces of America are
found to be venereal diseases, tuberculosis, infant and maternal
mortality, and malnutrition. The economic factor is the major problem. Upon its solution depends the improved health condition of
the nation.

Housing, for instance, is concomitant to the prevention of malnutrition, tuberculosis, infant and maternal mortality, venereal diseases, juvenile delinquency, immorality, and crime. About 18,000
Negroes throughout the United States have been recently housed in
the dwelling projects, so it seems that the housing program is making an approach to the needs of this particular low-income group.
This program not only contributes to the morale and general health,
but provides a means of participation for Negroes on its planning
boards and in work programs. Every housing plan includes adequate
recreation facilities for the inhabitants of the improved dwelling
project.

Consumer education may help people to discover new tech-
niques for the improvement of health, housing, and recreational
needs. Defense production has brought about the necessity for readjustment in the use of materials vital to defense; however, adequate substitutes for these materials have been made available.
The Office of Price Administration and Civilian Supply is concerned
with price control, expansion of supply for and distribution to consumers, and the consumer's protection. With the aid of O.P.A.C.S.
bulletins, the consumer may learn to spend money wisely and work
through cooperatives to increase his purchasing power. . . .

Farm Security

"Farming is both a business and a way of life for half of all the
Negroes in America," according to a study made by Mrs. Constance
Daniels of the Farm Security Administration. Ninety-five percent

of this number are farm operators living in the South, with more than three-quarters of them tenants. Half the number of all share-croppers are Negroes. The total number of Negro sharecroppers exceeds that of white croppers in Georgia, South Carolina, Arkansas, Louisiana, and Mississippi. Consequently, Negro children of sharecroppers growing to manhood and womanhood face the drudgery, neglect, and privation typical of all croppers' children plus the added handicap of discrimination because of race.

Farm Security has been a stepping-stone toward a new lease on life for approximately 50,000 Negro farm families. The F.S.A. is attempting to develop social and economic patterns in agriculture through the establishing of homestead projects. More than 1,800 Negro families are living on such projects. Rental cooperatives, debt adjustment services, migratory labor camps, the relocation of farmers situated on submarginal land, and aid to rural education are a part of the Farm Security Administration program.

To preserve the vitality of human resources of the nation through assistance and guidance to farming people in the use of the natural resources over which they have control is the problem of the Farm Security Administration. The agency realizes that there can be little real national security unless a means is found to secure and stabilize the lives of the lowest-income families of the country, of which the Negro is a significant part.

Women's Bureau of the Department of Labor

The Women's Bureau has sent agents into seven factories on the Atlantic seaboard, filing defense contracts, in order to observe their employment practices. Approximately 100,000 workers were employed in these seven plants; in three there were no women employed, and in the other four only a fraction of 1 percent. The need for workers in defense industries is mounting by leaps and bounds. Already in certain areas there is approaching an anticipated shortage of male labor, skilled or semiskilled. In an effort to mobilize all the nation's resources it is essential that some plan be made for the intelligent use of "woman power." While some gains have been made in restricted employment areas there is still needed an extensive training program for women.

It has been discovered that women do well in industry—where (1) care, alertness, and little physical exertion is required; (2) manipulative skill [is needed]; (3) skill rather than strain is required; and (4) on large machines employing the use of lifts. There is also the matter of "secondary defense" in which women can make a lasting contribution, such as: (1) conservation, (2) child care, (3) sanitation, and (4) clothing.

One of the chief difficulties with which Negro women are concerned is the lack of well-trained people to fill places, and so we are likely to be embarrassed unless we can begin immediately to supply sufficient trainees. While the women of America are mobilizing for inclusion in the defense program, definite recognition should be given to the mutual problems of Negro and white women alike so that both groups may share in the economic and social gains to be derived from any solution of the total problem.

Civil Liberties

Civil liberties of persons in the United States, citizens and noncitizens, are defined in the major documents of our land, yet there are certain limitations set up for all residents. The Negro suffers from widespread violation of these legal safeguards more than any other group. Chief among these violations are his right to security of life, person, and property, together with an absence of a general belief that the Creator has endowed him with any equal rights common to his fellows. His security of life is violated by lynching, his security of person by assault in lynching and in other ways, his security of property in instances where property bought and occupied in restricted areas becomes the target for destruction by the mob.

Freedom of speech and ideas, the right to work, the privilege of travel without the humiliation of segregated conveyances and accommodations, are all basic pillars of privilege in a democracy. The price of democracy in America has now become the degree of willingness to which America enforces the civil liberties of Negroes and every other minority group.

In this period of unlimited emergency it is more easily possible to create an uninformed public opinion that will not only permit suppression of civil liberties, but will take no notice of them. There arises, therefore, a necessity for the education of American people to the idea that America is a democracy, a composite of the contributions of many nations and races. During periods of prosperity, there are not so many problems involving civil liberties; but the struggle to preserve civil liberties now merges in the basic rights for democratic liberties. We have then to create an intelligent, enlightened public opinion that will militantly oppose the restriction of these American principles for every group, be it labor, education, employment, or racial minorities.

Youth

The youth of America looks with apprehension upon the rapid and ominous development of war in the world. In order to defend democracy effectively, youth appeals for support to all organizations of their own, and to the labor and farm movements, for a program safeguarding the welfare, security, and morale of youth in the armed forces of our nation. There are already 1,500,000 young men under arms and in training camps, these to be followed by other trainees. The welfare and morale of these youth are of vital concern to all Americans.

Recommendations

Health, Housing, Recreation, and Consumer Problems

The conference recognized that the health and well-being of the people is basic to the defense and maintenance of democratic institutions and that provision for incomes adequate for the support of health and decency is fundamental to the solution of problems of health, housing, nutrition, and related consumer needs. While these problems affect the general population their incidence is highest among those of lowest economic status and particularly among the Negro people.

A. COMMUNITY WELFARE

The conference therefore recommended: All support to and cooperation with labor organizations in the extension of free collective bargaining as the most effective and democratic means of raising the income levels of the low-income groups; that we oppose reduction of W.P.A., relief, and nondefense expenditures giving assistance to substandard groups; that we advocate the elimination of federal and local income taxes that bear disproportionately upon the lower-income groups.

Since adequate provisions for the protection of jobs, health, and safety have been recommended by:

    1. The White House Conference on Children in a Democracy, 1940 (Section Children in Minority Groups),

    2. The Nutrition Conference, May 1941 (Economic section),

    3. The President's Executive Order, June 25, 1941, banning discrimination in defense industries,

the conference urged that Negroes be placed on all policymaking committees of local, state, and federal agencies in order to further implement the benefits to be derived from the recommendations made by these conferences.

B. FIRST AID
    1. We propose that all local organizations secure informa-
tion concerning the establishment of first aid classes in all communities and organize such classes in communities where they
do not exist. . . .
    2. Volunteers are being called for to receive training that
will fit them for air-raid wardens; the conference therefore suggests that Negro women volunteer for this service immediately.
    3. Hospitalization. Adequate hospitalization is requisite to
the maintenance of efficiency, sound health practices, and the
reduction of the infant and maternal mortality rate. Therefore,
the conference pledged its support to the immediate passage of
the Senate Bill S. 1230, which will create a federal fund for
hospitals.
C. HOUSING AND RECREATION
    1. The conference urged local organizations to contact the
Chairman of the Housing Division of the State Defense Council and request a survey of housing conditions and changing
rents with the object of providing adequate housing facilities,
particularly for the lowest-income groups, through the construc-
tion of new federal housing projects and measures for rent control through the state and local boards.
    2. It is further recommended that adequate recreational fa-
cilities be included in every housing program, that allocation
of housing facilities be made without discrimination because
of race, creed, or color and on the basis of economic need rather
than on the basis of the percentage which any racial group bears
to the total population.
D. NUTRITION AND CONSUMER EDUCATION
    1. Organized labor through its many local organizations can
assist in the survey of low-income families. The conference
therefore recommends that such a survey be made so that higher
wages may be obtained and nutritional deficiencies met.
    2. Local groups may secure from the Consumer Division,
Office of Price Administration and Civilian Supply, pertinent
information that may be used to provide instruction in consumer
education. The conference further recommends that such material be secured.
    3. It is recommended that all persons cooperate with
local organizations concerned with consumer problems in

investigating and reporting sharp rises in prices in all commodities to local officials and the Office of Price Administration and Civilian Supply, Washington, D.C., for the purpose of taking appropriate action to curb price increases, to secure investigation, and to control monopolies engaged in the manufacture and distribution of consumer goods.

4. Be it further recommended that all local groups petition the Department of Agriculture to introduce the following measures for supplementing the diets of low-income families in the communities where these measures are not yet in force:

a) Distribution of penny milk and nickel milk
b) Free lunches for schoolchildren
c) Food-stamp plan.

Organized Labor and Training for Employment in Defense Industries

The conference recommended:

1. That committees be formed from this conference to survey and report upon the enforcement of the President's Executive Order of June 25, 1941, designed to eliminate discrimination in defense industries, and to cooperate with other groups active in seeing that defense industries comply with the order.

2. That we urge the support of national legislation for the inclusion of household and agricultural workers and workers in nonprofit organizations under the Social Security Act.

3. That we call upon all trade unions, and their women's auxiliaries, practicing discrimination against women, particularly Negro women, to eliminate this un-American practice and join with all progressive organized labor in supporting the nationwide appeal for jobs for Negro women in national defense.

4. In view of the fact that an executive ruling regarding discrimination has existed since May 1940, we recommend that government contracts be withdrawn from companies with defense contracts that discriminate against workers because of race, creed, or color.

5. We advocate the elimination of all discrimination against Negroes in government service and in the armed forces of the nation.

6. That Negro workers receive equal pay and equal work in all defense projects.

7. That the government consider seriously the problem of placement of persons over 40 years of age.

8. That contact committees be formed so that women in local communities may ally themselves with all movements now established in their respective communities for the purpose of obtaining and disseminating information from the proceedings of all civilian defense committees.

Training and Employment in Defense Industries

The conference recommended:

1. That information concerning training and employment opportunities supported by the federal government be secured from the state or local offices of:

    a) N.Y.A.

    b) W.P.A.

    c) Employment Service.

2. That communities, through the press, platform, and radio, sponsor an educational program that shall create a wholesome respect for the dignity of labor, as well as pride in promptness, honor, and efficiency on the job.

3. That communities work to increase opportunities for vocational training provided in cooperation with public schools through:

    a) School training

    b) Part-time apprenticeship training.

Youth

We recommend that the program which should be adopted at the forthcoming American Youth Congress, to be held in Philadelphia, Pennsylvania, July 4 to 6, be reported to the Findings Committee of the conference and circulated among the delegates and affiliated organizations.

Be it further recommended that Miss Pauline Myers, of Richmond, Virginia, be commissioned as our representative to fulfill the instructions as outlined above.

Civil Liberties

Fully cognizant of the fact that theoretically the rights and privileges of *All the People* are protected by the Bill of Rights, and the Thirteenth, Fourteenth, and Fifteenth Amendments of our Constitution, we are nonetheless aware of the many varied and subtle means of restriction that have been and are now operating in every area of American life to the detriment and deprivation of the Negro worker. The Negro Woman's Committee for Democracy in National Defense regrets that millions of our race are disfranchised and unable to protect themselves in that section of our land where the great majority live. We therefore recommend:

1. That local organizations be urged to acquaint themselves with legislative enactments which have been created for their protection, so that they may intelligently employ every agency at their disposal, that through such activity these laws may actually function as provided.

That this conference go on record as supporting the:

    a) Geyer Anti-Poll Tax Bill

    b) Gavagan Antilynch Bill

    c) Marcantonio Antidiscrimination Bill.

2. We further recommend that local organizations be urged to send communications to their congressmen and senators enlisting the support of such representatives for the immediate passage of these bills.

3. Because of the increasing war hysteria, we urge the attention of the people of America to a solemn rededication to the principles of democracy as embodied in the Bill of Rights and the Constitution of the United States, and further to reaffirm their determination to maintain academic freedom.

II In the Military

When the United States entered World War II in December 1941, opportunities for women to serve in the military were limited to registered nurses who qualified for membership in the Army or Navy Nurse Corps. As wartime casualties mounted, nurses met the demands for service, and a total of 76,000 women, representing 31.3 percent of all professional nurses, served in the armed forces by the end of the conflict.

By 1943 official women's branches had been established in the Army, Navy, Coast Guard, and Marines. During World War I, the Navy and Marines had enlisted "Yeomanettes" and "Marinettes" to act as secretaries, while the Army had contracted with women to serve as telephone operators and dietitians. However, these women had not been granted full military status, and, at the end of the war, they had been discharged from their duties. In the months prior to Pearl Harbor, as the nation stepped up its preparedness efforts, proponents of women in the military drew upon this World War I precedent as they campaigned for the establishment of official women's branches in the various military services. Prominent women who supported this campaign included Representatives Edith Nourse Rogers of Massachusetts and Margaret Chase Smith of Maine, as well as First Lady Eleanor Roosevelt.

The first women's military branch to be established, the Women's Army Auxiliary Corps (WAAC), was created by act of Congress on May 15, 1942. This organization gave women only partial military status. On July 1, 1943, Congress abolished the WAAC and created in its stead the Women's Army Corps (WAC). This new organization provided women the same rank, titles, and pay as their male counterparts. In total, 140,000 women served in the WAAC/WAC during the war years.

The women's branch of the Navy, the WAVES (Women Accepted for Volunteer Emergency Service), was created on July 30, 1942. By the end of the war, approximately 100,000 women had served in the WAVES. The Women's Reserve of the U.S. Coast

Guard, the SPARs (from the Coast Guard motto, *Semper Paratus*, "Always Ready"), was established on November 23, 1942, and 13,000 women eventually joined the Coast Guard. The Marine Corps Women's Reserve was founded on February 13, 1943, and some 23,000 women served in the Marine Corps during the war years. In addition, 1,000 women ferried aircraft of all types for the quasi-military organization, the Women Airforce Service Pilots (WASP). A total of 350,000 women served in the military during World War II.

Throughout the war, the U.S. military remained largely segregated. Of the original 440 women who reported to Fort Des Moines, Iowa, for WAAC officer candidate training in July 1942, 39 were black. These women were housed separately, assigned separate seats in classrooms, and required to eat at tables especially reserved for "Colored." This practice of segregation continued during the wartime years for WAAC/WAC enlisted personnel and officers.

Black women were not accepted into the WAVES and the SPARs until November 1944, a change that only occurred after substantial protest by progressive organizations. Near the end of the war, the Navy reported that there were 2 black officers and 72 enlisted women in the WAVES. The Coast Guard reported that 4 black women had been accepted into the SPARs. Both black WAVES and SPARs were integrated into their service branches. Neither the Women Marines nor the WASP accepted African Americans. When the war ended, approximately 500 black nurses were serving in the Army Nurse Corps on a segregated basis. Not until January 1945 were black nurses admitted to the Navy Nurse Corps. Only 4 black women served in the Navy Nurse Corps, and they were fully integrated into the Navy. Despite the segregation and discrimination suffered by blacks in the military, however, African-American women demonstrated a strong desire and willingness to come to the aid of their country in its time of great need.

4   Yes, Ma'am!: The Personal Papers of a WAAC Private

Elizabeth R. Pollock

On July 20, 1942, a group of 125 enlisted women arrived at Fort Des Moines, Iowa, to begin a four-week basic training course. Along with 440 officer candidates, they were the first women to train for the Army. Auxiliary Elizabeth R. Pollock was a member of the First Company of enlisted women to be trained at Fort Des Moines. The letters she wrote to her family, published in 1943 as Yes, Ma'am!: The Personal Papers of a WAAC Private, *depict her excitement at meeting other young women from throughout the United States and "having an experience we shall never forget."*

Sunday

Dear Mother:

GRADUALLY, NOW, I AM GETTING acquainted with my colleagues. The eighteen girls in my room come from New York, Arizona, Oregon, California, Virginia, and Pennsylvania. We are as different as the states we come from, and our pasts are as varied. There is a girl I like especially. Perhaps I have mentioned her before—the one whose husband is missing in the Philippines. She is one of my marching partners and says it's fun to march with me. I can say it is a real pleasure to have her as a pivot when we do column left. Now and then we all talk over our reasons for enlisting. With some, it was because they were separated from their husbands; with others, because they had gotten in a rut in their jobs and wanted to get out. Some of them are like me—they were asked to volunteer because their services were needed in Aircraft Warning. A lot of the girls are happily married, but joined up because they thought there was a job to do. Now that we're here, though, our purposes are all the same. And we all know we're having an experience we shall never forget.

From Auxiliary Elizabeth R. Pollock, *Yes, Ma'am!: The Personal Papers of a WAAC Private* (Philadelphia: J. B. Lippincott Co., 1943), 43–55.

Monday

Sorry I didn't finish this last evening, but it suddenly dawned on me that there was some studying to do. Also, my train of thought was interrupted by the daily "Coke riot." After dinner there is always a mad rush for Cokes, and hundreds of shrill cries of "Anyone got two nickels for a dime?" It is physically impossible to keep any change here.

We are now lying in our rooms waiting for a whistle to blow— probably for fire drill this time. At two o'clock we are to have another lecture on Defense against Chemical Warfare and then gas masks will be issued. This morning we all smelled the different gases from bottles, very carefully so as not to have any casualties. I'm afraid I am not suggestible. I thought the apple-blossom gas smelled just like the new-mown hay gas. No doubt, if I ever smell one of them when no one is around to tell me what to expect, I'll imagine orange blossoms.

There are millions of rumors floating around about us Aircraft Warning people. We call them L.R.s—latrine rumors. First, we were all prepared to be sent home this coming Saturday, after basic training. That rumor died down, and other grapevine news has us staying for four, six, or eight weeks more. No one seems to know. I rather hope we get our administrative training here even though at home I could get a more satisfactory hairdo.

In spite of the above, life is falling into more of a pattern. Sunday nights there are band concerts on the Parade Ground and people drive out from town to hear them. If we want, we can wander down and sit on the grass, but I haven't gone yet because we can hear pretty well from here. Also, there are movies here on the post which we can attend. All this, with Friday night dances, gives us an ample social life if you have the stamina for it. . . .

Much love, Lisbeth

Tuesday

Dear Family:

When I read your letter asking what we wear to the dances, I realized that it has become a matter of course to me to wear my uniform. You can't wear anything else on the post, unless you stay right in barracks. Some time I am going to reckon up the hours I save per week by not having to decide every morning and evening what to put on! In the evenings, when I stay inside, I usually wear slacks, but that doesn't involve any choice. We can wear civilian clothes to town, as I've said, but if one is coming back late at night, it's wiser not to until we get some kind of identification, as the guards might not let us in. I have a dreary vision of standing at the gate in a bit of fluff, trying to figure out the next step when the sentry says, "Stand forward and be recognized." Even if they searched, they'd get nowhere, as we don't have any dog tags yet.

Last night the Second Company of our regiment invited us to a party. Something about the army brings out latent talent, because the skits and singing were really excellent. It probably wouldn't have overcome an outsider with mirth, but it had us falling in the aisles. There were take-offs on inspection and our efforts to learn proper drilling, and on classes, with the inevitable auxiliary who "can't hear, sir." And every so often a flock of WAACs would tear across the stage frantically looking at their watches. Then one WAAC got up and did a really beautiful solo on her flute. At the end they had all their officers up on the stage. Their first sergeant was there, too, and as he is to be married soon, he received a special ode. He had to read the inscription, "To Sweetypie Sergeant"— and the expression on his face was wonderful to see. After that they gave us Cokes.

Our company is giving a party Friday night before the dance, and I hope we can at least come up to theirs. They seem to be a very jolly company, and won the commendation for marching last Saturday.

Barbara, one of the Aircraft Warning girls from Boston, the one who is a painter, invited me after this party to another one in her squad room, and we had a regular boarding school feast from S. S. Pierce [a gourmet food brand], flavored with other good things from Oregon that another girl in the same room had. The meals are so good and I eat so much at them that I wasn't very hungry, but it was fun. I remember Napoleon said that an army travels on its stomach. This army isn't traveling, yet, but we are certainly laying a base. . . .

Our regiment has voted to stand Retreat. We don't have to any longer, but we want to. Tonight we had the men's band down at our end of the Parade Ground taking orders from our trainee regimental commander. The women who take regimental commander's place have to yell. Their orders must be heard by three companies. They do it very well, really. We can understand their commands even

A scene in the WAAC squad room, where members gather during leisure periods on Saturday afternoon. The WAACs are using local hotels for their quarters, Daytona Beach, Florida, December 1942. *Courtesy Library of Congress*

better than the major's as their voices are clearer. The WAAC band went by, not playing, but marching with instruments. That apparently is the first step. . . .

There have been a whole lot of new movies and lectures this week, and I can't begin to tell you about them all. There was one very graphic movie with the moral: keep your mouth shut. This is a good place for that propaganda, certainly. The grapevine carries on much as usual, but then, most of the things we talk about would confuse our enemies more than it would help them.

Did I tell you we finally got paid? However, by the time they had deducted laundry and money for a defense bond—you see, I'm thinking of the future—and for pictures for identification and P.X. [Post Exchange] books, I didn't have so much left that I was tempted to go on a spree. Also, will you please broadcast it that anyone I haven't written to is not forgotten. I have to snatch time for these letters as it is. Lights are about to go out right now, and then mail call comes so often, or we have to fall out in front of the barracks for some reason or other, even in supposedly free time. . . . I hope people will understand.

They say bed check is in five minutes, so good night.

Love, Lisbeth

Friday

Dear Family:

Tomorrow ends our basic training and we will be told what we're going to do and where we're to go. Already some are assigned and starting to work in offices and Personnel. The Motor Corps girls appear in khaki overalls and look very pleased with themselves to be in there pitching, though I can tell they get a little tired now and then when they have a lot of benches and things to load and unload. The cooks are sprinkled in among the men cooks in the mess hall now. They have to get up at four in the morning. Some of them look very attractive in white, with big white caps. One little woman who has been sick and rather glum has a continual smile on her face now as she serves behind the counter. She says she's very happy. I'm always glad when people find themselves, even when it's in the kitchen.

Of course, we Aircraft Warning women are already assigned as far as our line of duty is concerned, but we don't know yet what our fate is to be. There's a new rumor out every hour on the hour, all "official," and getting wilder all the time. First a girl rushes in and says, "Have you heard the latest?" We all jump up with our eyes bulging and say, "No, what is it?" And the girl says, "Aircraft Warning will be sent to Alaska." So for awhile we plan arctic wardrobes and wonder how we'll keep from getting chilblains and how long the nights are up there. Then another WAAC will burst in, and this time it's Florida, or the Canal Zone, or Ulster.

Classes have been more interesting this week. I think the army is very clever to use movies so much in instruction. If they'd done that with mathematics when I was in school, I might not get into a cold sweat now every time I see figures. In the last few days we've seen movies on map-reading and chemical warfare, the way to put on gas masks and feminine hygiene. I told one of the ex-school-teachers in my room that after the war she might try doing Caesar's Gallic Wars in movies, with Lowell Thomas rendering the commentary in Latin. She seemed to consider it seriously.

Every time you turn a corner here you run into *Life* [magazine]. Someone has produced a new quip. "We have *Life, Liberty* [another magazine]—but what of the pursuit of happiness?" Everything we do, almost, is photographed. *Collier's* [magazine] turned up, too, with a lot of cameras. As we are the First Company, and I am in the first platoon of the First Company, I am generally out near the front. However, I am in the second row, so I may not be easily found. I guess we all look pretty much alike, as a matter of fact.

This afternoon we have been cleaning the barracks—every square inch of it. In fact, practically every *cubic* inch. I warn you, I'll probably be very critical of your housekeeping when I come home. I polished the fire extinguisher, dusted the molding above the windows, scrubbed the floor, and then helped disinfect the gas masks. I kept trying to imagine where I'd look for dust if I were the inspecting officer, then I cleaned there. We have to leave the place in perfect condition and even make beds for the officer candidates who are coming in. We plan to give them "short sheet" beds, just as the men did for us when we got here.

It's time to go to the Service Club for our company's show. From what I've heard of the rehearsals it should be good. . . .

Sorry to end so abruptly. I can't properly answer the letters I get. All I try to do is give some notion of what our days are like. By the way, everyone was terribly excited that our company won the honor of carrying the colors in our graduation parade tomorrow. We were best in Regimental Retreat tonight.

Much love, Lisbeth

1st WAAC Training Center Co.
Ft. Des Moines, Iowa

Sunday

Dear Mother:
Another turn of the wheel of chance, and I might be writing you from an "unknown destination." As a matter of fact, until Saturday our destination was unknown, and I wrote you of the vigorous and thriving crop of rumors that were raised as a consequence. Well, we moved all right, but we're only a stone's throw away from our old quarters—if the stone had a good right arm behind it, that is. We are now assigned to the refurbished stables that once were a home to the mounts of this cavalry post. As you see by the heading I'm now in another 1st Company. This is rather prosaic after the lurid tales we were told about our possible fate, but it is a con-

siderable change, just the same, and most of us are inwardly glad that it was no greater. We had made our adjustment to army life in the old barracks, and now we have moved a step further along the way. I guess it is like being a sophomore; the giddy feeling is gone and you find yourself committed completely to a particular undertaking.

Auxiliaries Ruth Wade and Lucille Mayo demonstrate their ability to service trucks as taught them during the processing period at Fort Des Moines and put into practice at Fort Huachuca, Arizona, December 8, 1942. *Courtesy National Archives*

Things moved into high on Saturday, with Parade and everything. We had personal inspection by Colonel Faith himself—but I didn't quail as much this time as at first—and then we posed for the Movietone News. On top of all this, Captain Menter brought some men through our room to show them what barracks inspection was. We heard they were Swedish noblemen on a tour, but they didn't look it. Maybe we didn't strike them as the flower of American womanhood either, though.

After lunch that day we moved to the new barracks. Tension was high, and voices a little shrill. Charlotte and Nancy Richards and I stood together—we're fairly near the same height—hoping to get beds together. Then, lo and behold, they counted us off in 3s!

Now Charlotte and Nancy are in the third platoon and I'm in the first, so I'm on the other side of this ex-stable from them. However, I did have some luck, as the nice Californian, Mary Jane, is next to me. We are in a little cubbyhole with four beds, open in the front, with lockers on either side. I wish they'd left the feed boxes in our stall—they'd come in handy! Charlotte and Nancy weren't so fortunate. They landed in a single line of beds right opposite the day room, and entirely exposed on all sides. They're rather far from the windows, too. I felt badly, as I was the one who instigated the plan of our being together, and now I am so cozily situated.

We've all talked of calling our families since we moved. I think we were a little homesick last night in our new quarters. I was really going to phone, but the booth was never empty and I didn't have change. I will call some night as you say it's all right to reverse the charges. I'm afraid I'll never collect enough quarters and dimes and nickels.

After our company play Friday night, which was excellent, quite professionally done, I went to the movies on the post with Barbara, the painter from Boston. We know a few people in common, and so get along rather well. We both have the same kind of restraint, though neither of us is the least bit tongue-tied. Barbara can talk easily and well without giving herself away. She manages rather successfully to keep her background intact, even in these alien surroundings. Now and then, though, she astounds me by having a burst of practical joking. It's never safe to pigeonhole people too readily. We topped off our party with a Creamsicle, and felt we had made a night of it. I'm not usually out of barracks so late, and I had the sensation of great daring.

Today I'm Charge of Quarters—C.Q.—for twenty-four hours, as it had come around to my turn. I've been acting in this capacity for two hours, and so far have done nothing but read over three letters I got. This is a slow day. C.Q. has authority when no noncoms [noncommissioned officers] or officers are around. Everyone asks you questions—even if you've just that minute pinned the arm band on—and you're supposed immediately to know all the answers. Do you remember your "thinking cap"? I always used to wish there was something one *could* put on and suddenly be wise.

Charge of Quarters has to check lights and plumbing, call everyone in the mornings at 5:30, and meet and salute the commanding officer when he arrives. She also has to do bed check, but I'm let out of that, since it isn't required Saturdays and Sundays. I like this job and feel more capable doing it than giving commands. I am pretty sure that if yelling commands in a "snappy" military manner is how you get to be an officer, I'll not make the grade. Our first sergeant has told me, though, that I'll have to march the Aircraft Warning people to class tomorrow morning. I guess I can handle that assignment without too much anguish.

There was another birthday party at the same restaurant in town. I was tired after the strain of moving but the girl was so anxious to have all of us from our old room that it would have been mean not to go. Ten of us sat at one table, and a man and his wife at the table next to us said they would be honored to have the other three sit with them. We were all in uniform, and I felt rather as if we were back in boarding school, especially when one of our lieutenants came up and spoke kindly to us. Afterwards we trooped over to a WAAC dance which was held at Younkers, the big department store here. Of course, there were the *Life* photographers, as busy as ever. I never thought I'd be in on a party that *Life* went to. I danced with lots of men, including a cook from the post and a nice Finnish boy from Minnesota, and some M.P.s from the Army War Show. I asked one soldier if he missed long dresses and flowers on his partners. He just chuckled and said, "I never argue with my luck. Girls are girls, whatever they dress themselves up in." Pretty soon he said, "Say, miss, what kind of a sergeant do you have?" And we were off! They were all engaging youths and seemed thrilled to walk around town afterwards with WAACs. They treated us to coffee, and I think it was just as well we decided to accept their invitation, because they profited from the coffee themselves. The Finnish boy had just been paid, and I think he might have gotten more of an edge on if we hadn't been around as a steadying influence. Maybe we are destined as the main support of the armed forces, but I believe prevention is more sensible than cure.

The cook paid our trolley fare back to the post. By that time there were only three of us left—the hardy girls!—and we got in at 2 A.M. and had quite a time finding our beds in the huge, dark, and unfamiliar barracks.

The three companies of our former regiment have been reshuffled now into two training companies. The smartest ones are in our company, we think. Along with all the other changes, we have a new captain, too—Captain Bardin, who is awfully nice. Most of the noncoms are the ones we had before, which gives us a homey feeling, but our instructors will be different. We'll have a little close-order drill three times a week, calisthenics twice, and classes from seven-thirty to Retreat the rest of the time.

One of the lieutenants has just been in here, in sports clothes, on his way to play golf, looking for a girl to give her some order or other. He entered cheerfully singing out, "Everybody works but father." It was hard for me to remember to be military and say, "Yes, sir."

Well, this has taken all afternoon, with questions and telephone calls interrupting. (That's what being a C.Q. does.) I certainly would love to see any or all of you, but I don't suppose anyone wants to come to Des Moines for vacation. All I can show you would be the Fort and the one night spot where we've had dinner every time I've been in town.

Could you send me my purple suit, brown pumps, purple beanie, white blouse, and navy blue sheer dress? There is no special hurry, but I'll be able to use them in September if I spend a weekend in Chicago. I'll send home the civilian things I haven't needed.

With love to all, Lisbeth

5   The WAVES: The Story of the Girls in Blue

Nancy Wilson Ross

Following the creation of the WAAC/WAC, WAVES, SPARs, and Women Marines, each of the service branches took specific steps to ensure that the public was well informed about admission requirements, training, and the duties of women in the military. Popular magazines and newspapers published hundreds of articles on these topics. Radio stations assisted with recruitment by broadcasting programs about the experiences of military women. The well-known writer Nancy Wilson Ross authored The WAVES: The Story of the Girls in Blue, *one of the books in this publicity campaign. In the following selection, Ross focuses on the wide array of occupations, ranging from accountants to X-ray technicians, open to women who joined the Navy.*

From Nancy Wilson Ross, *The WAVES: The Story of the Girls in Blue* (New York: Henry Holt and Co., 1943), 1–15. © 1942 by Nancy Wilson Ross. Reprinted by permission of Henry Holt and Co.

THE WAVES, THOSE TRIM GIRLS in the smart navy blue uniform, with its mixture of the romantic and the functional, are steadily increasing in numbers. The people who once stopped to stare at them now accept their part in the picture of America at war. Their stormy weather headgear, an approximation of the medieval wimple, is still enough, however, to slow traffic and to make small boys cry, "Oh, look—Arabs!" Actually the flattering folds date back to the Sepoy Rebellion [in India, 1857–58], when they protected Sir Henry Havelock's soldiers from the burning desert sun. Now the "havelocks" protect America's WAVES from rough weather, if not from the curious glances of their sometimes envious civilian sisters. We shall not speak here of the glances of their uniformed and civilian brothers, which is a longer matter.

The initials of the WAVES stand for the words "Women Accepted for Volunteer Emergency Service." WAVES is, however, the officially recognized title of the women's branch of the United States Naval Reserve, established by an act of Congress on July 30, 1942. A few months ago the very word WAVES was a kind of joke, and the thought of women in uniform was barely acceptable to the so-called protective male animal. But the organization is functioning

Saluting the colors. Captain Mildred H. McAfee, USNR, director of the Women's Reserve, accompanied by Rear Admiral George S. Bryan, USN, Hydrographer for the Navy, inspects the WAVES on duty at the Hydrographic Office, Suitland, Maryland, December 4, 1943. *Courtesy National Archives*

now, developing surely and fast, and wiping out laughter about itself as it goes.

Any account of what women must accept to become a part of the United States Navy proves that they know what they are doing, and why they are doing it. They haven't joined up in the hope of looking like so many [actress Marlene] Dietrichs in the desert, with Gary Cooper on the side. They have joined to release some shore-bound man for sea duty, and to perform any of the numerous tasks to which the Navy may assign them. How they live, eat, sleep in that period between the day when they arrive at some training center, "typically bewildered and reeking of gardenias"—as a writer in the Northampton, Massachusetts, *Wave Lengths* described them—to the day they go forth in their new uniforms, indoctrination behind them, forms a new picture for modern society to contemplate.

But the account of the duties and activities of the WAVES is not the whole story. No one can write about the WAVES—or any women in uniform, for that matter—without dealing to some extent with their thinking and their feeling in this emergency period when the relationship of women to society, and women to men, is so obviously changing. When large numbers of women are asked by an arm of the military to accept a responsibility equal to a man's, and for the first time in history with equal pay—accompanied by none of the old chivalric trimmings—you may be sure some subtle change is in the wind. It would be a bold prophet indeed who attempted to chart these changes, but it would be a blind human being who pretended not to see their shadows cast on the wall. Since it will be a good two decades, in all likelihood, before their emergent pattern may be traced in the social life of this century, no observer can do more than hint, suggest, question, point—and let each reader be his own Cassandra.

The WAVE in training who rises from her iron bunk with a guilty bounce at 0615 Navy time to worry all day about the polish on her shoes, Captain's Inspection, today's preventive shot for one of the deadly diseases against which she is being immunized, about the hang of her skirt, the fit of her jacket, the sixteen points of a naval court martial, or three points of [Alfred Thayer] Mahan's strategy, and how she can get it all done before taps at 2200, is making—whether she realizes it or not—another significant chapter in that history of women which has yet to be written.

Anyone who enters the Women's Reserve of the Navy for training must accept the fact that, henceforth, she is a member of the

Navy first, and a woman second. "Remember to be a lady, forget you are a woman," is one of the first pieces of advice given a new WAVE. To the United States Navy these women and girls are only so many potential seamen, yeomen, specialists, ensigns, and lieutenants. In time, if the emergency lasts that long, some of them may become lieutenant commanders—captains, even—though at present no woman has reached the rank of lieutenant commander except Miss Mildred McAfee, who left the presidency of Wellesley College to accept the leadership of the WAVES.

In the early days of the organization the problem of how to address a WAVE officer received some close attention. "Sir" was generally considered impossible, yet "ma'am" had a Victorian flavor not relished by the twentieth-century American female. Finally it was decided simply to address women officers by their rank or by the usual Miss or Mrs.

Emily Post must have felt this decision keenly. She had already gone on record with the urgent hope that the officers of the Women's Reserve of the Naval Reserve would see the golden opportunity presented to them. Wrote Mrs. Post in *This Week*, November 15, 1942:

> Quite apart from the military angle—although this has made it of real importance—it has been in my mind for a long time to find some way of re-instating "ma'am" in probably all sections of the country, except the South, as the accepted equivalent of "sir."
>
> That we should persist in thinking it "unstylish" to address a lady by the title that is in England used even for the Queen and members of the Royal Family is not sensible. And the perfect opportunity to establish the prestige of "ma'am" is in the hands of the officers of the Army and the Navy Women's Corps. They could so easily give this title the rank it deserves.

In spite of Mrs. Post's impassioned crusade, "ma'am" went into the discard as far as the Navy's WAVES are concerned.

Whether addressed as "Lieutenant," "Mrs.," or "Miss," the women and girls of the Naval Reserve receive men's pay, and men's training. They do men's work. Their initial course as future members of the Navy consists of a boiled down, highly concentrated, and very stiff dose of naval indoctrination, which gives them a working knowledge of the organization, personnel, administration, and operation of the Navy, as well as a thorough grounding in naval etiquette, customs, traditions, and usage.

Some follow their indoctrination course with intensive training in such special fields as naval communications, radio room procedure, fundamentals of radio, theory of electricity, the general communications instruments used by the Navy. Some with particular aptitudes are sent to schools where they learn to operate the Link Trainer (to teach pilots "blind" flying); to the first-of-its-kind Control Tower School in Atlanta, Georgia; or to be trained in synthetic gunnery. The Navy wants women in many capacities: as storekeepers, yeomen (stenographers), code receivers and senders, radio technicians, pharmacists' mates, aviation mechanics and metalsmiths, aerographers, parachute riggers—and for dozens of other jobs which they can do as well as men, and thus relieve men for active combat duty.

Thousands of women are needed, and the program to train and place them is steadily expanding. Captain H. W. Underwood, who is the commanding officer at the Naval Reserve Midshipmen's School (Women's Reserve) at Northampton, called the figures "staggering" when they were at the twenty-five thousand mark. And so they are when it is realized, as he pointed out, that they represent one half the number of officers and one sixth the number of enlisted men in the regular Navy just before Pearl Harbor. By the end of 1943 the number of WAVES is scheduled to be very near the fifty thousand mark. . . .

The list of billets to be filled by WAVES is, in itself, an eloquent commentary on the progress women have made in educating themselves in the less than one hundred years since their "higher education" has been deemed a public responsibility. When you read the long list of qualifications "necessary, desired, or helpful" prior to a WAVE's indoctrination, there come to mind at once the maligned females of the last century who fought for the right of education and inclusion in men's professions. Not many years ago Charlotte Brontë—bursting out in protest for her whole sex against its dull and circumscribed lot—wrote:

> Women feel just as men feel; they need exercise for their faculties and a field for their efforts as much as their brothers do; they suffer from too rigid a restraint, too absolute a stagnation, precisely as men would suffer; and it is narrow-minded in their more privileged fellow creatures to say that they ought to confine themselves to making puddings and knitting stockings, to playing on the piano and embroidering bags. It is thoughtless to condemn them, or laugh at them, if they seek to do more or learn more than custom has pronounced necessary to their sex.

When you see WAVES lying under Link Trainers with oil cans, or handling welding tools in a machinists' training course, you cannot help thinking of those unhappy "tomboys" of the immediate past who often went down to defeat in their private lives because society offered them no outlet for their natural talents. How they might have been inspired to study and work if there had ever been the slightest chance of their using any knowledge they might have picked up of astronomy, meteorology, or simple blueprint reading and practical mathematics!

Not that talents once considered "unwomanly" are the only ones of use to potential members of the Women's Reserve. More typically feminine abilities turn up in new and startling company. To

The first WAVES to qualify as instructors on electrically operated .50-cal. machine-gun turrets hand along their knowledge at the Naval Air Gunners School, Hollywood, Florida. Draped with belts of .50-cal. ammunition, Florence Johnson, Specialist 3/c, and Rosamund Small, Specialist 3/c, walk out to the target range, April 11, 1944. *Courtesy National Archives*

be a parachute rigger, for instance, you need not only manual dexterity (a phrase that appears often in the outline of qualifications), but it is desirable to have experience in fabric work, tailoring, or home sewing. Some of the enlisted women of the Naval Reserve who are taking over the responsible job of parachute rigging at Lakehurst, New Jersey, learned the necessary lightness and sureness of touch as hairdressers in civilian life. Although the Women's Reserve is interested in girls who have operated a "ham" short-wave radio set, or tinkered with rebuilding an old car, it is equally interested in girls who can cook and sew. There is a Specialist rating given to women of the Reserve who are especially qualified for housekeeping. The rating carries with it the designation of U, for Utility, and seamen who are assigned to housekeeping and mess duties may be designated as Seamen U if they show special aptitudes. So Charlotte Bronte's pudding makers need not confine their domestic talents to the home unless they wish to.

The Navy wants all girls who can do things, and who are willing to turn their aptitudes—large and small—to their country's service. The list of occupations open to women of Class V-10, as the enlisted women's group is called, when set out alphabetically in a long vertical row, challenges even the most feminist mind:

Accountants
Aerographers' mates (work with weather instruments)
Aviation machinists' mates (service and repair of engines)
Aviation metalsmiths
Bakers
Bookkeepers
Business machine operators
Chauffeurs
Cooks
Duplicating machine operators
Escort girls
File system clerks
Freight clerks
Information aides
Land line supervisors
Librarians
Line assistants (assisting at ground work in takeoff of planes,
    signaling, clearing fields, etc.)
Link Trainer operators (teaching blind flying)

Mail room clerks
Messengers
Office clerks
Pharmacists' mates (assistants to Medical Corps. Requires
    training in advanced first aid and home nursing)
Photographers (includes land and aerial photography; knowl-
    edge of developing, printing, sorting, splicing, assem-
    bling layout desired; experience needed as commercial
    artists, mechanical draftsmen, inkers, opaquers, and
    animated cartoonists)
Physiotherapists
Stewards
Telegraph operators
Telephone operators
Tower workers (stationed at control towers in air stations)
Waitresses
X-ray technicians

As short a time ago as the last war few women had been trained
for specialized fields, though the Navy enrolled in 1917 and 1918
almost 12,000 women as "Yeomanettes." They served for the most
part as clerks, stenographers, typists, and telephone operators—
which is the kind of work "yeomen" do in the Navy. Probably [Sec-
retary of the Navy] Josephus Daniels is directly responsible for the
creation of the WAVES in 1942, since it was he who asked in the
critical spring of 1917, when the Navy was desperately in need of
extra clerical assistance at shore stations: "Is there any law that
says a yeoman must be a man?" The law, he was told, did not specify
males, and the way was thus left open for the hiring of females,
which Secretary Daniels at once proceeded to do.

By the war's end these women were doing most of the immense
amount of clerical work in the Navy Department, besides acting as
translators, draftsmen, fingerprint experts, camouflage designers,
and recruiting agents. Five women even went overseas with the
Bureau of Medicine and Surgery to serve in hospital units in France.
One female actually served in an office of Naval Intelligence in
Puerto Rico.

Today the story is very different. Many women are being trusted
to act as cryptanalysts, signal workers, transmitters and receivers
of messages in code, packers and repairers of parachutes; to help
pilots to learn instrument flying with the aid of the Link Trainer,

and so on through the long list of highly technical and special assignments

The Navy, however, has laid down certain rules and qualifications for any young woman who wishes to join the WAVES and be entrusted with this responsible work. An applicant in Class V-10 must be at least twenty and not over thirty-six years of age. If unmarried when appointed, she must promise not to marry until her indoctrination and training periods are completed. She must have a good local reputation; she must be a graduate of a high school or a business school, or have taken business courses, which, in addition to practical business experience, could be considered the equivalent of a high-school education.

She must be at least five feet tall and weigh at least ninety-five pounds. She must be able to distinguish whispered words at fifteen feet, and her vision, if faulty, must be correctable with glasses to 20/20, which is to say that she must be able to read at twelve feet what perfect eyes can read at twenty.

Then she has to pass what are known as Aptitude Tests, to rate her general intelligence and give the Navy some idea of the kind of work for which she is fitted. If the applicant passes these tests and possesses the other qualifications, she is sworn in and ordered to active duty. The government then, at its own expense, sends her to one of the many training schools which now dot the country. She gets her general indoctrination at "boot" school (boot is the Navy word for "rookie") at Hunter College in New York City. If she is to be a yeoman she may be sent to Oklahoma Agricultural and Mechanical College at Stillwater, to the Georgia State College at Milledgeville, or to the Iowa State Teachers College at Cedar Falls. If she is to specialize as an aviation metalsmith she goes to Norman, Oklahoma, or to Memphis, Tennessee. Machinists' mates train in Norman also; storekeepers learn to keep stores at the University of Indiana; the Link Trainer School and the Control Tower School are both in Atlanta, Georgia. Parachute riggers and aerographers' mates receive technical instruction at Lakehurst, New Jersey. Medical training for future specialists is given at the Naval Hospitals in Bethesda, Maryland, and San Diego, California. In Detroit WAVES are learning some things about gunnery.

College graduates who aim at wearing those light blue stripes near the cuff, which stand for ensign or lieutenant in the Women's Reserve, go for their training to Smith College at Northampton, or to Mount Holyoke at South Hadley, only a few miles away. Entering as apprentice seamen, they become Reserve midshipmen at the end of a month, drawing pay equal to that of Annapolis midshipmen. At the end of two months some are commissioned and go forth to their jobs "anywhere in the shore establishment of the Navy, but not beyond the continental limits." Some remain for additional training in communications or other specialized work. A small percentage of highly trained women in given fields are granted probationary commissions before coming to Smith, and remain there only for the indoctrination period—that is, long enough to learn the basic facts about Navy organization, history, and personnel.

The daily time schedule for a group in training at boot camp or school follows a strict military routine. This routine completely fills a day that begins at 6:15 A.M. and ends at 10:00 P.M. with lights out, and no fooling! The schedule, with the time in Navy style, progresses around the clock French fashion, with no such nonsense as the hour after twelve noon becoming, irrationally enough, one o'clock instead of thirteen.

0615	Reveille
0645	Breakfast
0710–0745	Police rooms
0750	Form and march to recitation
0800–0850	First recitation period
0900–0950	Second recitation period
	Inspection of rooms in quarters
1000	Drill formation
1000–1030	Drill
1030–1200	Physical education and athletics
1200–1230	Lunch
1300–1450	Study period
1450	Form and march to recitation
1500–1550	Third recitation period
1600–1650	Fourth recitation period
1700–1745	Recreation
1745–1830	Dinner
1845–1930	Study period
1945–2050	Evening lecture, educational films, discussion period
2200	Taps

This is a brisk schedule and one that requires discipline. But thousands of modern women accept it.

Judging from statistics, few of the women and girls of the WAVES were suffering from ennui or boredom at the time they entered the service. Any study of the application papers of those training to be officers reveals an amazing range of activities in which they were employed in civilian life: anthropology, archaeology, geology, meteorology, social service, interior decoration, deanship in women's colleges, psychology, personnel work in department stores, electrical engineering, designing, teaching, library work.

There has been, inevitably, a certain element of escapism operating to swell the ranks of female volunteers, just as a percentage of male enlistment grew out of dissatisfaction with the narrowing circumstances of civilian life and the prospect of a familiar routine and environment stretching dully down the years. But many women have joined the WAVES because they want to be occupied in some patriotic activity while their men are away at war. Already among the WAVES are the widows, fiancées, and sisters of men who have lost their lives in the present conflict. Among these is the sister of the famous five Sullivan brothers who joined up together, trained together, and lost their lives together on the *Juneau*. The number of women who enter the service to take the place of a man reported missing or lost in action is bound to increase as the war goes on.

Some of the proudest of all WAVES are those whose mothers were Yeomanettes in the last war and who are carrying on a family tradition in the female line. A pretty, slender, and popular yellow-haired girl working in "communications" at Jacksonville, Florida, can boast of a Yeomanette mother and a father who was a sergeant in the last war. Training at Madison for radio work was also the daughter of a chief petty officer in the Yeomanettes of the last war, and another whose mother was an officer Army nurse. There are many daughters of Navy men who have offered themselves to their fathers' branch of the service out of a mixture of motives, some sound, some sentimental. . . .

The usefulness of the WAVES is daily becoming an accepted fact to the men of the Navy. There is no longer any doubt about it, the women of the Naval Reserve are doing a good job. If the on-looker—watching the girls in blue swinging so jauntily down the street—could know the story of their lives thus far, and the factors that have brought them to join the WAVES, he would have both a good picture and a good opinion of a great cross-section of American women in the 1940s.

6   Three Years Behind the Mast

Mary C. Lyne and Kay Arthur

*A wide variety of uniforms were proudly worn by women em-
ployed in military, quasi-military, and civilian jobs during World
War II. Indeed, the opportunity for women to don war-related
uniforms was abundant. However, the public often found it difficult to distinguish among the uniforms of the various service
branches. This was especially true for SPARs, who were often
mistaken for WAVES. The following excerpt, by former SPARs
Mary C. Lyne and Kay Arthur, describes the baffled responses
of civilians when they encountered SPARs.*

W E TRIED TO BE UNDERSTANDING, tried to tell ourselves that we
were once civilians too. But it didn't help. Civilians were
strange creatures who couldn't even tell the difference between a
WAVE and a SPAR. In fact, it seemed to us that civilians took a
keen, secret pleasure in remaining ignorant of the differences between uniforms, dismissing the whole subject with a simple, "I just
can't tell them apart!"

With many inward groans we would explain that although our
uniforms were basically the same as the WAVES, we were *not*
WAVES, nor WACs, nor nurses, nor yet WASPs or lady Marines.
We also grew accustomed to being addressed as "You Girls."

"How do You Girls like being in the service?"

"What do You Girls do all day long?"

"Don't You Girls get tired of wearing the same thing every day?"

"What do You Girls do in your spare time—march?—play
volleyball?"

By far the majority of civilians seemed to assume that we must
have been leading miserably dull lives before, or we never would
have plunged into uniform. At some time or other all of us were
cornered by at least one who asked in a give-me-the-lowdown tone
of voice, "Why did you join the service?" (Implying: "I don't understand it. You seem like such a nice girl, too.")

From Mary C. Lyne and Kay Arthur, *Three Years Behind the Mast: The Story
of the United States Coast Guard SPARs* ([Washington, DC]: n.p., [1946]), 77–
83.

Courtesy National Archives

To look the inquisitor squarely in the eye and answer, "Because in this emergency the government of the United States sent out an urgent call for all able-bodied women to volunteer" would have sounded like an insufficient reason. Nothing short of a job in an opium den, a wicked stepmother in our home, or an unhappy affair with [actor] Charles Boyer could satisfy these questioners about our motives for volunteering.

On the other hand, we sometimes ran into bus drivers who wouldn't take our nickels, shopkeepers who wanted to give us all the merchandise on their shelves because "you're in uniform and my son is over there," old ladies who pled with us to take their seats on the subway because "you're doing so much." Homo Civilian was a peculiar, unpredictable human animal.

In Salt Lake City a SPAR met one of them, a woman, who seized her by the Mainbocher [couturier who designed the SPAR uniform] lapels and cried, "You sent my son away!"

"Me?" the SPAR asked faintly.

"Yes, *you*. You released my son and sent him away."

The SPAR, a kindly, sympathetic girl who just happened to be between the ages of 20 and 36, tried to comfort the irate mother. She expressed hope that the son would be coming home soon. She explained that by joining the service she was undoubtedly helping to bring him home.

But the woman, unmoved, continued her reproaches.

"I won't see him for months and months now," she moaned, "and it's your fault."

The SPAR, envisioning a remote South Sea island, asked fearfully, "Where was he sent?"

"*IDAHO*," wailed the mother.

If our uniform baffled the public on sunny days, on rainy days they were mystified. That controversial object, the havelock, occasioned such comment as, "Look, Halloween!" or "What's the Foreign Legion doing around here?" or "Pardon me, Sister, do you mind if I smoke?" Had we carried pink parasols or sported sou'westers we should probably have passed unnoticed in the crowd. In our simple blue drapes we felt like Mata Hari between two flags.

Once explained, however, the havelock became greatly admired by civilians for its practicality if not its glamour.

"Very sensible idea," a deaf and rain-soaked old man once shouted to a SPAR on the subway, "it won't be long before everyone will be wearing those hassocks on their heads!"

We had to face it. To civilians we were figures of fun wherever we went. We grew accustomed gradually on streetcars, buses, and trains to the frank stares, the furtive scrutiny, even the smiles and giggles. Just walking down the street in our conservative navy blue, we were about as inconspicuous as a brass band.

We seemed to bring out a certain coyness in many civilians which was merely embarrassing to us at the beginning, but grew acutely boring as the years wore on. One classification of the plain-clothes gang tickled themselves pink shouting "Hup, hup" as we walked past, trying to keep out of step. Members of another group liked to yell, "Ahoy, mate!" from cars and trucks, or murmur, "Hello, Wavie" insinuatingly when they were closer at hand. It was all in the spirit of good clean fun, we knew, but somehow we resented having the uniform we honored the object of such humorous sallies. And if there was one thing we had never thoroughly appreciated before we joined the service, it was the joy of being inconspicuous.

On days when our spirits were high, we could even bear being mistaken for Persian WRENS [Women's Royal Naval Service, or WRNS]. But on bad days, sometimes a stray remark would be the last straw. One SPAR admits that she still feels guilty about the time a little five-year-old girl, walking along with her mother, simply said, "Oh, look, Mamma, a WAVE!" The SPAR, who had spent the entire day explaining that she wasn't a WAVE, turned fiercely on the poor little thing and yelled, "Oh, *shut up!*"

Doubtless misled by recruiting posters describing "the fresh-faced girl in the trim navy blue with her jaunty hat," civilians expected us at all times to maintain an attitude of cheerful briskness. This role was often exceedingly difficult. Yet we could not permit ourselves the luxury of sagging in public—even if we had been up since 0600, had put in a hard day at the salt mines, and had drawn the duty for that night. Normal expressions of fatigue were usually interpreted by civilians as signs of frustration, boredom, or dislike of regimentation. "The only thing I have against women in uniform," we often overheard, "is that they go around with such frozen faces!"

We were all quite aware of the fact that civilians reasoned about us from the particular to the general. We were constantly under surveillance by the public eye. Should one of our number have too much beer, ergo—"All SPARs are drunkards." Should one misfit express publicly dislike for her job, ergo—"All SPARs hate the service." SPARs as a group were judged, appraised, and compared with the other women's reserves as groups. When our white gloves and hat covers were dazzling and we were on our best behavior, we proclaimed loudly that we were SPARs, do you hear, *SPARs!* If anything went wrong, we consoled ourselves with the thought, of which only we could appreciate the irony, "Oh, well, they probably don't know what we are anyway."

Even members of our beloved families began to behave queerly—like civilians! Mamma's little baby had to explain many a time why she couldn't "just tell that old commander that Tuesday night would be *very* inconvenient." One officer was the recipient of regular letters from her father exhorting her to work extra hard and "get ahead," so that she wouldn't have to remain an ensign for the duration. In one letter he enclosed a picture of Captain [Dorothy] Stratton [the first director of the SPARs] with the attached note: "Now, she seems to have made the grade—*why not you?*"

We were lucky if we had families and friends who appreciated our craving for frothy lingerie, perfume, and elaborate cosmetics. But many of us were the victims of those "Presents for the Service Girl" signs in department stores at Christmas—and had to coo, "Just what I always wanted" over a shoeshine or first-aid kit! One SPAR was even given a pup tent by her little brother, and several others had to beam over nautical instruments.

The admiration of civilians, particularly our families, was dear to our hearts. She was the rarest SPAR of all who didn't think up some excuse to have her picture taken as soon as she found a SPAR hat and uniform approximately her size! We couldn't help preening and purring at the little remark we heard so often: "Your uniform is certainly the best-looking one."

On leave we descended on our homes like rockets from Mars. We were no longer the same girls who had gone away. Whether we had trained at Palm Beach, Florida, or Stillwater, Oklahoma, whether we had sailed on salt water or merely gargled it, to the old folks and the neighbors we were now—sailors.

Usually the explanation that we ourselves were not going in for active duty afloat but were releasing the men for sea duty was sufficient. But sometimes our families were hard to persuade, as in the case of the SPAR whose account of her trials is quoted in part.

"When I visited my sister Shirley on leave, after six months in the SPARs, all I had in mind was catching up on sleep, playing a little badminton, and getting a suntan. The report that I set their house afloat and made my brother-in-law walk the plank has caused considerable misunderstanding. It is high time to set forth the facts.

"When I arrived, Shirley said, 'Ahoy, mate!' and gazed disapprovingly at my suitcase. 'I thought you'd have a seabag.' (It was salty, coming from someone whose seafaring experience consisted of a ferryboat ride from Oakland to San Francisco.)

" 'Your sister,' said my brother-in-law, Leonard, 'is doing her best to make you feel at home.'

"He waved a hand toward the mantel, on which was a model of a clipper ship and a clock which looked like a ship's helm. It struck eight times in bell-like tones.

" 'Eight bells,' said Leonard dryly, 'or in my landlubber parlance four P.M. Looks like we've shoved off on a long cruise. And I've a feeling that when I get the bills I'll be seasick.'

"He carried my suitcase upstairs, and then departed for his workshop in the basement, where he builds furniture as a hobby. My sister lingered while I unpacked.

" 'Your lingerie!' she exclaimed. 'It's just the same!'

"I laughed. 'What did you expect?'

" 'I thought it would be labeled "U.S. Coast Guard" and have anchors. Isn't everything you wear G.I.?'

" 'Everything that shows,' I said, changing from my uniform to white sharkskin slacks.

" 'You look just like a civilian, dear.' My sister looked disappointed. 'What will the neighbors think?'

" 'I don't care what they think,' I retorted cheerfully. 'I'm on leave and I'm going to relax.'

"She sighed. I went out to the front yard to cut roses. I was still there when my nine-year-old nephew, Tony, came home from a game of sandlot baseball. His 'Hi!' was warmingly welcoming, then his grin faded.

" 'Gosh,' he said accusingly, 'nobody would know you've been to war. You look the same. That's just like a girl!'

" 'Well,' I said defensively, 'I am a girl.'

"I snipped roses in silence, dimly aware of a figure in khaki walking past on the sidewalk.

" 'That's the captain,' Tony said. 'He's visiting at Buddy Mason's house. He flew a bomber in Italy.' His tone was admiring and touched with awe. 'Aren't you going to salute him?'

"I felt guilty. 'We don't salute unless we're in uniform.'

"Tony gave me a disillusioned look, turned on his heel, and went into the house.

"My duty was clear. I went into the house and put on my uniform.

"When I came downstairs I encountered Tony sprawled on the floor reading the comics.

" 'Would you mind going topside for me?' I asked. 'I left some gear on my bunk, and my handkerchief is in the head. Don't slip on the ladder. That new varnish is slick.'

"He looked at me blankly. 'We call the bathroom the head,' I explained, 'and the stairs a ladder.'

"Then Tony looked at me with new respect. 'Sure—I mean, aye, aye, sir!' He flew up the stairs before I could have said 'shiver my timbers,' if ever I said shiver my timbers.

"There is such a thing as the armed forces letting down the people on the home front."

Men, all men, regarded as one great big awkward group, protested longly and loudly that they didn't care for "women in uniform." We knew that, and didn't expect them to care for us collectively. What man cares for women as a group anyway? Individual men cared for individual women in uniform, and that was all that mattered to us.

Men's prejudice often took the form of what in civilian life would be called slander. Attacks upon the morals of SPARs were common, and where there was little basis in fact for the charges, tales were invented and improved upon in the telling. Others, less aggravated and more literate cases, blew off steam by drafting letters to magazines and newspapers, secure in their knowledge that the general public, all too suspicious of any innovation, would applaud. Either we had to grin and bear it or fall into the trap of becoming embittered ourselves.

Actually, some of the men who yelled the loudest fell the hardest. True, many of them let us struggle with our own suitcases, and, resenting our intrusion into their world, often took delight in making us feel uncomfortable in many small ways. But, sooner or later, when it got down to the individuals, it was Boy meets Girl—uniform or no uniform. One by one they came around.

In spite of themselves, servicemen turned to us because they knew they would find sympathetic shell-pink ears beneath the Coast Guard blue brims. They might have thought it unromantic, but they were all full of the service and liked to talk about it. They didn't have to explain ratings, restrictions, liberty, duty nights, or extra watches to *us*—we knew. We shared their gripes with them, and when dances or service functions came up, somehow there was never any lack of uniformed men to attend them.

As far as the dates were concerned, blue braid was a distinct handicap, as all SPAR officers realized. The Braid's common lament is summed up in the following revealing verses:

R.H.I.P (Rank Has Its Privileges)
or
Lament of a Woman Officer

The streets of the city are crowded
With sailors so manly and cute,

I walk out expecting a whistle
And get—a snappy salute.
I date the plump, stuffy Major
And stifle my envious sighs
While my yeoman steps out with a bos'n
Who has passionate Boyer eyes.
While waltzing, I gaze most sedately
At my silver-haired three-striper date
And long to be tagged for a rhumba
By that handsome machinist's mate.
And so I dine with the Captain,
Or chat with the Colonel—alas,
And yearn to exchange my "privilege"
For fun as a seaman first class.

                    —Dorothy E. Bunyan, Lt., U.S.C.G.R.(W)

A high-ranking woman officer, one of the group sent to Hawaii to survey the situation before the enlisted girls were assigned, tells this story on herself. From the second she set foot on the island she was given a big rush by nearly every man in the place, constantly wined and dined and covered by leis. One evening, she tells us, when she was dancing to smooth music with a handsome officer, she was jerked abruptly out of seventh heaven by his ecstatic murmur in her ear: "If you're this good, *what*'ll the young ones be?"

It might have been expected that civilian men, especially 4-Fs [those classified as unfit for military service], would resent us. No doubt many of them did. But quite often they actually seemed to be fascinated by the fact that we were living a life so different from theirs and to feel that when dining or dancing with us they were more closely identified with the war effort.

After the war's end, new veterans often sought our company. They wanted to talk about their own experiences in the service, and the sight of our uniforms seemed to fill them with nostalgia. We had already noticed that veterans of the first world war invariably cottoned up to us. They would seize any slight opportunity to engage us in conversation, and they were always willing to treat us to food and drink if in return we didn't wince at the familiar opening: "Too old this time. Tried to get back in, told they couldn't use me. But listen, sailor girl, in the last war we . . ." On subways, buses, trains, and streetcars we noticed that when the men wore discharge pins they also wore an eager, wistful expression when they looked at us. Gone was the blank, hard, or sassy expression of former days. A small triumph, but our own!

Even after V-J Day we were quite often taken for WACs. And by that time if someone asked if we were WAVES, we almost answered in the affirmative. A tendency on the part of the public after V-J Day was to imagine that we had all served overseas in wild, desolate, and dangerous places. To disabuse civilians of this idea took diplomacy.

Riding on a bus one day, a SPAR got into conversation with the woman sitting next to her. After telling her seat companion about her two sons who had been fighting in the Pacific for several years, the voluble mother asked the SPAR where she had been stationed.

"Oh," the SPAR replied modestly, "I've been right here in New York all during the war."

The woman turned on her. "Shame on you!" she said.

Perhaps, after all, we and not civilians were the ones to be regarded as curiosities. But after our thorough indoctrination into a new way of life, we lost our perspective for awhile, forgot for the time being that actually we were a comparatively small, unique group. We learned how slowly new ideas trickle down into the public consciousness, for we were a new idea to America. Yet, when all is said and done, America finally responded with vigor to the phenomenon of women in uniform—even to the point of imagining tenderly that we had all been stationed either in jungle bivouacs or the tails of B-29s.

When the great histories of this war are written, historians will not overlook the part we played—but they'd better not call us WAVES or we'll sic our grandchildren on them!

7 Shakedown Cruise

E. Louise Stewart

The Marines were the last of the service branches to admit women. Indeed, their antipathy toward women in the military was quite strong, and, according to the standard work on the history of the Marines, "there was considerable unhappiness about making the Corps anything but a club for white men." Yet, following the admittance of women early in 1943, the

From Lieutenant E. Louise Stewart, "Shakedown Cruise," *Marine Corps Gazette* (May–June 1943): 36–38. Reprinted by permission of the *Marine Corps Gazette*.

commandant of the Marine Corps, General Thomas Holcomb, remarked, "There's hardly any work at our Marine stations women can't do as well as men. They do some work far better than men. What is more, they're real Marines. . . . They get their basic training in a Marine atmosphere, at a Marine post. They inherit the traditions of the Marines. They are Marines."

In February 1943, Lieutenant E. Louise Stewart joined Major Ruth Cheney Streeter, director of the Marine Corps Women's Reserve, on the first nationwide recruiting drive. Stewart proudly reported on this trip in "Shakedown Cruise," published in the Marine Corps Gazette. *A "shakedown cruise" is the first cruise for a vessel when it goes into commission or comes from the Navy yard after an overhaul. Its purpose is to troubleshoot problems. As Stewart remarks in her article, "Somewhere on the trip something happened to us. . . . We weren't women in uniform anymore. We were Marines."*

O N THE NIGHT OF FEBRUARY 18TH at exactly 2340—service time— a small band of Marines set out from New York's Pennsylvania Station. There were three of us, neatly labeled "Major Ruth Cheney Streeter's party," consisting of the Major, Director of the Marine Corps Women's Reserve, Captain Ward W. Hubbard, Public Relations Officer and self-termed "accompanist," and myself— another P.R.O. and acting aide to Major Streeter.

We were an advance guard in every sense of the word, sent out to soften up the public for the newly organized "lady Marines," to see for ourselves how and where men Marines live, work, and train, and to investigate the work, quarters, and reception in store for our women in uniform.

Technically we ourselves were Marines. Our newly inked commissions—two of the first four given women in the history of the Corps—announced as much, referring both to Major Streeter and me as "he," "him," or "his." We wore the traditional forestry green uniform with pointed cuffs and curved back seams. We boasted the traditional globe and anchor ornaments. And in our suitcases we carried the traditional *First Sergeant's Handbook*. But we were untraditionally unindoctrinated.

It is a great honor to be the first of anything—especially something as important as the Women's Reserve expects to be. But it's also a source of gray hairs. There we were, claiming that women of the Corps would be well trained in military rules and courtesies, when we ourselves were so recently civilians that we didn't even know who should get in and out of cars first. But the Marines we were to meet would expect us to know. It was like tossing raw recruits into the first wave of an invasion force. And—we admit it—we were nervous (no more nervous, we discovered later, than the Marines were about meeting *us*).

Fortunately the first part of our trip was devoted to publicity and recruiting, often in cities where Marine green was a strange sight. In Pittsburgh the entire town was turned over to us. Not only did Major Streeter receive the key to the city, but February 19th was designated by the Mayor's proclamation as "Marine Corps Day." Flags were flown on all public buildings, our pictures were in all the newspapers, and at 8:25 A.M. we were greeted at the [train] station by the president of the women's clubs, twenty uniformed representatives of service organizations, a movie star, reporters, and the recruiting officer with eight sideboys.

We were whisked—with motorcycle escort—to the William Penn Hotel, where we breakfasted with 75 people and where Major Streeter spoke a few words. After breakfast there was a press conference, a radio broadcast, and a very successful Victory Luncheon at the Duquesne Club, where Major Streeter spoke a few more words, this time to about 200. After lunch came another broadcast, and a speech and reception at the University of Pittsburgh, with a quick visit to the Officer Procurement Office tucked in between. From 5:45 to 6:15 we "rested." A dinner at the Twentieth Century Club preceded the main event, "Free a Man to Fight Night" at the William Penn, where nearly a thousand young business women were entertained from eight to eleven P.M. by an orchestra, movie stars, and variety acts. The evening reached its climax when Major Streeter swore in thirty-three enlistees of outstandingly high caliber. Then, Cinderella-like, and still with motorcycle escort and farewell committee, we were whisked back to the train, already held up for ten minutes.

By the time we left Pittsburgh, Pittsburgh was aware of the Marine women's uniform. And fully 50 percent of the women in that uniform (the Major and I) were aware of why Marines have to be tough.

Everywhere we went—Chicago, Omaha, Denver, and Seattle—our reception was the same. Everywhere we were greeted with enthusiasm and kindness, never for ourselves—they knew little about us—always because we bore the name and insignia of the Marines, because the Marines themselves had made us a part of their Corps. Traveling with civilians, seeing their pride in our name, we began to develop the well-known Marine *esprit de corps.*

Not everyone, of course, knew who we were. People on trains stared at us, asked questions, settled bets about us. We were called everything: WAACs, WAVES, SPARs, and Western Union messengers. But the Marines knew what we were. We spoke to all of them, naturally. We wanted their opinions, we wanted them to like us, we wanted them to be glad that we were going to take over their home work. One Corporal I chatted with hit the nail on the head. Wounded at Guadalcanal, then on his way home from the hospital, he said, "Well, I'll tell you. I was kinda sore about it at first. Then it began to make sense—though only if the girls are gonna be tops, understand."

His friend, a Sergeant, broke in. "Hell," he said, "they're gonna be Marines, aren't they? They gotta be tops!"

"Then you don't mind that we're called Marines?" I asked. "Wouldn't you rather have us called something like WAMS?"

"Sir, uh, Ma'am, uh, Lieutenant," said the Corporal, "if you'd been called WAMS we'd have never spoken to you."

About that time Marine fever really struck us. Every time we spotted a forest green uniform on the street we'd say, "Look, there's a Marine." We read our handbooks, practiced saluting, and plied Captain Hubbard with questions.

In San Francisco we also had our first chance to meet officers who would one day command women Marines. Major General William P. Upshur invited all commanding officers from the surrounding territory to a meeting in his office, where Major Streeter told them something about the work and training plans for the young women. After her talk the officers discussed their problems and ideas with Lieutenant Colonel John B. Hill, executive officer of the Division of Reserves, who had traveled ahead of us across the country.

In San Francisco we had our first chance to meet a large group of officers' wives—at a luncheon given by Mrs. Upshur. They told us a lot of things about the Corps we never knew before, and most of them had the same feeling of "belonging" that we had. We decided it must be catching.

San Diego opened the second phase of our trip. For the first time we were to meet Marines in their own backyard. Brigadier General Underhill took us on a tour of the Marine base, Major General Holland Smith and Brigadier General Kingman arranged for us to see Camp Elliott, and Major General Fegan escorted us around Camp Pendleton. We visited classes indoors and out. We tried our skill on the rifle range, we jumped from the parachute tower, flew with paratroopers making their first jump, rode in Jeeps, tanks, and anything else around. We got plenty dirty, and we loved it. This was what the men we were to replace would do. It was visual proof that the job for women would be an important one. Everything looked exciting to us, but we knew it wasn't exciting to the men. To them it was hard work—and the difference between life and death on some battlefield.

By this time Captain Lillian O'Malley Daly had joined us. A Marinette in the last war, she had been newly commissioned and assigned to Camp Pendleton. One morning Captain Daly and I said goodbye to friends on a troopship. It was early morning, the ship was crowded, the docks empty, and the stillness eerie. We walked to the single gangplank in silence. We knew that the men aboard ship had talked for months about seeing action. We knew that they wanted to go, and that this was what they had been trained for. But that last minute before sailing seemed very empty and lonely, and we couldn't help feeling depressed.

We found our friends, gave them a few odds and ends, and wished we could have brought something better. "Forget it," they told us, not sharing our depression. "We've got everything." "Yes, Ma'am," a voice called down from the main deck, "we've sure got everything!"

We felt better then. There's not much you can do to beat people like that.

In Los Angeles we switched back to our old routine with radio broadcasts, press conferences, and speeches. We visited a great many colleges where we told the young women about the Women's Reserve. But now we had something more to speak of than requirements for admission and details of training. We told them about our experiences. We explained that their hours would be long, their work hard and sometimes boring. We didn't try to paint a picture of glamour and a fancy uniform. But we did point out that we didn't know of a bigger job than to "free a Marine to fight."

After touring Texas, Louisiana, Florida, and Georgia—all sold solid on the Marine Corps—we went to Camp Lejeune and saw more Marines in training. Plans were discussed for women's barracks and schools, and Major General Julian Smith arranged to have

A member of the U.S. Marine Corps Women's Reserve, trained for duty to re-place a male member of the Corps for combat action, transmits a final weather report to a pilot before he prepares to take off from a Marine air base in the United States, July 15, 1943. *Courtesy National Archives*

us all taken out in amphibious tractors and landing boats, from which we climbed to the nets on the mock-ups. Camp Lejeune surprised us. We flew in, landed at Peterfield Point, and went by Tent City which looked the way we had expected the entire camp to look.

The red brick buildings and green lawns were a great and pleasant surprise.

It was hard to come back to Washington after being with the men and watching them work. But somewhere on the trip something happened to us. We didn't look any different. We still weren't completely used to military customs. But we weren't women in uniform anymore. We were Marines. We knew other Marines. And we had tried to discover what kind of women they wanted in the Corps—by stacking ourselves beside the men. We got our answer that day the troopship sailed from San Diego. The same day, after the ship pulled out, we went with Mrs. Underhill to visit the San Diego Naval Hospital. A great many Marines from Guadalcanal were there, and we figured they might have heard about us and be interested in what we looked like. We walked up and down the wards, joked with the men, let them try on our hats (they all thought they looked like Hirohito in them), and asked if we could take any messages to their families back east.

The others had seen wounded men before. Personally I had not. I was not curious, though I didn't know quite what to expect. One thing I did expect to feel was pity, and it struck me a little odd at the time that I didn't pity the men once I saw them. We all felt sick inside that they had suffered so much, but they were men, and you don't pity men, even when they're very young and very sick and very gay.

When we left the hospital that day we were angry that Marines had been shoved around as they had been. They weren't a censored number of wounded anymore. They were Marines we'd seen training at the parachute tower, the ones we'd watched qualify on the rifle range, the ones we'd waved goodbye to only a few hours earlier. And we felt with more intensity the purpose of our presence in the Corps.

When you came right down to it, the kind of women the men wanted were the kind the old Sergeant spoke of that day on the train. "Hell," he'd said, "they're gonna be Marines, aren't they? They gotta be tops."

Well, hell, that's how we feel about you too.

III At "Far-Flung" Fronts

Although U.S. women did not actively participate in combat during World War II, their roles as Army and Navy nurses, Red Cross workers, USO entertainers, war correspondents, and WAACs/WACs brought them close to the front lines of battle. In fact, more than two hundred Army and Navy nurses died while serving their country.

Military nurses stationed in Hawaii and the Philippines found themselves caught up in combat during the first waves of the Japanese attacks on American territory. Army nurses landed in North Africa on November 8, 1942, the day of the Allied invasion. On January 27, 1944, five days after troop landings on the Anzio beachhead in Italy, Army nurses went ashore. Four days after the Normandy invasion of June 6, 1944, Army nurses began staffing field and evacuation hospitals in France. Navy nurses stationed on hospital ships cared for the wounded who had been evacuated from the bloody fighting on islands and atolls in the Pacific. During the last months of fighting, specially trained Navy flight nurses landed on airstrips still under fire on Iwo Jima and Okinawa and evacuated critically wounded patients to hospitals on Guam and Hawaii.

Opportunities for African-American Army nurses to serve outside of the United States were limited. Their assignments included caring for German prisoners of war at the 168th Station Hospital in England and working in the Southwest Pacific with the 268th Station Hospital, the only all-black hospital in the U.S. Army.

Red Cross women who served overseas were sometimes stationed close to the front lines, where they drove clubmobiles, staffed Red Cross clubs, and worked in military hospitals. In addition, USO entertainers, "soldiers in greasepaint," provided diversion for embattled troops.

More than 150 American women correspondents filed dispatches from overseas during World War II. These women took tremendous risks in order to obtain exclusive stories. To cite just one example, on D-Day, June 6, 1944, Martha Gellhorn stowed away on one of the first English hospital ships to cross the Channel. On D-Day plus one she talked her way on board a water ambulance and went ashore in France. Her dispatches, published in *Collier's* magazine, reported on the invasion and the difficulties of transporting the wounded from the battlefields. Gellhorn was probably the first American woman on the Normandy beachhead.

WAACs began serving overseas late in 1942. They were employed as clerical workers, switchboard operators, automobile mechanics, and mail clerks. The first five WAAC officers arrived in North Africa on December 22, 1942. The transport ship carrying them was torpedoed one day out of port, and they spent a day in a lifeboat before being rescued by a British destroyer. A month later, enlisted WAAC personnel, "the first American Women's Expeditionary Force in history," landed in North Africa. In fact, WACs served in all of the theaters of war. However, the only African-American WAC unit to serve overseas was the 6888th Central Postal Directory Battalion, assigned to England and France in the spring of 1945.

Initially, WAVES, SPARs, and Women Marines were not permitted to serve outside the continental United States. In 1944, however, Representative Margaret Chase Smith introduced legislation in Congress that would allow Navy women to serve in Alaska, Hawaii, and the Caribbean. When a congressman suggested that they would undergo hardships that no American women should have to endure, Smith tersely replied, "In that case, we'd better bring all the nurses home." The bill was approved, and early in 1945 a few WAVES, SPARs, and Women Marines were assigned to duty in Hawaii and Alaska.

8 Navy Nurse

Page Cooper

In 1946, Page Cooper wrote a book that told the story of Navy nurses during World War II. Making extensive use of firsthand accounts, Navy Nurse *conveyed the spirit that motivated these courageous women. Included here are two excerpts. The first contains an account of the difficult challenges faced by Navy nurses stationed on board the newly refurbished hospital ship, the USS* Solace, *anchored at Pearl Harbor at the time of the Japanese attack in December 1941. The second one describes the dangerous work of Navy flight nurses as they evacuated the wounded from island battlefields in the Pacific.*

SITTING LIKE A SWAN IN A COVEY of dull gray ducks, the Navy hospital ship *Solace* rode at anchor in Pearl Harbor on that infamous Sunday morning. Her white paint glistened, the green band around her hull was as fresh as new grass, her cross as red as Christmas candy. Inside, her instruments, her dental chairs, X-ray machines, laboratory scales, floodlights over the operating tables, shone brightly. She was newly equipped, the first of her kind and the only hospital ship the Navy had commissioned since the end of the first World War. This was the finish of her shakedown cruise, a long one that had taken her down the Atlantic coast, through the [Panama] Canal, and to this first port of the Pacific.

A year earlier almost to the day, Grace Lally, her chief nurse, had first seen her in Brooklyn tied up at a dock in the Atlantic Basin. On a raw December morning she stared up at the dingy gray ship daubed with red lead that made her look as though she had the measles. Inside, the staterooms were stripped of all the cruise ship trimmings she had boasted when she was the S.S. *Iroquois* on the Florida run. Sawdust and steel filings, ripped-out partitions, the bare ribs of the ship sticking through new gashes in the bulkheads made her a skeleton. And Miss Lally wondered if she could ever become a real hospital.

Gradually as the work went on, the new ship began to emerge. In order that she might be at the end of the telephone to assist

From Page Cooper, *Navy Nurse* (New York: McGraw-Hill Co., 1946), 14–24, 167, 174–75.

Captain Jensen, the senior medical officer, Miss Lally was stationed at the Brooklyn Naval Hospital as assistant to Chief Nurse [Frances] Bonner. On bright afternoons the two bundled themselves against the wind and sloshed through the mud and snow to watch the progress. Sometimes Mary Benner, who taught in the corps school, joined them and the three exchanged reminiscences of former tours of duty in Cuba and Panama, the Philippines, Guam, Samoa, China, and, of course, Pearl Harbor. Every Navy nurse who had served overseas had either been stationed at Pearl Harbor or passed through it, staying long enough to enjoy the civilized pastimes of the country club of the Navy. They speculated about the destination of the ship. With the war in Europe involving us more deeply every hour, they guessed the Atlantic.

These three women had packed into their years of service in the Navy the experiences of a dozen lifetimes. Frances Bonner, a tiny, reserved Pennsylvanian, kind, wise, not easily impressed, had joined the Navy in 1915 when the Nurse Corps numbered fewer than a hundred members. Overseas service had taken her across the Pacific to the Philippines, China, Japan, Hawaii. Guam she considered one of the prettiest spots on earth, and Manila—every Navy nurse loved Manila. There was nothing pleasanter than to sit on the *lanai* [porch] of the quarters at Canacao and watch the fleet come in. As the wind tugged at her slight frame she was reminded that it was always summer in the Philippines.

Mary Benner was younger, plumper, brown-haired, brown-eyed, as natural as a hollyhock. She would have liked another tour of duty at Samoa. The Samoans both fascinated and baffled her because she could never be quite sure how much the native girls trained in the Navy hospital actually learned. They were so cleverly imitative, so eager to please, that she suspected they were like children humoring a kind stranger whose ways were curious but did no harm.

Grace Lally, "Tugboat Annie," her friends called her because she had spent so many years afloat, looked upon every new post with lively interest. This handsome gray-haired Irishwoman, as ready with a quip as a smile, had been an Army nurse during the first World War but "after she saw the light" she had joined the Navy Nurse Corps. She had served in the Philippines and had met a taste of war aboard the submarine tender U.S.S. *Canopus* when she sailed up the Yangtze in 1937 to bring out American refugees caught by the Japs, scattering destruction on their way to the China Sea.

The grubby, blistered ship before them could not escape adventure. But wherever she went, these three women knew that she would have the finest equipment which modern science had evolved.

In January, Captain Perlman, the skipper, came aboard and from then until the last surgical instrument was packed, the last barrel of plaster rolled aboard, the work hummed. When the *Solace* was commissioned in August 1941, she carried medical supplies to last a year and provisions for six months, refrigerators full of frozen meat, and Birdseye cabinets with fresh fruits and vegetables, and enough strawberries and raspberries for ice cream every day.

Grace Lally stood in the August midday sun, watched the seven-starred pennant climb the flagpole and listened to Admiral Oman's voice while the electricians worked steadily on the upper deck. She thought to herself that no ship seemed quite finished at the commissioning. Her twelve nurses were aboard and had stowed their books, bathing suits, ukuleles, and evening dresses in the chests of drawers by their berths or in their big footlockers. Proudly they showed the visitors the diet kitchen, the electrically heated chow carts, and the four hundred hospital beds.

"Shall we hang this on the quarterdeck?" Captain Jensen and Grace Lally were discussing the proper place for the letter that the staff of the old *Solace*, one of the famous ships of the first World War, had written to the staff of her successor. This gleaming new ship had a great tradition behind her. Miss Lally imagined that she felt a twinge of pity for the old Navy hospital ship *Comfort* which was sitting not far away in the back channel of the Navy yard, worn out and idle, her once white sides painted yellow.

Soon after this the *Solace* sailed down the coast while the nurses cut bandages, piled up field sheets and sponges against what might be ahead. Two weeks in Norfolk, a month through the Canal, two weeks in Long Beach, then the *Solace* headed into the Pacific. In port she stayed away from the dock. As yet there had been no patients to take to base hospitals so there was no need of tying up at a noisy dock and listening all day to the riveters. Sometimes the crew grumbled because it was inconvenient to get ashore, but Captain Perlman said he had spent three months getting the ship clean and wasn't going to see her fouled up with grime and rats and roaches.

On Navy Day, the twenty-seventh of October, the *Solace* dropped anchor off Ford Island in the midst of the most impressive concentration of warships those aboard had ever seen. For the first time the girls encountered submarine nets, huge barrels dragging enormous chains. At sundown little boats chugged out, pulled them together, and in the morning pushed them back to the open harbor, but there was nothing disturbing about them. Every other afternoon the girls shopped in Honolulu, swam at the beach, wore their prettiest frocks to tea dances at the Moana or the Royal Hawaiian Hotel.

At church call on Sunday mornings the Protestant nurses attended services on deck, looking off to the cloud-crested hills across the water. As there was no Catholic chaplain on board, the Catholics went to services on the other ships, *Oklahoma* or one of the aircraft carriers. On that Sunday of December 7, a chaplain had arranged to hold services on board. Miss Lally was in her cabin waiting for Mass to start. The sharp rattle of a machine gun made her raise her eyes to the window. Something splashed in the water. On the battleship *Nevada* anchored next to the *Solace* the boys were fishing over the side. A plane zoomed down on them, machine-gunning the deck. Miss Lally ran into the wardroom which had windows on three sides and found the paymaster standing at one of them. As though they were looking at a newsreel they saw a dive bomber hit the *Arizona*'s stack. The harbor rocked as the enormous battleship blew up with an explosion that sent ammunition and smoke and splintered boiler plate into the sky; in a moment what was left of her rolled over and sank in a pool of burning oil.

"Japanese!" Miss Lally had seen those red disks on planes over Shanghai. She and the paymaster started headlong to the doorway, Miss Lally to report to the officer on deck.

"Set up the emergency wards," he ordered.

Already the corpsmen were rolling double-decker beds into the officers' lounge and fastening them with stanchions. As she made the rounds and gave her orders, Miss Lally found everybody at battle stations. Her senior nurse was already clearing the wards, and the nurse in the surgery was breaking out supplies of sterile dressings. Most of the nurses were steady although a bit white about the mouth. One of the younger girls stood at a porthole shaking, on the verge of hysteria. Crazily, Miss Lally's mind raced back to the sinking of the *Titanic*. She remembered that as that ship had started to sink, the orchestra had played "Nearer, My God, to Thee."

Shall I sing hymns to the girl or slap her, she wondered. She abandoned both ideas in favor of a hot cup of coffee and noticed as she went on that the nurse had herself in hand.

The *Solace* had lowered her lifeboats before the first flight of Japs had disappeared. Within twenty minutes the casualties began to come aboard from every sort of boat, hoisted up from the small boats to the gangway; there was no time to swing the Stokes stretchers over the side. The doctor at the head of the gangway examined and assigned the casualties, with a nurse beside him writing tags. The men were so caked with black oil and blood that it was difficult to tell the wounded from the whole.

All morning the nurses in the operating rooms sterilized trays of instruments and gave anesthetics while the doctors set fractures, amputated, and probed for shrapnel. In the burn wards the floors were slippery with tannic acid with which the corpsmen drenched dressings. In every ward, nurses and doctors were giving plasma. Everybody wanted to help; the supply officer made the rounds with towels, toothbrushes, toothpaste; the chaplain gave spoonfuls of water to those who would take it; seamen brought pails of fresh water and carted away caked, oil-soaked clothes and reeking dressings. When a second flight of bombers attacked the *Oklahoma* and the *Nevada*, nobody looked up.

Late in the morning Miss Lally went down to the galley to see how the supply of hot coffee was holding out. In the mess room the breakfast dishes were still on the table, unwashed, and the frightened mess attendants huddled in the galley.

"You've got to help," she told them. "We need sandwiches and coffee, plenty of coffee, and it must be hot for every man who comes aboard. And we'll have dinner tonight as usual. It will help to keep up our morale."

The boys began to clear the table. Afterward there was never a lack of sandwiches and strong hot coffee.

Even in the confusion of those first few hours certain of the wounded caught the imagination of the whole ship. One of them was an officer from a battleship, some said the *Nevada*, others the *West Virginia*, who volunteered to go ashore for ammunition. An explosion tossed him from the ship's boat into the harbor, but he managed to swim to the dock. Returning with a load of shells, he was blown into the water again. This time he was picked up unconscious, wounded with shrapnel. The doctors removed the shrapnel, but he had inhaled fumes and lay unconscious; but by a miracle, worked perhaps by everybody's hopes, he pulled through.

Red Cross nurses from Honolulu helped. Ten arrived before noon on that first day and stayed the night, sleeping on cots in the wardroom. By evening the casualties—nearly three hundred—had been cleaned up, given emergency operations, plasma, and put to bed, but it was an uneasy night. Even the patients who had minor injuries went into delirium or shock when the antiaircraft guns sounded. And this in spite of general anesthesia. But the shock of seeing their friends blown to shreds before their eyes left them so stricken that they could not make the effort to recover.

Miss Lally left the operating room before midnight and lay down on her bed for a few minutes in her uniform. She dozed off hearing distant bombing. Presently she shivered, and half-asleep turned off the electric fan. She laughed herself wide awake—the bombing had stopped with the fan.

A few minutes later an alert sounded; she grabbed her life jacket and went into the wardroom. There was no more sleep that night, so she poured hot coffee and opened a can of cookies that her sister had sent from home. They had been so shaken that they were nothing but crumbs, yet they tasted good. "Survey cookies" (not up to the Navy's standard), the chaplain commented as he took another handful. The coffee and cookies had helped so much that Miss Lally ordered the cook to keep them always in the wardroom for alerts.

The doctors and nurses moved about by blued-out flashlights although the *Arizona* was burning like a torch. Occasionally someone went on deck for a breath of air and reported fantastic things in the harbor, conjuring all sorts of objects out of the floating wreckage. Destroyers nosed about on patrol. Occasionally P.T. [patrol torpedo] boats challenged each other. When a submarine alert sounded, a pack of them rushed up, dropping depth charges that went off with a bang and shot up a geyser of spray. On the starboard side the water was covered with huge bubbles as big as a washtub.

"The devils *would* hide under us," grumbled one of the doctors. He and several others circled the *Solace* in a boat, dragging grappling hooks, but they didn't snag a thing.

Every time a light appeared in the harbor someone was sure the Japs had landed on the island. Several nurses remembered advertisements in the Saturday evening paper which might have been communications to the Japanese command: one a decorator's announcement, a picture of an overstuffed chair with the tufts arranged to make a map of the airfields; another a sale of silks with such queer names as "Yippee" and such unusual prices as seventy-five cents a yard. A young doctor topped all these yarns by insisting that the Japs were trying to decode the "Hutsut" song [a popular song (1939) that used supposedly Swedish words]. The doctors and nurses laughed at their own credulity but in their mood nothing seemed incredible, not even the rumor that Admiral [Chester] Nimitz was going to order all the ships to steam out so that he could dynamite the submarines in the harbor. If someone had said that the Japanese Army was marching on Honolulu with bamboo pipes like the chorus of a Gilbert and Sullivan opera, he would have found a believer.

By the next day the routine of the *Solace* had been restored except for alerts. It seemed to the girls that they always had to stop and grab their Mae Wests [life jackets, named for the buxom movie star] at the most inconvenient moment, even though the menace was nothing but "washing-machine Charley," the sailors' name for a Jap solo bomber. The nurses had been battle tested and had settled down to the work they had been trained to do—the patching and healing of human bodies—and, though they did not talk about it as part of their job, the healing of unsettled minds and emotions.

In the nurses' quarters the girls stuck closely to the rule that they had established for themselves: never to talk shop. They didn't want to go stale or emotional lest their patients suffer for it. So, shutting out the chaos and the destruction, they smiled and joked, repeated funny stories, laughed at them even if they weren't funny, powdered their noses, freshened their lipsticks, and carried on. What these men needed most was a sense of security, an assurance of life going on in the ordinary way, so the girls determined that the atmosphere on their wards should not be grim. Within twenty-four hours the *Solace* was a cheerful ship.

The fact that most of the patients were too ill to look out of the windows helped, for the harbor was like a futurist's dream of the Day of Judgment; it was so full of black oil and charred wreckage that it would have been mass murder to drop a lighted match overboard. Not until weeks later did someone think of drawing off the oil by suction and using it on the dirt roads of the island.

Every morning the patrol boats came out with the tide to nose through the floating tennis rackets, cameras, shoes, and picture frames, looking for bodies that might have floated loose from the mud. Miss Lally went out on one of the boats to see the wrecked *Arizona*, hoping fervently no body would come up that day. In the part of the hulk that was above water gaped an enormous hole covered with oil. She and the officers climbed aboard. Near the gun

emplacements were a few helmets, little mounds of ashes, and fragments of bones, mute evidence of the intensity of the heat. One of
the doctors picked up a blackened piece of metal that had been a
chaplain's shoulder cross. An officer climbed on the conning tower
on which nothing remained but a few buttons and the binoculars of
the officer of the day.

It was quiet, so quiet that you could hear your own heart beat.
By a sudden quirk of memory Miss Lally recalled a day in China in
1937 when she had stood in the heart of just such a desolate silence. She and a nurse from the *Canopus* had been exploring the
site of the bombing in Chapai. It was bitter cold, and the odor of the
glue in their hastily purchased fur coats was almost sickening. They
stood shivering in front of an apothecary's shop, the front of which
had been blown in. The other nurse, a veteran souvenir hunter, picked
up from a shelf a fancy cloth-covered box filled with pills that looked
like miniature ping-pong balls. In the corner she saw a stack of thin
china bowls and wanted one, but hesitated to step in this empty
street of death. Finally she ventured to enter on her toes and stretched
out her hand. The pile of bowls toppled over and crashed to the
floor, breaking that dead stillness with a crash that sounded like a
shriek of protest against this desecration of the dead. Miss Lally
held her breath expecting to hear some hideous sound in the harbor,
but there was nothing but the swish-swish of a P.T. boat streaking
back and forth.

As the days wore on, the company aboard the *Solace* grew accustomed to the throbbing of the engines (with the declaration of
war she was ordered to keep up steam) and became such veterans
that instead of cringing when the submarine alarm sounded, they
rushed on deck—all who could get there—to look for the "feather"
[the wake of the periscope moving through the water]. They weren't
even ruffled when the ship moved anchorage one morning, to offer
a less conspicuous target for the Charleys, and they discovered that
the nearest neighbor was an ammunition ship.

By Christmas the patients who lived had improved; their burns
were healing and the dead skin had begun to slough off in patches,
leaving a bright pink underskin. According to the Navy tradition
that a Christmas tree shall adorn the mast of every ship, no matter
where she is, the *Solace* raised hers on Christmas Eve, not much of
a tree but the best that could be found in Honolulu. In addition to
the gifts that the Red Cross brought, the nurses managed a few
extra surprises: an angel food cake for the boy from Ohio with gas

in his lungs—because his mother used to make one every Sunday (there was no angel-cake pan aboard but a paper cup from the dental clinic served well enough to make the hole in the center); and butter-pecan ice cream for the curly-headed runt from Texas whose leg was in traction.

In the new year the boys began to pack up their bomb fragments and bullets, their souvenirs, for a move to the naval hospital ashore, and eventually to a transport for San Francisco. Many of them had no personal belongings, not a wallet or a snapshot or a fountain pen—nothing but the bullets the surgeons had picked out of their flesh, but it didn't matter because they were going home.

By the middle of February the *Solace* was scrubbed and clean inside. She had won her citation—an honor that is usually reserved for individuals—and she was following what was left of the fleet into the South Pacific. But her spotless sides were stained with oil and grime. The proud white lady had become a tramp.

~

San Francisco, the war's glamour city, is not only the port of embarkation for overseas but the home of the Navy Flight Nurse School which ranks even higher among the nurses' preferred services than duty in Pearl Harbor or on a hospital ship. However, the requirements for admission to the school are so arduous and the number so limited that not more than a fifth of the girls who volunteered have been accepted. . . . .

Twenty-three-year-old Jane Kendeigh, "Candy," the boys call her, one of the eight girls of the first graduating class who arrived at Guam [in early 1945], made the first trips to both Iwo Jima and Okinawa. On her flight to Iwo her plane arrived while the Japs were attacking the airfield. As her plane came in she looked down on the American invasion fleet off the island, so many ships that they fairly cluttered up the sea. They were firing at the island, and on the airstrip the antiaircraft was so busy that the pilot circled for an hour and a half before he could land. When the plane was back at sea with the wounded safely aboard, the corpsman asked Candy, "Were you frightened by the firing?" There hadn't been time to think about it at the moment but then she remembered how her knees had quaked and her breath came short.

On Okinawa she landed on Love Day plus six to bring out sixteen stretcher cases and four ambulatory patients, most of them with serious gunshot wounds. When she stepped out of the plane, and the embattled Marines saw the pretty, dark-eyed girl with the flight cap sitting on the back of her curls, they forgot their wounds and whistled. But she wasn't there to be a pinup girl. Her job was to get her wounded aboard and to Guam as quickly as possible. It was necessary to give plasma on the way home but she got her boys to the hospital in good condition.

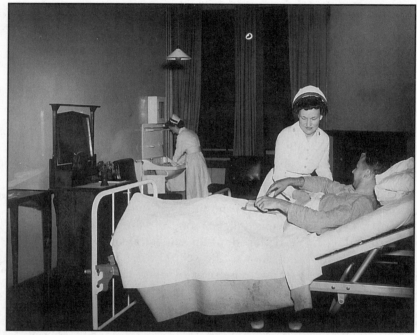

Lieutenant (j.g.) John W. Banzer, Jr., USNR, with Lieutenant (j.g.) Augusta Powell and Ensign Esther Nelson, U.S. Naval Base, Netley, England. *Courtesy National Archives*

That was the first. Now the girls fly in and out of Okinawa and Kwajalein, Guam, Pearl Harbor, and San Francisco on the big, silver, four-engined Douglas land planes that are designed to be the clippers of the future. They have become accustomed to the admiring glances of the passengers in the big Naval Air Training Station at Pearl Harbor and the high dignitaries who come down to see the loading of the planes. The ambulances pull up from the hospitals. One after another they unload while the flight surgeon checks the patients with the physician from the hospital. The corpsmen load them on the platform hoist, two stretchers at a time. The boy on the outside puts up his arm to shield his head, the platform is raised by an electric hoist and slides into the open doors of the plane, missing the sides by not more than an inch.

While the corpsmen lift the stretchers into their strap hangers, three in a tier, the nurse checks her manifest which lists name, rank, injury, what medication the patient has had, what he is to have. The flight surgeon says O.K., the ambulances drive off, the huge plane closes its doors and taxis to the end of the field. She zooms down the runway, the longest in the world, and is off over the sunny hills of Oahu . . . [to] San Francisco.

9   I Served on Bataan

Juanita Redmond

Juanita Redmond, author of I Served on Bataan, *was an Army nurse stationed in the Philippines when the war began. She was one of the last nurses to be evacuated from Corregidor by submarine before the U.S. surrender to the Japanese on May 6, 1942. Some sixty-seven Army nurses and eleven Navy nurses serving in the Philippines were captured and imprisoned at the Santo Tomás and Los Baños internment camps until their liberation in February 1945. In this selection, Redmond describes her last days on Bataan.*

A T TEN O'CLOCK ON EASTER MONDAY the first wave of bombers struck us.

Someone yelled, "Planes overhead!" But those had become such familiar words that most of us paid them little attention. I went on pouring medications, and then the drone of the planes was lost in the shrill crescendo and roar of a crashing bomb.

It landed at the hospital entrance and blew up an ammunition truck that was passing. The concussion threw me to the floor. There was a spattering of shrapnel and pebbles and earth on the tin roof. Then silence for a few minutes.

I heard the corpsmen rushing out with litters, and I pulled myself to my feet. Precious medicines were dripping to the ground from the shattered dressing carts, and I tried to salvage as much as possible.

From Juanita Redmond, *I Served on Bataan* (Philadelphia: J. B. Lippincott Co., 1943), 106–22.

The first casualties came in. The boys in the ammunition truck had been killed, but the two guards at the hospital gate had jumped into their foxholes. By the time they were extricated from the debris that filled up the holes they were both shell-shock cases.

There were plenty of others.

Outside the shed a guard yelled, "They're coming back!"

They were after us, all right.

In the Orthopedic ward nurses and corpsmen began to cut the traction ropes so that the patients could roll out of bed if necessary, broken bones and all. In my ward several of the men became hysterical; I would have joined them if I could. It was all I could do to go on being calm and acting as if everything were all right and I had everything under control.

"Where's Miss Redmond? Is Miss Redmond alive?"

He was being carried out; fortunately, he had rolled out of bed and, though he had been covered with debris, except for a few scratches he was unhurt.

Father Cummins said calmly: "Somebody take over. I'm wounded." He had shrapnel in his shoulder.

Only one small section of my ward remained standing. Part of the roof had been blown into the jungle. There were mangled bodies under the ruins; a blood-stained hand stuck up through a pile of scrap; arms and legs had been ripped off and flung among the rubbish. Some of the mangled torsos were almost impossible to identify. One of the few corpsmen who had survived unhurt climbed a tree to bring down a body blown into the top branches. Blankets, mattresses, pajama tops hung in the shattered trees.

We worked wildly to get to the men who might be buried, still alive, under the mass of wreckage, tearing apart the smashed beds to reach the wounded and the dead. These men were our patients, our responsibility; I think we were all tortured by an instinctive, irrational feeling that we had failed them.

The bombing had stopped, but the air was rent by the awful screams of the new wounded and the dying; trees were still crashing in the jungle, and when one nearby fell on the remaining segment of the tin roof it sounded like shellfire. We were shaking and sick at our stomachs, but none of us who was able to go on dared to stop even for a moment.

I saw Rosemary Hogan being helped from her ward. Blood streamed from her face and her shoulder; she looked ghastly.

"Hogan," I called, "Hogan, is it bad?"

She managed to wave her good arm at me.

"Just a little nosebleed," she said cheerfully. That was Hogan, all right. "How about you?"

"I'm okay."

The corpsmen led her off to Surgery, which luckily was still standing.

Then Rita Palmer was taken from her ward.

Her face and arms had been cut and her skirt and G.I. shirt had been blown off.

I asked a doctor about the other nurses.

"They're all safe," he said.

But there was no time for thankfulness; we were driven by a terrible urgency to save the twice-wounded patients who were still living; to save the medical aids that would keep them alive.

Kitchen utensils from the destroyed mess were strewn over the grounds. From the shattered Receiving ward case records blew about like confetti. The pharmacy had been hit and most of the drugs were gone, but some cabinets were found to be not too badly smashed and there was a swift desperate search for bottles and boxes that could be salvaged. . . .

With the doctors, each of the nurses on ward duty made a survey and a record of the living and the dead from her ward. Several of my boys had died of shock; they hadn't been hit, they had been too weak to live through the explosion.

There had been about sixteen hundred beds, or makeshift beds, in our hospital. Now there were only sixty-five left standing. The nearby camps were sending us help, men, and supplies, trucks and buses and other vehicles since most of ours were destroyed, and we transferred most of the patients to Hospital No. 2, keeping only those too badly injured to move. Rosemary Hogan and Rita Palmer were taken to Corregidor.

Perhaps I am making this sound as if it all took a long time. It didn't; it was all in the same day of the bombing. And the bombers were still strafing us, though never as they had in the morning. We placed as many patients as we dared near, or even in, the foxholes; but there were those whom it was too dangerous to move, and we had to leave them in the beds we had cleaned out in the section of the shed still standing.

The corpsmen tried to make the nurses stay near the foxholes while they cleaned up the grounds and attended to the patients.

"We can run faster than you can," they said.

However, it was impossible to do much work that afternoon. We waited for darkness, and then the entire staff pitched in. We gathered together as many records as we could find and sorted out the wreckage for every scrap of material and supplies that could be salvaged. There were holes to avoid and tin roofing that might collapse at any moment, and we had to work by flashlight. We still uncovered arms and legs and mutilated bodies.

That night there were many burials.

Standing in the jungle clearing that is their Bataan home, these three U.S. Army nurses exemplify the part that medical workers played in Philippine resistance, April 14, 1942. *Courtesy National Archives*

Usually the dead were buried as quickly and quietly and reverently as possible. A grave registration unit was attached to each hospital which attended to all the details and kept the records. We tried not to disturb the other patients in the wards, but the beds were so close that even by moving the deceased patient at night, someone was bound to hear. Night nurses often found that the patient in the next bed had disappeared, especially if he were a Filipino, and was hiding under some other bed. If he stayed in his own bed, he would explain, he would be the next to die.

But this was wholesale burial. We tried not to hear the scraping of the spades or the thud of earth thrown on earth, but we couldn't get away from it. We couldn't be impersonal or detached.

That night we stayed in our foxholes. I didn't sleep. We hadn't eaten since breakfast, but I wasn't hungry. We were like hunted animals, waiting for the kill, almost hoping it would happen quickly so that the torment of waiting would end. But stronger than that was anger: anger and hate and a hot desire to fight back, to avenge our dead.

What kind of human beings would deliberately bomb a hospital, defenseless, openly marked for what it was, filled with the wounded and the sick?

I don't know. The only answer I had found when I crawled out of my hole in the morning, my head aching, a crick in my back, my legs cramped, was not an answer but a conviction. This isn't a war in which anybody—*anybody*—is let off. Each single individual of us is in it and each must give everything he has to give. An enemy that will bomb hospitals and undefended cities—sick and injured men, or women and children and helpless old people—isn't an enemy you can ever come to terms with; not in the usual meaning of the phrase. The war must end without compromise.

It wasn't particularly original thinking, I know, but somehow it comforted me to have it clear and simple in my own mind. I could put the long thoughts of the people I would never see again into the background and go on about my work.

The bombers were aiming at nearby targets all morning, and we gave medications between leaps into the foxholes. I kept running back and forth between my ward and the trench until Alice Zwicker shouted after me:

"Red, for heaven's sake, stop running around out there. They're coming over again. You get back here and put your helmet on."

It was crowded, damp, and dark in the foxhole, but I jumped in obediently as the planes circled over us. Zwick kept saying over and over, "Oh, God, send them away. Oh, God, send them away." Finally they flew off, and instantly Zwick jumped up and shook her fist at them.

"You'd better not come back!" she yelled after them, and followed that warning with an angry stream of very fancy swear words. We all shrieked with laughter, and she turned on us furiously.

"What are you laughing at?" she demanded. "I don't see a damn thing that's funny."

"Do you really want to know?" I said.

"I certainly do. It seems to me you have a queer sense of humor."

I explained, "Just a few minutes ago you were praying so earnestly and then you turn around and in the same breath give the Japs unholy what-for in some of the finest cuss words I ever heard."

She was horrified. "I did no such thing," she said.

"Oh yes, you did."

"But I *didn't*."

"Never mind," said one of the girls soothingly. "If I go first, I'll put in a good word for you."

We managed to get together some sort of meal that day, and slowly, under great handicaps, the hospital began to function again. The dressing carts were far from complete, but we made out with what we had as best we could. We concocted many substitutes, rather proud of our ingenuity, and set the Filipinos' clever hands to work making others, such as applicators, for instance, which they made out of stems stripped from the branch of a tree, and then whittled and smoothed into shape.

We wouldn't have been surprised to hear that the hospital site was to be abandoned, but evidently this was not planned, for carpenters were soon busy tacking oilcloth and black paper over the blasted Surgery windows, and we heard that engineers were to be sent out to help us reestablish the hospital.

But that evening of April 7th at six o'clock heavy artillery shells burst through the jungles around our base. Still unknown to us, Bataan was falling. Fort Drum, Fort Hughes, and Corregidor were firing on Bataan beyond our retreating troops, trying to hold back the Japanese forces.

A little over an hour later, the nurses were ordered to be ready to leave in fifteen minutes. There was a bus provided for us, and Captain Nelson would drive down with us to the docks where we would embark for Corregidor.

There was too much to be done and said in so little time. We wanted to discuss certain details about our patients; we wanted to leave careful instructions for the care of those we were particularly worried about; we wanted to know what was happening, why we were being ordered out. . . .

It hurt to say good-bye. All the doctors and corpsmen were there to see us off, and some of them kept saying it wasn't good-bye; in a few days we'd be back again, but nobody believed them. They said it had been good working with us. They said we'd been brave soldiers.

"We'll be seeing you," they all repeated firmly.

10   G.I. Nightingale

Theresa Archard

Theresa Archard's memoir of her Army nursing career, G.I. Nightingale, is the source for the next selection. As a member of the 48th Surgical Hospital, Archard landed in North Africa on the day of the Allied invasion. She provides a chilling account of what it was like to be part of the invasion convoy as it approached Algeria on November 8, 1942, as well as a description of the trauma experienced by Army nurses as they cared for the wounded on the battlefield near Gafsa, Tunisia, in March 1943.

ALL OF US WERE SPECULATING about where we were going. . . . Rumors flowed thick and fast, and they became more and more fantastic. And then the day came when we were handed leaflets that contained instructions as to how we should conduct ourselves when we reached North Africa. What a stir that news created!

North Africa—of all places. "Why, I didn't even know Africa was civilized," cried one of the nurses. To most of us Africa meant jungles, Livingstone, the Belgian Congo, and Fuzzy-Wuzzies in general. We forgot about Algiers, Tunis, Constantine, and Casablanca.

We were called together . . . and given instructions as to the method of disembarking. Three medical officers, twenty enlisted men, and five nurses were assigned to each group. We were to line up on the decks, and when our numbers were called we were to go have our packs ready, keep the front of our harness open, have our shoes unlaced and our helmets on our heads untied. If we were hit and had to go overboard, we were to slip out of the pack and kick our shoes and helmets off. Then we would have a chance to save ourselves. Incidentally, our life belts were under this regalia, so that the girls who could not swim would be able to stay afloat until help came.

"Do all of you girls swim?"

"I don't," spoke up Gladys Self. Whereupon two enlisted men, good swimmers, were assigned to take care of her.

Without a flicker of an eyelash all this was told to us. Many of us had sinking hearts but pretended we were not afraid. Some said outright that they had a cold feeling in the pit of their stomachs. But it was too late now to do anything about it, and we all decided not to think too much about what was ahead.

It was evening, and we were agog with excitement. We were seeing lights for the first time as we passed Tangiers. To our eyes, accustomed by now to the blackout, the effect was like something out of fairyland. We gazed back at it until we could see no more. . . .

The time was drawing closer. The convoy had been large even when we left Scotland. Now ships stretched as far as the eye could see, and it seemed as if it were all ships and no ocean. We were told we had picked up a convoy that had come straight from the States and that [Air Force General] Jimmy Doolittle and his boys were going to provide an umbrella of planes for us.

"Nothing to worry about now," we told each other. "This will be a pushover for the boys."

We were informed that night that we would disembark the next day. We had almost arrived at our destination. The chaplains told their respective flocks that religious services would be held in the early morning.

There was very little sleep that night—we were all keyed up waiting for what was to happen. Our musette bags [knapsacks] were in readiness. We had three days' supply of food—hash, beans, stew, and coffee, plus three chocolate bars—D and C Rations. How much we were to treasure them in the next few days!

November 8, 1942. Invasion Day! Just before dawn the guns started booming. Explosion followed explosion, and the noise was monstrous. This was it! We were invading North Africa, and each of us wondered what our part would be.

With the coming of daylight we could see ships all around us. A voice blared forth from a loudspeaker, pouring out orders. Commando boats drew up alongside the ships which disgorged their cargo of men, tanks, guns, and equipment. Sergeants barked orders, enlisted men followed each other over the sides of the ships, the gunfire offshore becoming more and more deafening. We were two miles from land. Perhaps because of the formidable noise coming from it, the little town, so peaceful under that blue sky, looked more lovely than it was, the grass greener, the red earth and white stucco buildings reminding us of happier days when ships sailed to such ports in safety. Now the shores were alive with creeping men.

Hours passed, and then it was our turn to leave. . . . Boat by boat we were taken off the ship. It was horrible gazing down at that swaying ladder, our helmets like iron on our heads, full packs on our backs, our shoes untied, and the roar of guns all around us. Suddenly there was an especially heavy explosion and then, somehow, with the help of that Providence which watches over us all, we were in the commando boat. If Florence Nightingale could see us now!

Toward the shore we raced, but the boat didn't quite make it. We had to wade in—some of the good-looking girls were carried in by enlisted men. The thought passed through my mind that men were the same the world over—a pretty smile could get you anywhere, even off a commando boat during an invasion. Wet to our waists, we floundered up the beach.

A new land—but what a landing!

~

It was two o'clock in the afternoon and hot as blazes when we arrived at our next hospital area, two miles from Gafsa. The boys were still fighting there. Our trucks were lined up by the side of the road—not too far over, as only a certain number of feet had been cleared of mines.

"Why haven't the tents been set up?" I asked Colonel Wiley, and his answer nearly floored me.

"Well, you see, they haven't taken the mines out of that field and we're waiting for the engineers to do it."

Sure enough, in came the engineers with their queer equipment, a long-handled pole with a disk at the end. Inside that disk was some intricate mechanism. A needle on the disk would fluctuate wildly when it came near metal, and the whereabouts of the mines would be disclosed.

After lovely Montesque and even Bou Chebta [both in Algeria], this place was a desert, wild and forlorn. Dust was everywhere and there was no letup from the wind.

As the area was cleared, tents were erected. We (dopes) had infinite faith in the integrity of the Germans as far as the Geneva Pact was concerned, and so our tents were grouped together. Nearest the entrance was the receiving tent, where all patients were admitted. Homemade tables in the center held our sterile supplies, blood pressure apparatus, and whatever was needed to reinforce dressings on patients who were not to be admitted but were to be transported back to the evacuation hospitals. Directly behind these tents were the shock wards—later renamed resuscitation wards because the word shock had an unfortunate effect on the boys, and it took time to explain to them exactly what a shock ward was. These wards were for patients too badly wounded to be operated on at once. The operating tents were over to the side of the resuscitation tents, with preoperative and X-ray and ward tents adjacent. On the outskirts of the ward tents stood our supply tents, holding all the supplies not in use—plasma, saline, extra blankets, enamelware, and surgical instruments. And finally, the kitchen and special-diet tents were set up as near to the wards as possible, but that was an eighth of a mile away.

Within an hour and a half we were ready to operate. Patients were coming in. Badly wounded boys—the worse yet—serious belly wounds from mine explosions, head and chest wounds. The head wounds were really bad, brains oozing from some of them. The sucking chest wounds gave up frothy, bright red blood with each exhalation.

This time it was not a question of receiving ten or twenty patients at a time. Sometimes as many as twenty ambulances pulled up every few hours, which usually meant eighty patients. At first we had two sets of sawhorses in the receiving tent to support the litter cases, but the doctors preferred to look the patients over while the litters were on the floor rather than wait for one litter to be removed and another placed upon the trestle. The seriously wounded and those in shock were sent to the resuscitation wards. No time was lost; their clothing was not removed. The litters were placed on the bed and treatment started immediately—plasma, saline, whole blood, sulfadiazine given intravenously. This went on until the patients were in condition to be operated on. Only then were they undressed, and usually their clothing was in such bad condition that it had to be cut off.

Patients who were not in shock were undressed in the receiving tent, pajamas put on them, their clothing placed in a barracks bag. All the necessary information was taken from their field medical records—a square, glazed, water-repellent envelope had been tied to their jackets or clothing. Reports were typed by two of our men, who sat with portable typewriters, going at it for dear life.

The admitting officer decided what was to be done to each patient. If he needed an operation, he went to the preoperative tent and there awaited his turn. In the meantime, he was fluoroscoped and the site of the shell fragment marked, so that no time would be wasted in the operating room.

Those operating rooms! Ten tables going night and day, no sleep for the doctors—they worked the clock around. The girls had had the foresight to accumulate packing boxes full of supplies, all sterilized. We would not run out of them—we had plenty.

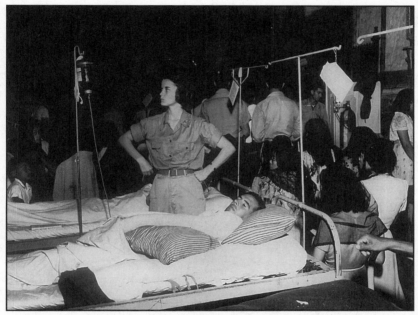

First Lieutenant Phyllis Hocking monitors the glucose injection apparatus for a G.I. patient in the 36th Evacuation Hospital, Palo, Leyte, Philippines, quartered in the Church of the Transfiguration, as the congregation kneels during Christmas Eve services, December 24, 1944. *Courtesy National Archives*

Abdominal cases, bad ones, had to have suction or Wangensteen tubes. We had none of the pretty gadgets the nurses had used in the States, the kind you just flipped to have them working beautifully. Ours were made of empty saline bottles, and we used the extra rubber tubing from the plasma sets. Dozens of those Wangensteens were going at one time, easing the pain of abdominal wounds, but we had only eight standards. We had to find a good method of suspending those sets, along with the plasma and saline.

I had a corpsman sink four extra tent poles along the side of the beds toward the head. To the top of the poles he strung wire, the ends of which were countersunk to afford greater stability. It worked wonderfully. Sometimes as many as twenty bottles were suspended from that wire. The suction apparatus, a three-bottle affair, was a little more complicated than the two-bottle one. But then, one didn't have to worry so much if in setting it up one got a positive pressure instead of a negative one.

Those tents were something to see—a double row of beds or cots in each tent, sixteen beds or twenty to twenty-five cots. There were no tables, chairs, or miscellaneous furniture. A packing case served as cupboard, desk, and catchall. Our chlorinated-water supply stood there in five-gallon cans. One little potbellied stove was in the middle of the tent, and on this we heated water for baths and hot-water bottles. . . .

And those baths! We didn't give them in the morning and call it a day. Like the brook they went on and on. Sometime during the twenty-four hours, all those boys would get bathed. It was necessary to work like that. Our turnover was so rapid we had to get the baths in whenever we could.

When one of the very sick boys told us that for three days he hadn't had anything to eat except grass, we thought he was a little light-headed. But it turned out to be the truth—the suction apparatus had got clogged and needed to be cleaned; when we dislodged the plug we found bright green grass!

The nurses worked eighteen and twenty hours a day; the corpsmen worked the clock around. Few of us rested. There was no time to think or cry—we just had to hang on and see that those boys got good care. The nurses still tried valiantly to get the baths in. We had a reputation to maintain. The corps surgeon had told us that the evacuation hospitals in the rear were sore at us—our patients were so spoiled when they left us. So the baths went on, night and day, never a patient going back who hadn't been bathed.

The corpsmen had donated all the blood they could spare. Nurses offered but were refused. The doctors couldn't afford to give blood—they had to keep going, all of them. Colonel Wiley hit upon a solution. He got in contact with Ordnance and Quartermasters [providers of weapons and supplies, respectively] and asked them for blood donors. Within two hours thirty men had been sent to our area. They were to rest in an empty ward tent, and as blood was needed they were called. The blood given the patients was of the same type but we cross-matched it, too. We could take no chances on their getting chills—they were too sick to stand any more than they had to.

We had a mixture of patients now, German and Italian prisoners along with our own boys, seriously wounded and getting the same heroic treatment. The Italians would come in screaming that they were our friends; the Germans were sullen and afraid. They had been told they would be horribly treated if taken prisoner. Vilma Volger, Father Powers, and Lieutenant Schwade tried to assure them, in German, that they would be well treated, but that it was necessary to operate on them. We finally got their consent, but what an ordeal!

Later on, as they recovered, the Germans took to boasting. "You Americans have taken Maknassy and El Guettar," they told us, "but that is all you'll get. Wait until we get to Oran, Algiers, and Casablanca. We'll take care of you then."

The poor men—they knew only what their leaders wished them to hear. They didn't know Oran and Casablanca had been taken the previous November. We had to keep them under guard, but otherwise one would never have known they were the enemy—a hospital is a place of refuge.

The nights were bad with the noise from reinforcements and supplies being sent along the highway to the front. Patients came in by the hundreds—there seemed to be no letup. We were situated between an ammunition dump and an airfield—a good target for those Heinkel bombers overhead. The sky was alight with flares dropped at intervals. Tracer bullets made huge necklaces in the sky. The noise was nerve shattering.

Many of the patients returning from the front had been treated by the Battalion Aid men and could be sent on from the 48th Surgical back to the evacuation hospital. Those evacuation hospitals were one hundred miles to the rear of us, and the ambulances were doing twenty-four-hour duty, in complete blackout. Patients admitted to our hospital were looked over by the receiving officer. If in good condition, they were sent to the cafeteria and later evacuated.

That cafeteria was Colonel Wiley's brainchild. A ward tent was set up parallel to the receiving tent. Cots were placed around the sides for the sitting patients, and the center was left empty for the litter cases. Over at one side Helen Hobson, assisted by two corpsmen, prepared coffee, soup, cocoa, and crackers. Every patient going through our hospital was fed. Fortified by a hot drink, a little food, and perhaps a sedative, they were grateful for the break in the journey that eased them on the long trek back. They never complained at being sent on, knowing that the boys admitted were in far more serious condition. . . .

The fatality list was very low, one good reason for it being prompt treatment. The people most responsible for seeing that the wounded got immediate treatment were the litter bearers and ambulance drivers. We nurses have been called Angels of Mercy; if we are, then the ambulance drivers and litter bearers are Archangels of Mercy. It's one thing to be up at the front with a gun in one's hand; at least a man has a chance. But those brave men removing the wounded from the field of battle went in under fire, taking chances every minute of being blown to pieces. They worked day and night, coming back to us gray faced and haggard looking, but always going back to recover more patients. We gave them hot coffee and food and begged them to rest—afraid lest they go off the sides of the road from complete exhaustion. But they were determined to go on. We were filled with respect for such gallant men, and from then on they were our pinup boys.

11   Home Away from Home

Julia M. H. Carson

On April 17, 1941, six volunteer organizations—the Young Men's Christian Association, the Young Women's Christian Association, the National Catholic Community Service, the Salvation Army, the National Jewish Welfare Board, and the National Travelers Aid Association—met in Washington, DC, and founded the United Service Organizations (USO). According to the official history of the USO, it was established for the purpose of "serving the religious, spiritual, welfare, and educational needs of men and women in the Armed Services . . . and, in general, to contribute to the maintenance of morale in American communities and elsewhere."

All over the world, American women and men in the military were touched by the work of the USO. Stage and screen stars, most notably Martha Raye and Bob Hope, volunteered

From Julia M. H. Carson, *Home Away from Home: The Story of the USO* (New York: Harper and Brothers, 1946), 124–30. © 1946 and 1974 by Julia M. H. Carson. Reprinted by permission of HarperCollins Publishers.

their talents for USO Camp Shows that dazzled the troops. However, the names of the more than five thousand Camp Show entertainers who traveled with small "tabloid units" have long since been forgotten. The following letter, written from New Guinea by an anonymous Camp Show trouper, was published in Julia M. H. Carson's 1946 work, Home Away from Home: The Story of the USO.

Dear People:

HERE BUT A FEW DEGREES from the Equator it is, if I may say so, very warm for Thanksgiving. But climate notwithstanding, turkey and all the home fixins taste just as good or better than usual, as can be attested to by the fact that I'm distributing myself over three Thanksgiving dinners today.

To those of you who are interested, I have never had less sleep, never felt healthier, certainly never happier, and certainly never so full of respect, admiration, and pride in my fellow Americans, that walk this part of the earth. For that jaded faith in humankind, the best thing I could wish anyone is a trip to the Southwest Pacific theater of war. . . .

To go 'way back, three short months ago—on my birthday, to be exact—we waved farewell to the Golden Gate for a destination unknown to any of us. "Now it can be told" we have traveled in a Dutch merchant ship, the Dutch crew of which left their homes five years ago for what was supposed to be their routine run from the Netherlands to Cape Town. They were shunted to the South Pacific and haven't seen their homes since. Many of them know they may no longer have homes. It's a fairly small ship—a combination luxury liner and troopship.

One other USO unit—a concert troupe of two men and three girls—was aboard. If you think life for six girls among so many men is hard to take, try it sometime, you gals. Here we got our first taste of the unprecedented popularity which had been ours in this man's world—and which, I'm afraid, has spoiled us forever for back home, where the man-woman ratio works the other way. But here, too, almost unconsciously, one sets a course of policy, as it were, to guide one in the topsy-turvy social scheme of one girl to thousands of men. . . .

Days began at sunrise and ended whenever you could tear yourself away from that last look at the Pacific sky, so unbelievably

Sergeant George Camblair and his girl sit out a number at a USO dance while he is home on a weekend furlough, Washington, DC, September 1942. *Courtesy Library of Congress*

covered with stars. But they were never long enough to do all the "fun" things that as grand a bunch of men as ever lived could find for you to do. Perhaps the shortest way and the only way to tell it is simply to list a series of unforgettable impressions: the dense black-out to which you became so accustomed that on a night when some-one forgot and lit a cigarette, it took on all the proportions of a burning skyscraper. Playing the show (we did it three times) on the open deck with the wind blowing you about and the deck heaving under your feet; the evening songfests when hundreds of fine, strong men's voices thrilled you more than any concert ever will. The church services in the men's mess . . . closing with a prayer that choked you—not because it was a very good prayer, but because you knew what every man prayed for.

Neptune Day—the crossing of the Equator—and the fabulous ceremony that attended it (curtailed a bit because there's a war on and also because there were six women aboard), where men were "spotted" by the Royal Family for head shaving, rotten egg baths, and dunking in an improvised pool, and where all six girls were royally dunked, too. That night when, as a gesture of feminine pro-test, we wore dinner dresses, only to find that that night was the first of the evening stand-tos [drills for repelling possible enemy attacks] and the first gas mask drill, and at sunset we stood for fifty minutes in long dresses, topped by Mae Wests, and for part of the time, grotesque gas masks. . . .

The day the first plane was sighted, general quarters was called, the gun crew rushed to man the guns, the plane was recognized as friendly, and a half-relieved, half-excited shout went up from all hands. The first rain, when the troops on the deck below soaped themselves to the waist, only to have the shower stop. . . .

The first glimpse of our destination, the long, thrilling process of landing, the first native fuzzy-wuzzie (kinky hair dyed yellow with peroxide—they'd give you New Guinea for a bottle of it), and our first sight of an American Army base in a beautiful land that you'd scarcely heard of before the war, but which was to become the site of a nearly three-year-long battle and the lonely home of thousands and thousands of American men. The gangplank and your feet on land again after three weeks of a ship's deck. The first coconuts, presented to me by dozens of G.I.s hungry for the sight of someone fresh from the States. . . .

Our first stop in New Guinea found us (three girls) situated with the Red Cross girls—in barracks that shot up almost overnight like a mushroom to house us, sharing one shower, one latrine, and one ironing board, with some eighty girls. In a day we dropped all hope of privacy. We were in the Army! Here those sharp uniforms issued us by the USO and the colored cotton dresses we'd been told to buy in great numbers were literally torn from our backs, and we were poured into G.I. trousers and shirts (sleeves rolled down) and flat-heeled nurses' shoes—standard garb for health reasons and general practicability throughout this theater of war. . . .

Since this first base, we have traveled by C-47s from one end of New Guinea to the other with a split week in New Britain. We've been quartered in hospitals with board walls and floors, or with nipa [palm] walls and no floors; in a PT base in a specially constructed tent complete with hot and cold running water, surrounded by a stockade and protected by an armed guard. Now we find ourselves in a pyramidal tent among the WACs, sole furnishing of which are three Army cots, sans mattresses, sans pillows, sans sheets. But we're still a long way from a foxhole.

Since that first day in New Guinea, I've eaten C Rations, and I've eaten steak and ice cream, dehydrated potatoes and eggs, and the ever-present Spam and bully beef, and I've drunk unforgettable glasses of milk flown in from Australia. Life is cheap in New Guinea as compared to a glass of milk and a green salad. I've stood in chow lines handling my mess gear with the best of them, and I've eaten in mess halls far more picturesque than any atmospheric job in New York City.

I've ridden in and driven Jeeps, peeps [small Jeeps], weapons' carriers, command cars, tanks, ducks [amphibious trucks], M8s [trucks], and LSTVs [landing ship tank vehicles]. I've flown in P-38s, A-20s, and Piper Cubs. I've broadcast from jungle radio stations. . . . I've been wakened in the middle of the night by a rat scampering across my face. . . . I've tramped through the jungle, cutting our way with a machete (never understanding how men can fight an enemy through it when I can scarcely walk through it); I've stood in mud up to my ankles with the dust blowing thick around my head. . . .

All this is on the "fun" side, but, believe me, the work is even more thrilling and soul satisfying. We're driven in Jeeps and command cars anywhere from five miles to thirty, bouncing over the rough roads in a cloud of black dust, as the case may be, so thick the driver can scarcely see the way, or through a downpour so wet he can scarcely stay on the road. We learned what the G.I. meant by, "Oh, my aching back!" Now we're immune to even black and blue spots. We've played in "theaters" that were only a board platform, and the rest was left to our stage manager and his detail of G.I.s. We've dressed in tents in mud to our ankles, and we've dressed in dressing rooms graced with the now-familiar parachute ceiling and a real, though hastily constructed, dressing table. And often there were flowers in our dressing rooms!

We've played to audiences, many of them ankle deep in mud, huddled under their ponchos in the pouring rain (it breaks your heart the first two or three times to see men so hungry for entertainment). We've played on uncovered stages, when we, as well as the audience, got rain soaked. We've played with huge tropical bugs flying in our hair and faces; we've played to audiences of thousands of men, audiences spreading from our very feet to far up a hillside, and many sitting in the trees (last night two native children sat perched throughout the performance on a corner of the stage. How much they understood, I don't know, but they laughed and clapped like crazy). We've played with a tropical moon shining through the palm trees full in our faces.

We've played to audiences in small units of five hundred or so, and much more often to audiences of eight to ten thousand. Every night we play in a different place. Certain audience cracks have become an accepted part of the show—we wait for them. Wisecracks are frequent but always friendly, and they've long since ceased to faze us. If G.I. Joe wants to enjoy a show that way, let him. Quicker to resent him are his fellows if he gets too exuberant. Twenty-five miles in blinding dust is a small price to pay for the yells of laughter and the roars of applause that have definitely spoiled us for a New York or Chicago audience.

But don't ever fool yourself that the G.I. audience in the Southwest Pacific, hungry for entertainment as it is, is not a discriminating and a smart one. Don't let yourself slip. Don't try to fool a G.I. with a Hollywood face and very little talent; above all, don't underestimate him by thinking all he wants is a leg show and dirty cracks. He talks and listens to "man" talk day in and day out. Every woman back home wears a halo now, and those who represent her had better keep theirs on, too. I've heard a girl swear out here and sensed a roomful of men freeze for a second. Give them laughs, but see that they are good laughs. Give them plays. They love them—from Tom of Arkansas, who's never seen one, to Harry from New York, who was brought up on Broadway.

And the gratitude of them to you for coming out here is as pathetic as it is undeserved and embarrassing. . . . USO work in the South Pacific is *fun*. And it is just as true in a sense that USO fun is work. Not really, but it is the social life so eagerly supplied by masculine New Guinea that can really knock you out if you don't take a day off now and then for "sack duty," just to catch up. A very important part of the work and fun is trying to be with the enlisted men as much as possible. . . . Their appreciation is again embarrassing when you mess with them instead of with the officers or when you meet them in their recreation halls, wherever they have them. . . .

And the hospitals. I can neither sing nor dance for the men. Often we cannot, because of the lack of facilities, play for the hospitals, but difficult as it is at first, every visit to a hospital ward just to talk is maybe the finest thing you can do out here. . . .

In hospitals or out, with everyone from a three-star general to Private Pete, the conversation begins with an invariable pattern: "Where are you from? How long have you been here? How do you like New Guinea?"... and then, "What's it like back in the States? Do they know there's a war out here?" And you try to tell them. But the real telling will come with what we do for them and with them when they're home once more. . . .

They've fought a battle against the jungle, the climate, disease, and, perhaps worst of all, monotony. . . . These men have faced realities—the hard, cold facts of a comfortless existence, and they're going to be sharp to penetrate the camouflage of flowery words and vague promises. And I think the toughest job of the home front is that of doing all we can to make our political and social scheme come up to our fighting men's ideal of America. They're not complaining now—not bitterly, that is (a certain amount of griping is part of the Army game)—and there's not one that doesn't say, "It's the boys in Europe or the boys up the line that are really taking it on the chin."

The good old American sense of humor is still functioning and strong. That's the eternal wonder of them, that makes you so proud of them you could "bust." They don't wave flags, they don't talk about the ideals they're fighting for. It has resolved itself into a job to do. They fight because the guy in the next foxhole fights. They kill because they've seen their buddies killed. But the homeland to return to—the ultimate goal of all they've been through—had better be worth it when they get back. And they can't be fooled.

With which sermon I'd better begin to draw to a close. . . . I hope some of you write, but if you haven't time for everybody, and you know someone out here, write to him instead.

12   I Knew Your Soldier

Eleanor "Bumpy" Stevenson

Like military nurses, American Red Cross women often went ashore soon after initial troop landings. On September 21, 1943, American Red Cross worker Eleanor "Bumpy" Stevenson arrived in Salerno, Italy, just twelve days after the invasion. Stevenson wrote about her experiences in Italy, as well as in England and North Africa, in I Knew Your Soldier, *published in 1944. Here she describes volunteering in an evacuation hos-*

From Eleanor "Bumpy" Stevenson and Pete Martin, *I Knew Your Soldier* (Washington, DC, and New York: Infantry Journal, Penguin Books [1945]), 41–54.

pital in Salerno and dispensing doughnuts from a Red Cross
clubmobile to men of the 45th Infantry Division.

E ARLY IN THE WAR there was a certain amount of controversy as
to whether or not Army nurses should go in immediately following a beachhead landing. There was a school of thought that
said, "They'd be more trouble than they're worth, and the hospital
ward boys could do the job as well." This kind of thinking was
disproved once and for all at Salerno, where the 16th Evacuation
Hospital unit, staffed with personnel from the Michael Reese Hospital in Chicago, was set up. Although the hospital was crowded
with patients, there were no nurses or Red Cross girls there at first,
because on their way over the ship carrying them had been bombed.
The hospital was operating without them, but there was moaning
and groaning from everyone, from ward boys to patients and doctors, because they weren't there.

A hundred times a day men would ask, "When will they come?
What in the name of all that is holy is holding them up?" And when
at last they arrived, cheers rent the air.

The evac hospital unit, without the women, went in on D-day
plus three; we got there on D plus twelve.

We had persuaded General [Mark] Clark to let a Fifth Army
clubmobile unit go into Salerno on the heels of the invasion, and he
had promised to wire us when he thought it was time for us to make
the move. Then, when almost simultaneously with D-day we heard
that Italy had surrendered, we arranged to go in on a troopship slated
to go to Naples. But our optimism was premature, and the invasion
dropped behind schedule.

The night before we sailed from Oran [in Algeria] I went with
Bill [Eleanor's husband, a Red Cross official in England, North
Africa, and Italy] to see General Ryder, who told him, "I don't know
where your wife's ship will land now, but if you still want her to go,
it's O.K. with me."

A few nights later we were climbing down landing nets into a
landing craft at Paestum, below Salerno. We were feeling a little
nervous, since the enemy was not too many miles away, and a little
awkward, too, since we were loaded down with helmets and musette bags and were wearing fatigue uniforms which are bulky and
cumbersome.

On the ship with us were the Fifth Army moneybags—really,
money boxes—containing five million dollars to finance the Army.

We landed about eight o'clock at night and prepared to sleep in a ditch bordering a field near the beach.

Responsibility ashore for me and the other two Red Cross girls was given to Major Newton, the finance officer in charge of the money. He was a practical man, and to save guards he put us to bed next to the money boxes—"killing two birds with one stone," as he put it.

Somebody must have been jittery about that gold, for in the middle of the night trucks came for it, and we climbed on the trucks, too.

All around it was completely black. To me one of the mysteries of this war has always been how the Army truck drivers go roaring along, apparently suspended in a sea of solid ink, without even those little slitted headlights they call "snake eyes" to guide them.

When we reached Fifth Army Headquarters in an orchard I felt that we were uninvited guests, and when I found that the Germans were only twelve miles away I was apprehensive over the fact that we hadn't waited to receive the wire from General Clark telling us to come. The headquarters itself had been forced to move back down the road from Salerno because of the intense German fire, and that moment was one of the few times during the war when the rear echelon was ahead of the forward one.

I suggested that we Red Cross girls go to the 16th Evac Hospital, which was nearby. When we got there, Colonel Bauspies—now in the Medical Corps of the VI Corps—greeted us with open arms. To us he seemed a saint sent straight from heaven; for when we asked him if he could put us up, he pointed at the tents his nurses would sleep in when they arrived and said, "See those tents? I haven't got a nurse in any of them. Help yourselves."

We pitched in and did all we could do to fill the gap left by the missing nurses, although the three of us who did arrive were just a drop in the bucket to twelve hundred patients needing attention. But we washed them, rushed bedpans, held aloft bottles of blood plasma while it ran into their veins, shaved them, kidded them, and generally ran our legs off. However, we were trying to substitute for a hundred trained hands, and it was a pretty hopeless undertaking.

On September 28th the whole hospital blew down. There was a real hurricane—the kind of wind which leans against you and really pushes you. Afterward there were only two or three tents left standing out of the hundred that had been there before. A group of men glued to the end of guy ropes stood there all night holding up the X-ray tent. When morning came, there was an unbelievable litter of cots, blankets, and ropes all over the place.

During the storm we went from one heap of canvas to another, peered under, and asked anxiously, "How're you doing?" until a feeble "O.K." came back to us. Then we'd crawl under to the wounded, and they would start joking and saying, "Hey, this is worse than bombing. This thing is everywhere."

One pneumonia patient who had a temperature of 103 degrees got up and tried to help us bundle men into trucks to move them to a nearby warehouse. I worried about him and wondered if his exertions would prove fatal, but the next day his fever was gone. The excitement and hard labor had dealt his pneumococci a knockout punch, but it is not a treatment I would recommend to the average pneumonia patient.

Toward morning the wind died down, and the whole unit pitched in and started to put the tents back up again. We served two or three thousand hot soups and coffees that night. The warehouse we moved into was the Quartermaster Supply Depot for the Fifth Army, and we were told we could help ourselves to any of the stores we found there.

The item we needed most was clothing, for most of the men had lost their pants and shoes, and what clothes they had were soaking wet. Then and there I noticed that men who can stand almost any hardship quail and grow querulous when they lose their pants. Such a loss must be a kind of masculine Achilles' heel, for the only complaining we heard were plaintive cries of, "I want my pants. Ain't that just like the Red Cross? They give us cigarettes when all we want is pants."

In early October we had doughnut machines operating with some divisions, but after an inspection trip to the front Bill discovered that the 45th Infantry Division, largely made up of men from Oklahoma and New Mexico, and including a lot of full-blooded Indians, was in for a brief rest period at Telese and had never seen a Red Cross girl.

He said to us, "Four of you girls get up there, but fast. It's a great outfit, and it will cooperate with you a hundred percent." He had talked to General [Troy] Middleton about it, and the general had agreed it was a good idea for us to go. But by the time we arrived, we found that we had only a week in which to serve them before they went back into action. We buckled down, and the doughnuts, although perhaps not as light as confetti, flew like it. We served fifteen thousand men in five days, averaging as many as three thousand a day, which meant more doughnuts than that, for there is no such thing as a single doughnut in the Army.

Then the 45th was ordered back into line at Presenzano, and we said to the colonel [in command], "Look, we haven't finished with your division. We haven't had a chance to see all of them, and passing over some men and taking care of others is worse than not having come up at all. What will we do?"

"Why don't you come along?" he asked. We were thrilled almost to tears, as it was the first chance the Red Cross girls had ever had to work with troops in action. We bivouacked with the Ordnance Company in tents and housed our doughnut machine in a tent, too. Those machines really grind out doughnuts. They have a

The Red Cross's Miss Georgianna Tucker, serving, and Miss Mary Burton Wallis, at checkerboard, U.S. Naval Base, Netley, England. *Courtesy National Archives*

capacity of four hundred an hour. And in a pinch they can produce more than four thousand a day.

About then there was a German counteroffensive, but [the colonel] didn't take it very seriously and comforted us by saying, "Don't worry, girls, tomorrow we'll drive the Jerries back and everything will be O.K."

That night we were under fire, but fortunately for our peace of mind we didn't know what was going on. I was sharing a tent with Betty Coxe, a clubmobile girl from Haverford, Pennsylvania, and when the whistle of shells and the crash of explosions began outside, she raised up in bed and said, "Coach, aren't our boys doing a lot of firing tonight?"

"Yes, they seem to be," I told her, and we dozed off again.

I had been given that "coach" nickname because the girls seemed to regard me as a mother superior, and asked me for advice and guidance in personal matters. Also, Bill had used me from time to time as a troubleshooter. His pet phrase for describing my operations of that nature was that I was good at "infiltrating." When he wanted something, he said he could send me to see the brass hats [high-ranking officers], and I'd usually come back with whatever he wanted in my mouth, like a well-trained retriever. Every time we accomplished something with a division, I saved it up in my mind, and when we ran into stumbling blocks or we had new problems in diplomacy to solve, I was able to quote those previous successes as precedents. It seemed to have an impressive effect on new divisional commanders. The idea of having a woman for a spearhead was a novel one, but Bill said I did a good job.

Presently, Betty cocked her head once more and said, "Coach, what's that funny whistling noise? We must be using a new kind of gun."

The next morning when we woke we found thirty shells had landed in our immediate vicinity, and the Ordnance Company was packing up to go. But the next night we were still there because our truck couldn't get in or out of the new area, owing to the mud. The clubmobiles we were using then weren't very mobile. They had no four-wheel drive and wouldn't go through deep mud or around bombed-out bridges.

Most of the time our doughnut machines were operated by G.I.s who had been given limited service while convalescing from wounds or shock. We had one with us named Clyde who roused me during that second night by saying, "Bumpy, get up, the Jerries is coming. You'll have to get yourself a German doughnut boy, because I'm retreatin'." After which he took off down the road. I don't know where he went, but he came back in the morning.

Every time a shell landed, another doughnut boy, named Skipper Maillard, who was always saying something to lighten the drudgery, said, "Mama Maria, I want my mama. I want somebody's mama," and dove into a foxhole. He'd sit there in three or four inches of water and finally say, "I'll give the Jerries just ten more minutes, and if no shells come over then I'm going back to bed." We helped him clock it, and at the end of ten minutes we'd tell him, "Time's up, Skipper." But no sooner had he ducked back between his blankets than another shell would land, and Skipper would dive back into the mud and water in his foxhole.

Finally, things got so bad the boys insisted that we Red Cross girls get into the clubmobile and go six miles down the road out of shell range, where we sat until daylight. Strangely enough, when we retreated the only one who stayed behind was Clyde, who had become quiet, calm, cool, and collected. He had worked up a philosophy to take care of the situation and told us, "I was scared because I didn't know what the shells were, but now that I know what they are, Jerry shells don't bother me and I'm not scared anymore."

When we set up housekeeping again, it was pouring, and there were three or four inches of soupy, watery mud in the tent housing the doughnut machine. As the G.I.s say, "We have running water in our tents, but not the kind you can turn off with a tap." We Red Cross girls tried to hack out drainage ditches, but we didn't do very well, for every ditch we dug seemed to lead the water right back into the tent. We felt it certainly would have been a great help if only one of us had majored in engineering before coming overseas.

In the midst of all that muck and goo, General Clark's aide arrived on the scene and warned us, "The general wants to see you. He's having lunch with General [Troy] Middleton now, but he'll be over right afterward."

We feared the worst. I could just hear his first words, "What are you doing up here?" And I was afraid he'd be very angry to find us so near all that excitement.

I'd been at Oudjda [in Morocco] for six weeks when the general was starting the Fifth Army, and while he had been very cooperative with us there, I knew he could get pretty annoyed if he thought circumstances warranted it.

When the general showed up, a pounding rain was drumming down outside, but our doughnut machine, despite the fact that it was up to its knees in water, was turning out doughnuts under full steam. He took one look at us, and instead of asking what we meant by being there, he said, "Why haven't you got Red Cross girls with the other divisions up here?"

When the idea filtered through our heads at last that we weren't going to be sent to the rear, I almost fainted. When I came out of it, I said, "General, we have girls assigned to all the other divisions, but some of the other commanding officers don't want them along when the men are in combat."

"I'm the general of the Fifth Army, and I want them there," he said.

That was my biggest moment overseas. "When you finish with this division," he went on, "I want you to go to the 3rd, who have had a tough time and are coming out of the lines very soon."

So we went back and lived with the quartermaster of the 3rd Division for a while, then moved on to the 34th.

Among the hours and moments packed into a cluttered jumble in my memory—some sharply etched and others fuzzy—is the last night we spent with the 45th on the twenty-eighth of November, while they were fighting around before the Battle of Mignano. Once again pouring rain slatted down on us in sheets. There were Betty Coxe, Lois Berney, Ed Kowslowski, field director, and I. We had only one truck and had been serving the last of the 45th Division units. When we came back we found that our two G.I.s detached to help us operate the doughnut machine were gone, and with them, the food stores. There was no gas and no water. Two nights before we had retreated and had come back. The previous night we had been under the heaviest shelling of all.

Betty Coxe had a rattling, wheezing chest cold, and we went to the 45th hospital clearing station to see if we could get a cot for the night—a cot, we prayed to God, not directly under shellfire. At the entrance to the clearing station our clubmobile was grounded by the clinging mud. Wading through the dark, we found a group of Medical Corps boys who yanked us out with an ambulance tow.

There were so many wounded that the clearing station didn't have an extra stretcher we could use as a cot, and scarcely a spot to put a stretcher down if they had had it. The kitchen was closed, so we trudged back toward our clubmobile. Twice I fell flat on my face in viscous goo, and Berney pancaked three times. Halfway back into the area where we had left our tents, our clubmobile stuck for good and all. I think it was the lowest moment in my whole life. Shells started arriving. They were antipersonnel shells that threw up mud and shrapnel. One landed squarely on our latrine twenty yards away. Some of the shrapnel went through the tent that housed our doughnut machine.

Our other truck came around in the morning and took us off to the 3rd Division, who were in rest near Riardo. On the way we caught up with our lunch, or rather our dinner, lunch, and breakfast combined. General Clark had asked us to go to the 3rd, because it had just been pulled out of the front after being there forty-three straight days.

We had a tough time getting accommodations. Bill Stephens, Red Cross representative with the Fifth Army, took us to the nicest house in town. As usual, it had no bath. We were used to that, but for some reason we chose that time to ask, "Don't the people here ever take baths?" The interpreter with us said, "Of course, they take baths. Every two months, when they need one, they go to Naples."

The housewives in the homes we tried—by us, I mean Lois Berney, Betty Coxe, Isabelle Hughes, and Eleanor Preble—looked at us coldly, and it was quite clear that they thought us camp followers in uniform. We kept on looking. Finally, we found a woman who would rent us two rooms. Her family consisted of a boy of fourteen, a girl of seventeen, and a smaller girl somewhere between eight and nine years old. There was only one other bedroom, and we could never figure where the rest of the family slept.

The smallest child was dying for an Army blanket. We scrounged one for her, and her mother ran up a suit for her out of the blanketing.

Although our laundry was not of the simple variety—it was made up of such things as G.I. pants, combat jackets, and Army shirts—the mother did all of it for us and would take no money for it. Her husband was away in Rome in the Carabinieri.

The Army gave us a potbellied stove. We removed a pane of window glass and cut a hole in a wooden shutter for an outlet. We were blacked out at night and had to have the shutter closed, stove or no stove.

We also had a washstand, but the running water we used in it only ran out of G. I. water cans lugged up to our room. I have never seen a girl enjoy water as much as Betty Coxe. She flung it on herself with joyous abandon, not caring whether or not she splashed it on the floor in her exuberance. We soon began to call our room Lake Coxe and tried to make her take her baths last, so we could escape before the flood set in.

Our routine, while we lived in Lake Coxe, was hitting the chow line at six-thirty in the morning and being blacked out at five-thirty at night. Between chow line and blackout, it was our job to drive to different units, eight or ten miles away, through what seemed to be a slowly flowing river of mud. I can't seem to remember when it wasn't raining during those drives, or when we weren't being pulled out of ditches into which we had slithered. In no time at all, the doughnuts became gray and soggy. Everything seemed to be open and exposed. Most of the kitchens were in six-by-six trucks with fly tents attached to the back. The fly would pick up a load of water until it sagged downward like a pudding bag. It was supposed to be a great joke to poke it when that happened, and let the water it held cascade earthward down an exposed neck.

My worst day there, I think, was when I started out with Field Director Ed Kowslowski, from Bridgeport, Connecticut, to pick up some doughnuts from a machine at VI Corps. We had gone twelve miles and had just crossed the Volturno River on a pontoon bridge in a rain that came down from the sky in straight lines, like endless strands of transparent spaghetti. No sooner were we over the pontoon when we had a flat and left the car by the side of the road. After a ten-minute wait, an Army truck picked us up. It wasn't going all the way to the VI Corps, where our doughnut machine was, but it took us five miles in the right direction.

We got out and waited another ten minutes, until another truck going toward the corps headquarters gave us a lift and let us out a quarter of a mile away from it. We squished the rest of the way. Once there, we found Bill Stephens, who worked out a scheme of putting the doughnuts into the Jeep for us to take back.

We packed four thousand doughnuts into empty K-Ration cartons. Finding containers and boxes was one of our biggest brain twisters. Sometimes we used bomb boxes—although they seemed to weigh a couple of tons even when empty. Bofors boxes [originally home to antiaircraft guns] were the best. They were made of tin and had handles.

The other girls in the clubmobile unit were waiting for us at the Seventh Infantry Regiment headquarters at Baia Latina ready to hand out the doughnuts when we arrived with them. As we approached Baia Latina—Ed Kowslowski and four thousand doughnuts and me sitting between the Jeep seats on a helmet—we were told that the bridge ahead was washed out. Bill Stephens had to leave us there. It was then six o'clock at night and too late to serve the doughnuts anyhow even if we had gotten there, but we made arrangements to be on hand early the next morning.

There were two ways in which we might be able to make it home for the night. One was the long, difficult route through the 3rd Division Headquarters; the other, a not-so-long but forbiddingly mountainous route that took us past the spot where the 15th Infantry was bivouacked. Unfortunately, we chose the latter. We climbed mountains and went down the far sides of them, all the time being maddeningly in sight of home on the other side of the river—until we reached the bridge. We waited at that bridge while another Jeep went over it. Just as it cleared the far end, the bridge was swept away behind it by the rushing water, and we had to turn around and retrace our tortuous route back up the mountain. We had no headlights, and our only means of illumination was a flashlight which we poked out of the window every now and then to show us the winding, slippery, high-crowned road.

Sometime later—it seemed ten or fifteen years later, during that night—we found the 15th Infantry kitchen. Somehow they produced a meal for us. It seemed to me one of the finest meals I'd ever tucked away, for at that point even our old friend Spam would have tasted like Chicken Tetrazzini to us.

After that feast, we did more backtracking and finally reached home at two o'clock in the morning. We slept as if someone had bopped us on the head with a quart of phenobarbital. Then, at five o'clock that morning, we got wearily to our feet and started in to do the whole thing over again.

Working with each division brought its own problems. We never knew in advance what those problems were going to be. One outfit wouldn't give us any limited-service G.I.s to help make doughnuts, with the result that the girls worked over those machines all day and had no time to visit the units. Another outfit wouldn't let any girls drive motorized vehicles, although they had proved that they could double-clutch almost as well as any G.I. truck driver. Another unit wouldn't permit our girls to bivouac with them and insisted that they live with a hospital miles away. But Bill claims his girls always won out in the end. "Just wait," he said, "they'll wear down the opposition"—and they did.

13   Shooting the Russian War

Margaret Bourke-White

Margaret Bourke-White earned a remarkable reputation as a top-flight photographer in the 1930s. Her cover photographs for Life *magazine are recognized as a high point in American graphic art. The following selection is taken from her 1942 book,* Shooting the Russian War, *which describes life and death on the Russian front during the fall of 1941.* Shooting the Russian War *is illustrated with extraordinary photographs taken by Bourke-White, the first accredited female war correspondent from the United States to go overseas.*

T HE DAYS ALTERNATED BETWEEN TRIPS through the eternal mud and banquets within the sound of enemy guns. The nights were spent in a bewildering succession of field headquarters, sometimes under canvas and sometimes under thatched roofs. Once we slept on the floor of a little resort cottage above the swollen Dnieper, near the fire-gutted town of Dorogobuzh. We slept all together in a room so small that we lay elbow to elbow, our feet against the head of the row of men in front of us. Erskine [Caldwell, the novelist and husband of Bourke-White] rolled me in my blanket over against the far wall and took his place beside me to give me a maximum of privacy. Occasionally I woke up and saw the sentry, bayonet in hand, guarding us, while a single candle flickered on his immobile face.

Often at dawn I would slip out ahead of the others so as to use the valuable early hours before we started on the move. There were always interesting types among the soldiers: Mongols, Ukrainians, Siberians, Uzbeks, Kazakhs, and Turkmenians, their faces wet under their dripping raincapes. And it was always raining.

I used flashbulbs to augment the weak light. One by one, my shutters began sticking in that helpless, half-open way which is the worst sight that ever confronts a photographer. And as each lens in

From Margaret Bourke-White, *Shooting the Russian War* (New York: Simon and Schuster, 1942), 253–55, 257–59, 261, 263, 265, 267, 269–70. Reprinted by permission of the author and the author's agents, the Scott Meredith Literary Agency, L.P., 845 Third Avenue, New York, NY 10022.

its crippled shutter went out of commission, I drew reluctantly on the dry ones which I was saving in my camera case.

These morning hours were often the only times that we were stationary during daylight long enough for me to make character studies and photograph soldiers doing their daily camp tasks. I usually worked until one of the correspondents would stick his head out between the flaps of the mess tent, coffee cup in hand, and call, "Come on, Peggy. Everybody's starting now. Don't hold us up the way you did yesterday," and I would hurry my equipment into the car and we would be off.

Once we were under way Erskine would slip his hand into his overcoat pocket and bring out something salvaged from breakfast. The morning he handed me the long, strong drumstick of a goose I was pleased indeed.

Sometimes the feast time, later in the day, gave me a little more time, and I developed a certain banquet technique. As soon as the toasts had begun I would steal away, a piece of black bread in my hand loaded with salt herring or a slab of cheese, and scout around for photographic subjects.

Once, when I came back at the end of a luncheon, there had been such enthusiastic toasting of Anglo-American-Soviet friendship that it was a small wonder one of the correspondents had slipped unobtrusively under the table. We were being piled into cars and were about to be taken to a group of field batteries directly on the first firing line when my husband missed him.

"Don't leave him behind," said Erskine, "he'll never get over it when he finds out what he's missed." So my husband raised the unconscious correspondent in his arms and placed him in the back of one of the cars, where he was brought along, quite unaware that he was being carried to the very brink of no-man's-land.

The completeness of his coma lasted until far into the night, which we were spending, packed tight as crackers in a box, on the floor of a tent. Suddenly we were startled awake, for our reviving companion, still under his spell, was chuckling and laughing to himself.

"Shut up and let us go to sleep," somebody called. "There's only one of you and there's a dozen of us."

"If there's a dozen of you I'll take you all to the baker," he announced, after which there was complete silence until dawn. At breakfast our correspondent could hardly believe he had been taken almost within a vodka breath of the German lines. He wrote up his story from the notes the other correspondents lent him.

Finally, a difficulty developed that worried me more than the weather. Some of the correspondents decided they had had enough of the rain and the mud and the disproportionate amount of time it took to go from one place to the next. They wanted to return to Moscow. It took so long to travel along the front, they argued, that they might as well start back and write up the things they had seen. The things they had not seen they could imagine. The simple solution of dividing forces and letting those who wished to see more of the front do so, and those who so elected go back home, was immediately rejected: that might give a scoop to those who remained.

The front faction and the home faction were about evenly divided. Erskine and two or three of the other Americans . . . were steadfast supporters of the front group; but otherwise the membership fluctuated so frequently that when matters grew crucial, I stuck around because my vote might be needed. Whenever I set forth my side of the case, that we had been promised we would be shown many more interesting subjects, and that surely if we kept on I would get my break of sunlight sooner or later, I was reminded that the needs of photographers are different from the needs of journalists. Well, they *are* different. No doubt about it. Quite different. And there was only one of me and ten of them.

The homing instinct reached its peak over one of the raw-fish breakfasts. The discussion grew so lively that the Russian officers accompanying us had retired, along with the censor, to the next room, to allow us to decide that matter for ourselves. (I often wondered what those army officers thought of our discussions. They had been so hospitable.)

And then it was one of the medical sisters who really swayed the vote. We looked up from our plates of raw fish to see her coming into the room with a steaming mound of mashed potatoes. Golden pools of butter were nestling in the hollows. Everyone's spirits rose, and the vote was cast to continue on through the mud and rain and see whatever the Russians were willing to show us.

I was overjoyed, because I had a deep feeling that I was going to get my break at last.

I always had interesting little adventures on the evenings that I slipped away from the banquet table. Once the soldiers showed me a big cache of captured German mechanized equipment hidden under the fir trees: some Skoda reconnaissance cars, a huge troop carrier with its caterpillar treads blown partially off, a Mercedes gun hauler, field guns, machine guns, and disabled tanks with swastikas painted on their sides.

Once a tankist returning from a battle where several enemy tanks had been surrounded and captured told me how the enemy tank drivers had filled every available bit of space around their feet, inside the tanks, with women's clothing which they had rifled from Russian villages. One tank, he said, was filled with women's underwear and another was crammed full of peasant embroideries, taken, I suppose, as souvenirs for German soldiers' wives. I was glad they had recaptured that tankload of embroidered scarves and blouses, for Russian peasant handiwork has a richness that is hard to match in any part of the world today. I would not have liked to see it go to the enemy.

Frequently, groups of pilots would return from the fight and show me their captured trophies, for a pilot always saves his enemy's medals if he is able to get them. Each of these pilots had his captured Iron Cross, and one of them had seven of them. "All the Fascist pilots want to get Iron Crosses," he said to me, "but we give them crosses of wood."

I was interested to learn that the Soviet fliers frequently recognized captured German pilots who had parachuted to safety when their planes were shot down. The *Luftwaffe* evidently made full use of the men who had flown passenger planes over the commercial line operating between Berlin and Moscow in peacetime—men who were thoroughly familiar with the route. Sometimes the Russians knew these captives well enough to call them by their first names. The Germans, however, never showed a sign of recognition.

Sometimes I talked with scouts who had penetrated far enough back of the enemy lines to make contact with the guerrillas, for the Red Army maintains connections with partisan troops wherever it can. Wherever possible, the regular army smuggles guns to the partisans. One returned scout told me about a group of villagers who were successful in halting an oncoming munitions train by tossing burning trees across the railroad tracks. When the German soldiers ran up to try clear the tracks, the villagers shot at them from an embankment with the only two rifles they had, and when those gave out they threw rocks at the Germans. In the end more of the partisans than the German soldiers were killed, but the enemy had been delayed.

Another scout came from a region beyond Smolensk, where a detachment of partisans had hidden in the tall grass along the highway, waited until a group of tanks came opposite, and tossed bottles of flaming gasoline at them, disabling three tanks. As this scout worked his way back, he passed through a town where a group of partisans had actually fallen on two invading tanks with hammers and axes. Machine-gun fire from the tanks killed several of the villagers, but finally, led by the village blacksmith, they managed to bend the machine guns out of commission and then, beating on the armored walls, they created so much din and dust that the tank crews had to surrender.

One of the scouts had come from a tiny village, nine miles behind the lines, with a report of how when the Germans moved in, the men went back into the woods, believing the Nazis would be less suspicious of the women. The German officers took up their quarters in a log schoolhouse, and at midnight the peasant women set fire to it with gasoline-soaked hay. Then, when the officers rushed half dressed out of the burning building, the women set on them with pitchforks.

In the Soviet Union, when territory is captured one does not see the swarms of refugees which have clogged the roads of other invaded countries. The government has previously instructed civilians to stay and become partisans. They have been given directions in the art of sniping and in guerrilla warfare, and if their village is captured they know just what they are expected to do. Guerrillas cannot win a war, but they can do a great deal to make the enemy uncomfortable.

The person whom I remember the most vividly among the Russians I came to know at the front was Tanya. Tanya was a nurse, with widely spaced blue eyes, honey-colored curls that spilled down shoulder length, and a strong, chunky little body. We were in the Yartsevo sector when I met her, not far from Smolensk, and Tanya had been born here. She knew every footpath, and at night, as soon as it grew completely dark, she would buckle on her sidearms and go crawling on her hands and knees through the long grass and low shrubbery, across to the German lines. There, behind the lines, she would learn what she could about the movements of the enemy and the location of German guns, and creep back just before daybreak to report on what she had seen. Then she would sleep a few hours, go to the hospital tent to help tend the wounded, and at night if she was needed she would be off again.

The area she was working in had changed hands many times between the Germans and the Russians, so she was much needed. It is a sector that is still changing hands, and as I write this today I believe it is being regained by the Russians. So the experience of scouts like Tanya has great value.

Later, the night that I met her, we were allowed to visit an action point. We were led to the edge of our little wood and told that we could run across an open meadow to another grove of trees about a quarter of a mile away. We were instructed to run single file and keep three meters apart. As we reached the middle of the meadow the whole horizon was ringed with light, and there was a sound of thunder above us. It was the Soviet battery firing over our heads, and the Germans began answering toward us with machine-gun fire. We quickened our pace, and as we approached the grove for which we were headed the Germans began sending up star shells, to light the front lines so as to be able to see scouts who might be slipping across. Even as I ran I could not help but notice what a brilliant glow the star shells threw on the ghost-white birch trunks. I hoped that Tanya, wherever she might be at that moment, was sufficiently hidden. And then, in an instant, we were inside the grove.

The action point was less than a quarter of a mile from the Germans. We had to walk on tiptoe and talk in whispers. Here, of course, I was not able to take pictures, because flashbulbs would have revealed our position. Under cover of the darkness, the battery crew moved like clockwork, loading and operating their big guns.

When we returned and started on to another section of the front, it was a little past midnight, much too early for me to find out if Tanya had made the journey safely. I shall always wonder about her.

The next day, we had left the woods and groves behind. We were approaching the great battlefields of Yelnya, where war had lashed back and forth in all its fury, the land sometimes in enemy hands, sometimes in Russian hands, until at the end of six weeks of some of the most savage fighting that the world has perhaps ever seen, the Russians had reclaimed it again. This was sacred soil, for this was the first land to be won back for the Soviet flag, and we arrived directly on the heels of this victory. Here there were no picnic groves, no little woods of fir and birch. We were entering a manmade desert.

The fields were chewed up with the treads of tanks, and we were passing "scorched-earth" villages, with only patches of ashes darkening the ground to show where homes had stood. On the side of a hill, above a small stream and facing the road, was something that looked like a Zuni village. Just as our American Indians built their hole-like houses, tier above tier, up the sides of the mesa, so as to be able to see and face the enemy as he approached, so the Germans had dug themselves into the hillside of Ustinov. And they had dug in with them several tanks which they could use as pillboxes [fixed artillery positions]. Communication trenches had been dug, joining links with forward positions and command posts. Each little cell-like dugout was banked with sandbags and braced with timber, and inside were metal cartons and wicker baskets which still contained hand grenades and land mines bedded in straw. The Germans must have been driven from this hill suddenly, for large stores of ammunition had been left behind for the Russians.

I heard Erskine shouting to me from the top of the hill. He was waving a German helmet, so I picked up one of my own. There were plenty to choose from; hundreds of them, savagely gashed and broken or riddled with bullets, were lying around in heaps. The metal they were made of was thin, much lighter than the heavy mushroom-shaped casques that protected Russian heads. I selected one that was fairly intact. The owner's name, Herbst, was lettered in white inside, and a single bullet hole over the left ear showed how Herr Herbst had met his end. I have the helmet at home now, in Connecticut.

We went along the windswept road, between bursts of rain and hail, and late in the afternoon we came to Ushakovo, where the great battles of Yelnya had been fought.

There was none of the sylvan character we had seen in our earlier views of the front when we reached the battlefield of Yelnya. Here the Germans had poured across the fields, filling up this area like breath being blown into an expanding balloon. After six weeks of fighting, through August and September, the Russians had managed to snip off the balloon and deal with the captives within the Nazi bulge. And now the place looked like the end of the world.

Here were the ghosts of blasted trees, great trunks split and smashed as though a giant hand had picked them up in bundles and dropped them broken back to earth. As far as the eye could reach was wasteland, pitted with shell holes, channeled with trenches, littered with the remains of war which had swept in concentrated fury back and forth across it during those desperate weeks.

The Russian dead had been buried in a common grave, marked with newly planted firs and surrounded by a fence topped with red-painted tin stars. Field asters still showed touches of lavender and purple where they had been laid on the freshly piled mound of earth. The Germans had been hastily shoveled into their own trenches, unmarked—many thousands had been dug into the ten-mile-square battlefield where they had fallen. Like hundreds of empty turtle shells lay the German helmets, some decorated with little swastikas painted in white, many cracked viciously through the top where the metal had given way during battle.

Erskine called me and pointed to a zigzag trench. The bottom was sprinkled unaccountably with dead mice.

Everywhere was the paraphernalia of life—a torn sleeve, the piece of a boot, a tattered raincoat, fragments of a rain-soaked German newspaper. Erskine stooped over and pulled out a handle projecting from the ground. It was an officer's broken sword.

We had to be careful where we walked because the ground was full of unexploded mines and shells. Once I stepped on something soft, and a green cloud rose into my face. It was a heap of moldy bread which still retained the shape of loaves, so recently had men been breathing and eating there. Nearby was a chased-silver samovar, pierced with a bullet hole, which raised an image of Russians drinking tea in what seemed like a bygone age.

When we reached the town of Yelnya, fighting was still going on nearby. The front was only a few kilometers away, and the rattle of machine guns and the deep roar of artillery sounded restlessly to the west. Yelnya had had an estimated population of five thousand, and now it was a ghost town. When we drove into its ruined streets I knew that here at last I had the pictures I wanted, pictures that would look like war. It was almost twilight, but the clouds, as though they had heard my prayers at last, began lifting, and the rays of the setting sun poured down on the skeletons that had once been homes.

I jumped out of the car and hastily set up a camera. I had just begun work when one of the reporters, a member of the home faction, dashed past me, notebook in hand. "Hurry up, Peggy," he called. "We're clearing out of here in five minutes, and we'll be halfway back to Moscow tonight."

It was too much—all the hopes and disappointments, all the fighting to salvage something through the mud and rain, all the arrivals at the most interesting places after dark, the tearing away in the mornings before I could complete my job. "I can't work this crazy way," I said aloud to the empty road. And I began to cry.

Crying doesn't do much good, because it interrupts focusing. I knew this, but I only stood there weeping, wasting my time. And then the censor came along and guessed what the trouble was, proving that there is some use for censors after all.

I shall never forget how he gathered a squad of soldiers to help me and instructed the officer in command of the town that I should be given all the help I needed. The plan was to have the correspondents go on to a banquet that was waiting for them sixty miles back on the road toward Moscow. Erskine would stay with me, of course. And the censor put a little pile of chocolates in the backseat of our car, cautioned me not to take too long, because the sound of the guns was rising, and the crowd was off.

Darkness was beginning to fall now, but the soldiers helped me string out my extension cords so we could light up portions of the road with flashbulbs. As it grew darker I brought all three of my flashguns into use, each with extension wires, and the soldiers strung out with them along the road, watching me for signals while I capped and uncapped the lens. It was too late to get instantaneous exposures, but it worked.

I was interested to see that the only building left even partially intact was the cathedral with its coppery-green dome, now being used as a Red Army barracks. But for the most part the town had been reduced to a collection of skeleton fingers, pointed toward the sky. These were the central chimneys, some of them still smooth with the polished tiles that are characteristic of peasant dwellings. Still, wherever two walls came together, or wherever there was a scrap of roof, people were creeping back to their homes, so resilient is the human race. Sometimes they were welcomed back by their cats, which have a way of lingering around the house even after bombing, although dogs turn wild and run away.

It was getting late now, and the garrison commander thought we should be on our way. Erskine was talking with a group of soldiers by the church, and I took one last walk, down a side street, and watched some people cooking food, which the soldiers had given them, over what remained of their brick and plaster ovens. They were setting up housekeeping in the midst of the ruins, and I noticed that they were using strange cooking utensils. I examined these utensils more closely. They were not mere pots and pans bent out of shape from bombing. They were pieces of wrecked German planes and portions of metal sheeting from captured enemy tanks. Bent into shallow shapes, they served well enough as baking tins or broiling pans.

The officer and my husband were both calling me now, and their voices were almost drowned out with the rising thunder of guns. The star shells that soared over the front lines to the west were gleaming in a cobalt-blue sky. It was time to go.

But as I walked back to the car I paused to look at a woman borrowing some hot charcoals from the fire of a neighbor. "What is she carrying them in?" I wondered, as I watched her heading homeward. The shape was familiar. She was bringing home hot coals in a Nazi helmet.

IV On the Home Front

Early in 1943, Max Lerner, the well-known author and journalist, writing for the New York newspaper *PM*, predicted that "when the classic work on the history of women is written, the biggest force for change in their lives will turn out to have been war. Curiously, war produces more dislocations in the lives of women who stay at home than of men who go off to fight."

The transformations that occurred in the lives of American women on the home front were truly immense. Rationing, shortages, war bond campaigns, blood drives, blackouts, and air-raid drills became a way of life. Women rolled bandages for the Red Cross, joined military mothers' clubs, volunteered their time at the local USO, and planted vegetable, or victory, gardens.

Many aspects of day-to-day life were accelerated by the war. This was especially true for young people in love. For servicemen who were stationed Stateside, the telephone occasionally helped to close the distances that often separated sweethearts. But for many courting couples, letter writing became the chief means of getting acquainted and nurturing their love. In the midst of the wartime emergency, young people took time out to write "miles of sentences" as they conducted courtships by mail. In fact, there were approximately one million more marriages between 1940 and 1943 than would have been expected at prewar rates.

War brides often traveled thousands of miles to be with their husbands at distant postings. A reporter for the *New York Times Magazine* described these young women as "wandering members of a huge unorganized club" who recognized each other on sight, exchanged views on living quarters, babies, and allotments, and helped each other in times of difficulty. The camaraderie experienced by war brides at informal gatherings where they "swapped stories" made life, if not pleasant, at least tolerable.

With their husbands away in the service, war wives almost always experienced a reduction in family income. In order to make ends meet, they moved in with other war wives, took in boarders,

Courtesy National Archives

returned to their childhood homes to live, and sometimes sought war work. One mother, writing to her son in combat, gave a succinct description of their situation: "These poor little war brides, they are finding life a confused and perplexing situation, too. It's pretty tough to have to fight a battle like they are doing. . . . But such is war."

Women whose men were wounded in battle, taken prisoner of war, or killed in action were required to draw upon an inner strength that many did not know they had. Assuaging sorrow and dealing with the loss of a loved one took much effort. Mothers, wives, fiancées, sisters, and friends continued to pray for those who had sacrificed their lives for the war. For many of these Gold Star women, the war has not yet come to an end. The price of victory is still being exacted.

14   Camp Follower

Barbara Klaw

Barbara Klaw, in her widely read book Camp Follower: The Story of a Soldier's Wife, *provided a comprehensive account of the experiences of service wives who crisscrossed the nation as they followed their husbands from posting to posting. Over fifteen million civilians moved during the war years in one of the greatest migrations in the history of the United States. People hurried to new jobs opening up in shipyards and war plants. War wives joined in this migration as they sought out precious time with their husbands at the military bases where they were stationed.*

In Camp Follower, *Klaw reported on train travel, the difficulty of finding hotel rooms, the shortage of rental rooms, and the camaraderie she experienced with other women in the same circumstances. The war wives whom Klaw wrote about banded together, giving each other baby showers, sharing information, doing anything to fill what she termed "the daytime void."*

Klaw, like most other service wives, found wartime housing grossly inadequate, and she described in detail her search for a room in a crowded military town. Camp Follower *was serialized in the* Atlantic Monthly *in October, November, and December 1943. It was also made into a play and broadcast on the wartime radio program, "Words at War."*

NEVER VERY GOOD AT FOLLOWING directions—particularly the "Oh, you can't miss it" kind—I walked around the central square of Neosho, Missouri, three times before I spotted the Travelers Aid office.

I had already been room hunting along the residential streets for two hours that morning, ever since my bus from Joplin landed me in town. I had found nothing but advice, freely given by friendly homeowners, who had themselves no vacancies. All of them had told me to go to the Travelers Aid—the official housing agency for Army wives, and I had been directed to the square.

From Barbara Klaw, *Camp Followers: The Story of a Soldier's Wife* (New York: Random House, 1944), 18–33. Reprinted by permission of the author.

On my first lap, I was looking so hard for signs that I didn't notice much about the shops behind them. The second time around I began to get some impression of the town's business district, its clean, modern town hall in the center making the squat little shops around the sides look untidy. I noticed barred windows on the top floor of the town hall, high above the surrounding buildings. "That's the county jail," a Neoshoan told me sometime later. "The prisoners get a fine view of the town from up there."

On my third lap of the square, I stopped thinking about my room hunt long enough to wonder at the peculiar array of shops Neosho housed. There were the usual businesses—the groceries, the department store (which advertised belligerently, "If we don't have it, you don't want it"), the five and tens, the beer joints, and the movie house—but in addition there were at least ten military stores, and almost as many jewelers.

It was obvious that the military stores had moved in to get the Camp Crowder trade. When I examined one of the window displays of cheap jewelry stamped with Signal Corps insignia, I realized that the jewelry stores must have come to town for the same purpose.

Later, Spence and I were to see these shops crowded on Saturday night with soldiers laying down hunks of their monthly pay for gifts that had little more than souvenir value. For themselves, the soldiers frequently bought useful things such as watches, but they also bought expensive identification bracelets and silver dog-tag chains—the kind of ornamental gadgets that I suspect most of them would have scorned in civilian life. "The G.I. substitute for a red tie," Spence called these ornaments.

I had almost forgotten what I was looking for when I finally spotted the red, white, and blue Travelers Aid sign down a narrow side street. I found the office sandwiched between a drugstore and a cleaning establishment, at the top of a flight of echoing wooden steps.

The office was mobbed with girls when I went in, some of them obviously well-seasoned room hunters. They sat in the few camp chairs along the walls, and stood in rough queues at the desk, waiting to talk to the girl attendant. The only unfilled space in the room was a wide swath around a rotund stove which was radiating fiercely into the already overheated room.

The girl at the desk was talking to a small blonde with a husky, brown-eyed little girl at her side.

"How was that place on Wood Street you looked at?" she asked.

"Same story," the mother said. "She didn't want kids. Patty scares 'em all, don't you, baby?"

"I'm an awful nuisance," the little girl said matter-of-factly.

"You'd think it was a sin for a soldier's wife to have a child," the mother said.

"Well, it makes it tough, all right," the worker agreed. "I may have something this afternoon, though, Mrs. Huston. Drop in then, will you?"

We all wanted the same thing, and we were all told that there might be some vacancies reported by afternoon. Each newcomer was urged to live in Joplin, and each felt as I did that it was too far from camp. I lit a cigarette, sat down as far from the stove as possible, and lingered after the others had gone, hating to hit the pavements again. I introduced myself to the girl at the desk, who was calm and efficient and pleasant. Her name was Margaret Lewis.

"Is your office always as crowded as this?" I asked.

"No, Monday's the worst day," Margaret said. "The wives come for the weekend, and decide to stay."

A soldier came in—red in the face, and obviously in a hurry.

"Can I leave a message here?" he asked. "I imagine my girl will come by here sooner or later. Her name's Lydia."

"Certainly," Margaret said. "What's the message?"

"Just tell her to leave my hat here, that I'll be in to pick it up later."

"All right. What's her last name?"

The soldier thought a moment.

"Lydia, Lydia something. It begins with a P—Lydia Pinkham," the soldier said. "That's it, Lydia Pinkham."

Margaret looked up at him. "You're sure?" she asked.

The soldier grinned. "No," he said. "But it sounds familiar. Anyway, she's got my hat. Tell her for God's sake that it isn't funny, and I've got to get that hat back. I've been dodging M.P.s [military policemen] all day." Without the slightest change of expression, Margaret wrote the message on a pad, with the Lydia Pinkham underlined.

"Don't forget my message now," the soldier warned, and he rushed out, his G.I. shoes clattering on the wooden steps. Margaret filed the message under P in her message file.

Just then the phone rang. Margaret wrote as she listened, and then said: "Yes, certainly, I will, Mrs. Upton. Thanks so much for calling us." She copied what she had written on another piece of paper and handed it to me.

"You might try this one," she said. "I don't know what it's like, but it's a vacancy, at least. She won't be home till four, so try after that. Let me know what happens, will you? The woman has refused to rent the room to the last five girls I've sent over." She didn't explain further than that, and I took the slip eagerly.

On the way out I passed a girl sitting on the stairs, holding one of her shoes in one hand and rubbing her foot with the other.

"God, this town!" she said crossly. "My feet's killing me."

My feet were killing me, too, in another two hours. Margaret had told me that I might try the cabin courts [motels] on the edge of town, and with a mental picture of Spencer and me setting up housekeeping in a cozy little one-room house of our own, I trudged out the long street to look at some of them.

They were clustered on the main highway entering Neosho, interspersed with diners, groceries, the town's bowling alley, and the Army prophylactic station.

The station was a clean, square little building, set back from the road, with a brightly painted sign reaching out to announce it. Over the door was a naked green light. Stop and go, I thought, all done in lights. Very neat.

Two of the cabin courts had "No Vacancy" signs up, but the third—advertising "10 cabins, all strictly modern, 10"—had two vacancies, I found on digging the manager out from under a bed where she was cleaning.

Her name was Mrs. Morris, and she showed me around her establishment with obvious pride.

"Now, this one here," she said, "is one of my very nicest. We just remodeled it, too. Careful of wet paint." The cabin was charming at first glance, with three large windows and baby-blue walls.

"And Venetian blinds," she said, pulling them up and down rapidly. "I just got them up, they make it pretty, don't they? They're mighty hard to get nowadays."

The bathroom was as spotless as the cabin, and almost as lacking in essential equipment. The furniture in the neat little room consisted of a bed, a straight chair holding an ashtray, and a small gas heater in one corner.

"The girls that've lived in here have just made themselves right at home," Mrs. Morris said. "The last one brought a radio and a little bedside lamp, and it was real cute."

"Where did she put her clothes?" I asked. There was no dresser in the room.

"Now, I don't really know," Mrs. Morris said cheerfully. "I never noticed. I guess she kept them in her suitcases."

"Could I see the closet?" I asked.

"Well, as a matter of fact, we haven't got around to putting a closet in this cabin yet," Mrs. Morris said. "Most of the girls hang up their dresses on those hooks there." She pointed to two sagging hooks on the wall. She stood in the middle of the room, and looked around with satisfaction.

"It's cute, isn't it?" she said. I agreed that it was, and remembering the swarm of girls in Margaret's office, asking for rooms—rooms of any kind—I asked the price.

"Well," Mrs. Morris said, "I used to charge sixteen a week for this one, but now with the Venetian blinds, I'll have to charge seventeen." I multiplied quickly and found that the rent amounted to considerably more than we had paid for a whole apartment in Washington.

"Do you have a cabin without Venetian blinds?" I asked.

The next cabin—which cost fifteen a week— had both dresser and closet, but Mrs. Morris obviously looked down on it.

"Of course, this one hasn't just been remodeled," she said. It, too, was scrupulously clean with orange and blue linoleum on the floor. I told her I wanted to look around a little more, but persuaded her to hold it for me until five when I'd call. Fifteen dollars appalled me, but it was cheaper than the hotel in Joplin, and Neosho was closer to camp.

Talking about rents, I later asked Margaret if the O.P.A. [Office of Price Administration] hadn't ever noticed Neosho.

"Sure," she said. "They came in here, and clamped down ceilings kind of indiscriminately, and people took their rooms off the market. Frankly, we were relieved when they went away. The cabin courts can't be touched anyway because they simply multiply their daily rate by seven to get a weekly rate."

On the way back to town, I stopped at an ugly but spacious stone house, set high on a bank which ran up from the sidewalk.

The woman who answered the door was so fat she had to sidle out onto the porch. Making her round face look even rounder, she had a thick braid of gray hair wound around her head, which had slipped rakishly over one ear.

"Well, I do have a girl moving out today," she said, when I asked if she had any vacancies. "But she's promised the room to a friend, I think." She turned laboriously and shouted back into the house.

"Gloria, that little girl from Atlantic City is taking your room, isn't she?"

From upstairs, Gloria shouted back that she was.

I heard a thump, like a shoe dropping, followed by a burst of laughter. The landlady smiled affectionately, and poked at the lopsided braid.

"I've got such a nice bunch," she said. "Five couples, and all of them just as sweet as they can be." I wondered automatically if the Missouri wind had messed my hair, and was glad that I had on my sole remaining pair of nylons.

"Well," she said, "I'm sorry I can't help you. I try to do everything I can for the Army wives, but I'm just full up to the rafters." I caught a glimpse of an unmade bed in the living room, imperfectly shielded by a screen, and wondered if one of her five couples lived there.

As she started to shut the door, Gloria shouted down the stairs.

"Mrs. Thompson, where are those panties I washed out yesterday?"

"They're in the kitchen, dear," Mrs. Thompson called. "I took them in off the line for you." She turned to me. "Gloria's so excited," she said tolerantly. "Her husband has a ten-day furlough before reporting to his new post." She suddenly remembered me. "I certainly hope you find something nice," she said.

I patiently covered whole streets of houses that afternoon, chatting with landladies and incumbent Army wives. The people were all friendly and talkative, but with one exception the answer was always no. The exception was a temporary room. I could have it for a week, the lady told me, but the couple, who had gone on furlough, would want it back after that.

"I have a lot of girls here," she said, leading me up the stairs. "When I first started renting, I put in a game room in the attic for them. This room is right off the game room."

It was, as a matter of fact, hardly off the game room. A partition that reached not quite to the top of my head cut off one corner of the large bare attic.

"The girls use the game room during the day, but it's very private up here at night," the landlady assured me.

"What about light?" I asked, noticing none in the room.

"Well, I let the couple keep on the light in the game room," she said, "and it gives them plenty."

She explained the bylaws of the house. "The bathroom's on the first floor," she said. "I don't let the girls use my kitchen, it just makes too much confusion, you know, and I don't like any radios in the house. Also, I don't like smoking, but I don't suppose you smoke, do you?" She didn't wait for an answer, and I hid the slightly tobacco-stained two fingers of my right hand, and decided it would be good for me to give up cigarettes, for a while, anyway. The room was eight dollars a week, and I said I'd call her back that afternoon.

"Well," she said as I left, "I hope for your sake that you find something permanent, dear, but if not you can stay here while you look around." It was phrased like an invitation—eight dollars a week and no smoking.

As I came down the steps of the house, a cab coasting languidly along the street pulled up beside me.

"You look as though you're room hunting," the driver said. I told him I was. "Well, most all the girls in Neosho are," he said. He was a good-looking young man, and I involuntarily wondered— hating myself for the thought—why he wasn't in the Army.

"I know of a nice room," he said. "Right on the square. Want me to take you there? I'm going that way, anyway. I won't charge you."

Thinking how extraordinarily nice all Neoshoans were, I said hopefully, "Do you really know of a room?"

"Sure," he said. "Just like I said. A nice one."

"Look," I said, ready to grab at any chance. "Could you possibly give me the address, and I'll go by there later? I want to finish up this street first."

"Well, I can't remember the address, but I could drive you right there." He sounded a little devious.

"Which side of the square is it on?"

"Come on, hop in," the man said. "It only takes a minute in the cab." I refused, cursing myself for a suspicious fool when the young man shrugged his shoulders and drove away. But I was right, I discovered when I talked to Margaret about it later.

"Yes," she said. "I've heard of that stunt. Those places on the square are colorful spots. That's where most of the syphilis that the camp authorities have a fit about starts. I guess some of the cab drivers are in cahoots with the houses." I never saw a girl coming down the steps of one of the houses on the square after that without wondering.

By the time it was four, my feet and head ached, and I could feel a hole growing in the toe of my left stocking. As nervous as though I were looking for a job, I stopped in at the bus station, the only public place I knew, to clean up before going to the house Margaret had told me about. I walked over there—directed by my U.S.O. map of Neosho—with my head held stiffly, trying to keep the wind from mussing my hair.

A boy of high-school age answered the door, and I asked him if they had a room for rent.

"Have we got a room for rent, Mom?" he yelled back into the house. His mother called him, and when he came back, he asked, "Did the U.S.O. send you?"

I told him that they had, and he moved the bicycle which partially blocked the door, and invited me in.

His mother, Mrs. Upton, was lying on a bed in the dining room in a housecoat and hairnet, with cold cream on her face.

"Excuse the way I look," she said. "I just got back from work." I could see that her hair was pure black under her hairnet, and her features were handsome and energetic, but beginning to be blurred by lines and excess flesh. She quizzed me about where I came from, how long I wanted the room for, and what my husband's schedule was. I felt more and more as though I were job hunting.

Finally, I figured I had passed the first inspection because she got up, walking as though her feet ached, and led me back into the room.

"It isn't much," she said. "But here it is." The room, in the back of the house across from the kitchen, seemed almost too good to be true. It was light, with an honest-to-God rug on the floor, a closet, dresser, double bed, which sagged only slightly, a card table covered with a fresh cloth, and a private entrance, opening out onto a concrete porch on the side of the house. I told her I thought it was wonderful.

"Oh, it isn't much," she insisted, "but the girls always seem to like it." We sat on the bed, with an ashtray between us, and talked it over.

"The girls here take care of their own rooms, and we all share the bathroom," she said. "It's right next door to this room. You use linen as you want; it's in a cabinet in the bathroom. And it's all live and let live. We're just an ordinary family, an ordinary American family, and we do what we want and let other people do what they want. We won't bother you, and I know you won't bother us." A girl, younger than the boy, and strikingly pretty, appeared in the doorway.

"Mother, is this dress all right to wear to the party?" she asked, after looking me over.

"You know it's all right. Go on away, Patricia," Mrs. Upton said. She pronounced it Patreecia. A small dog came into the room, sliding between the girl's legs.

"I hope you like dogs," Patricia said. I assured her I did, and she disappeared.

"You use your own entrance," Mrs. Upton went on, "and go your own way, and we'll get along fine. The kids make a lot of noise, but we're just ordinary people, and Mr. Upton and I work very hard." I found my mind jumping to follow her transitions, and noticed that her voice carried just the edge of a whine. "I want to do everything I can for you Army wives, and the girls who've lived here have always seemed to like it. They still write me, all of them, every girl that's ever lived in this house still writes me."

Patricia appeared in the doorway again, just to look this time.

"Go on about your business, Pat," Mrs. Upton said. "You know you're just showing off." There was a hearty yell from the next room.

"That's Ralph, my son," Mrs. Upton told me. "He's just showing off, too. My third one, Shirley, isn't here now. Shirley's my baby," she added, using the affectionate words matter-of-factly.

She asked me how long I had been in Neosho, and what I thought of it. I said I hadn't seen much except the square and a few of the residential streets.

"You've seen it all," she said. "All there is to see. That's Neosho, the whole town. We aren't natives, of course," she added emphatically. "We come from St. Louis. But Mr. Upton is in business down here."

"Oh, it's a terrible mess, this town," she exclaimed. "All these soldiers. I'm afraid for Patricia and Shirley. I really am. I tell you I'm afraid to let them go out in the streets at night." I shook my head sympathetically, wishing that we'd get back to the subject of the room, wondering if all this meant that she was going to take me. She got up and walked over to the doorway, and I followed, ready to admire anything she pointed out. Clotheslines were laced across the porch, and concrete steps led into the obviously untended part of the yard.

"Now, you see those are your steps," she said. I looked obediently at the steps and noticed a worn-out broom leaning against the pipe balustrade.

"Did the U.S.O. tell you what I charge?" she asked. They hadn't, and she went on. "Well, I charge eight a week. I could get thirteen with this private entrance, thirteen dollars, but I wouldn't want to take it from the girls." I didn't know then how often I was to hear about that thirteen dollars she could get. I came to wonder if there was some kind of chart where "private entrance equals thirteen dollars" was listed.

"Well," I said, trying not to sound too eager. "I'd like to take it, if it's all right."

"Yes, it's all right," she said. "You'll find we're just ordinary people. When will you move in?"

I explained that my baggage was up in Joplin, and that I'd move down tomorrow, "if that's all right with you."

"Sure, any time, any time," Mrs. Upton assured me. "I don't give kitchen privileges, you understand. I'd like to because I know it's hard for you girls, but I just don't want to make any more bother for the girl who works for me. Of course, as for coffee in the morning, that's all right, and if you want to keep milk or beer in the icebox, well, that's all right, too. But no cooking, because though I'd like to help you out, I just can't have it."

Her ground rules sounded pleasantly lax, and I accepted them gratefully.

"Would you like me to pay you now?" I asked.

"Oh, now, any time, it doesn't matter," she said. I gave her the money, anxious to get it into her hands and have the deal closed. "We'll count this as of tomorrow," she said, fingering the bills expertly.

"Are you going to live here?" Patricia asked, this time all the way in the room.

"Yes, she is," Mrs. Upton said. "Though what business it is of yours, I can't imagine."

"That's swell," Patricia said.

Ten minutes later, I went out of my own door, locked it after me with my own key, and walked down my own porch steps. I set off for the bus station where I was to meet Spencer, looking over the town with the newly possessive eye of a resident. I felt as though I had won a major victory.

15   If Your Baby Must Travel in Wartime

U.S. Department of Labor, Children's Bureau

The Children's Bureau, established in 1912, did more to promote the health and well-being of American children than any other federal agency during the first half of the twentieth century. Led by prominent female social reformers, including Katharine F. Lenroot, the director during World War II, the Bureau published hundreds of widely disseminated pamphlets and booklets on the health care of children.

If Your Baby Must Travel in Wartime is one of many Bureau publications on caring for children. It emphasizes the special hazards of traveling with youngsters and includes helpful hints for mothers planning journeys on crowded trains and buses.

Going by Train

YOU WILL NEED TO MAKE your train reservations early. Select the first or middle of the week for traveling. Stay off trains on weekends or holidays. Travel then is like a bargain-counter rush.

Travel arrangements of any kind are hard to make nowadays. Railroads are geared to military needs, and civilians take what is left over.

If you are going on a very long trip, try by all means to arrange for a stopover or two with relatives or friends. It will give you a chance to rest and get things in order again.

If you are traveling by coach, let us hope you are in one of the up-to-date coaches with comfortable reclining seats rather than in one of the not-so-modern coaches found on other trains.

If it is a de luxe coach and if your child is 2 or 3 years of age, you may be able to get a seat reservation for him. Otherwise you will have to hold him on your lap.

From *If Your Baby Must Travel in Wartime* (Washington, DC: U.S. Department of Labor, Children's Bureau, Bureau Publication 307, [1944]), 5–24.

Remember, too, if you have trouble, that the Travelers Aid is always willing to help. Its workers can help you locate friends or relatives. They can help you if you lose your tickets or your money, or if any similar emergencies occur while you are en route. They can get a doctor for you if you or your baby become ill. They can tell you of good restaurants to eat in or of places where you can rest or feed your baby. You can even arrange by telegram with the Travelers Aid to have someone meet you at the station from which you are leaving or at which you are arriving to help you. If you are a serviceman's wife, the USO can help you, too.

Plan well and travel light—After you have made all your travel arrangements, gather your forces at home. Write out in detail your youngster's schedule, and list the food, clothes, and other supplies needed.

Travel light, so far as your own personal belongings are concerned, lighter than you've ever imagined you could.

Your aim is to take on the train enough for essential comfort and not one item more.

Limit yourself to one dark dress or suit. Many mothers have found an apron a convenience, one that could be slipped over their dresses when they were caring for their babies. Additional clothing for yourself can be checked and sent on ahead.

Clothes, diapers, and such—Carry an abundance of changes for the baby or toddler. But plan to dress him simply in clothes that are easy to put on and take off.

Remember, weather may change, and many trains are air cooled. So take along a warm outer garment, preferably a sweater, and a blanket for the baby.

Unless your baby has completely mastered the art of keeping dry, use disposable diapers if you can possibly get them. If you cannot get them, then the next best bet is a supply of standard diaper linings—specially treated papers about the size of ordinary cleaning tissues, used with cloth diapers.

Many mothers prefer to use cloth diapers at night. Some babies become badly chafed if only paper diapers are used. Used cloth diapers can be wrapped in wax paper and repacked in your suitcase or put into a waterproof bag.

If your baby is sufficiently trained to use his own toilet seat, by all means take it along. He is less likely to be frightened if there is this one familiar thing in his strange surroundings. Some toilet seats come with a carrying case. If the one you have did not, then use a canvas laundry case or a shopping bag for this purpose.

Pack the baby's clothes, diapers, and blankets into a special suitcase or bag. Keep it unlocked and easily accessible on the train.

Milk for the baby—If the baby is breast fed, feeding him is relatively easy. Food for babies who are not breast fed presents a difficult problem.

For traveling, the simplest formula is one of evaporated milk. Milk can be obtained in small cans, and an individual feeding can be made up when feeding time comes. Then no refrigeration is needed. For such a feeding you will need to carry the following equipment, all of which should be assembled in one container, such as a heavy shopping bag or a medium-sized duffle bag:

Bottles and caps—boiled and ready for use. Take enough for all feedings during the trip, plus some extras for water. Wrap each bottle separately.

Nipples—boiled and put in a boiled jar with a lid.

Can opener (or some other instrument to open small cans of evaporated milk).

Milk in small cans. The cans should be washed off before you leave home.

Vacuum bottle containing boiled water. Sugar or syrup may be added to the water if desired.

Funnel—to put water into bottles. This should be boiled and wrapped in clean paper.

If your baby has not been on evaporated milk, and your doctor agrees that it is satisfactory for him, you should introduce him to it, several days or even a week before you start on your trip if he gets used to new things slowly.

Before you leave home, you can prepare the mixture of hot boiled water, with or without sugar or syrup, and carry it in a vacuum jug on the train. Then mix this mixture and the evaporated milk as you need it. Your doctor will tell you the correct proportions.

Usually the hot water in the vacuum bottle, when added to the milk, will make the feeding the right temperature for the baby. Carry small cans of milk, using whatever is needed for one feeding only.

Perhaps you can drink what is left in the can yourself or give it to a fellow traveler. Do not save it to use later.

The one thing you cannot do is to run the risk of giving your baby contaminated or sour milk. Never attempt to carry the milk warm in a vacuum jug. If you do, the bacteria that are present in milk will multiply many times, with the result that when the milk is fed to the baby, it will make him sick.

You can carry boiled nipples in a jar, as already suggested, or you can use nursing bottles with caps that make it possible to reverse the nipples into the bottle and thus keep them sterile.

Water for the baby—For baby's protection, it is very important that you do not give him water that has not been boiled. Usually it is better to take several bottles of boiled water from home even though you may find it possible to obtain boiled water on the train. Or plan to use the boiled water from the vacuum jug.

Other food for the baby—Orange juice and cod-liver oil usually cannot be carried conveniently. There is no harm in letting your baby go without these during the time when you will be traveling.

Unless your baby is on a special diet, don't load yourself down with canned foods under present traveling conditions. Your baby can get along for a few days on his milk. Plan to use as little food as you think you can get by with.

If your baby is a hearty eater, and you fear that he will miss his cereal, then carry dry ready-prepared baby cereal, to which you can add hot water from the vacuum bottle. You will need to take a dish and a spoon in the shopping or duffle bag. Foods that require heating will have to be omitted. Some children do not object to cold food. If yours does not, and if he has a big appetite, you can take canned vegetables or fruits, which he can eat from the can. Take rusks or crackers along for emergency use.

In planning these solid foods, remember that nothing can be heated except by the addition of hot water from your vacuum jug, and that no utensils can be washed on the train.

Food for young children—Meals for toddlers are not so much of a problem as meals for babies are.

Packing a lunch of customary foods will not be difficult for the short trip. This may include bread-and-butter sandwiches, wrapped in wax paper; cookies or crackers; canned tomato or fruit juice; and canned evaporated milk. (Several large paper bags to be used as "waste baskets" are a convenience.)

But for a long trip you may have to rely on getting your meals in the diner even though this is more expensive. Some railroads, however, don't serve meals to civilians until after servicemen are fed, so you may need to take along some food even though you are planning to use the diner. Be sure to go to meals early.

Most little children are thrilled at the idea of eating on the train and tell about the experience for many days afterward. For a toddler's diet the railroads even now can usually supply cooked cereals, baked potatoes, green vegetables, well-cooked meats, fruits, and milk.

Some dining cars provide half portions for children, but if they don't, no one will object if you order a meal for yourself and give part of it to Junior. But in case you are unable to get into the diner, it is wise to take some simple things for your toddler and yourself to eat.

Keeping baby clean—Mothers sometimes attempt to bathe babies on a train in the washroom basins. Don't do it. It isn't sanitary. It is better to let your baby go unbathed during the trip than to run the risk of infection. Clean his face and hands off with cold cream and cleansing tissues, and let it go at that.

When changing diapers, use oil and cotton and cleansing tissues. Change the baby where he lies instead of trying to take him back to the dressing room.

Keep handy at all times a small emergency diaper kit in a rubber-lined bag, so you can stop anywhere and take care of the baby if necessary.

Keeping baby comfortable—Adjustable canvas seats are available, chiefly for use in automobiles, but they are very helpful for train travel, too. They are light and can be folded and put in a suitcase. Some come in their own carrying cases. They give the child a restful change from the car seat.

Sleeping in the coach—If you travel by coach, the chances are you are going to have to sleep with your baby cradled in your arms. You may be able to rent a pillow, which will make the night more comfortable for you and your baby.

In most coaches lights are turned down at night, and often babies sleep undisturbed. The night trip will be harder on you than it is on the baby.

There is far more space and better service in Pullman accommodations, and if there is any way that you can manage to have them, you should do it for your own and your baby's sake. Accommodations on the Pullman are worth the extra cash, if you have the cash.

Even though you may be unable to reserve a lower berth in advance, it may be possible to arrange with the Pullman conductor to exchange your upper for a lower. The greater convenience of a lower berth is worth the extra cost.

If your baby is very tiny (under 3 months), he can travel by basket if you go by Pullman. For your baby's food, it is wise to use an evaporated-milk formula as [previously] described. . . . For any type of travel this formula is probably the safest and the easiest.

For a short daytime trip or an overnight trip, you may be able to arrange ahead of time to keep the bottles in the refrigerator of the dining car. If you do so, you must be very sure, though, that the dining car is not to be taken off the train at any point before you reach your destination. If you can safely use the refrigerator of the diner, you can prepare your feedings before you leave. Chill them thoroughly, carry the bottles containing the milk mixture in your sterilizer, and, as you board the train, hand it to the porter to put into the refrigerator. When baby is ready for food, the porter will heat a bottle and bring it to you. Don't forget to include a few bottles of boiled water in your quota of bottles.

If you are traveling in the Pullman, you can put the baby or young child to bed at his regular time and expect him to sleep soundly until morning.

If your baby is very young, you may use the basket for sleeping purposes. Berths are wide and long, and you can keep the baby, basket and all, with you at night. Change and feed the baby in the berth each morning before getting him up.

Put the older child in the half of the berth next to the window, carefully padding the window sill and window with a pillow to prevent head bumping and in winter to keep the youngster warm.

Carry along a waterproof sheet to give the porter when he makes up the berth. If the child is under 4, this is a wise precaution even though he may be perfectly trained at home.

Entertaining the young child—Little children get tired on a long trip, and who can blame them? You can keep them entertained if you take along a few carefully selected toys: colored crayons, pencils, tablets, a favorite doll, and storybooks. A familiar toy should be included, as new ones are not so comforting.

Children like books under such circumstances, and you should have several small ones with you. Books about trains and engines will be good fun.

Keep a small toy or two in your purse for odd moments—when you are waiting for your meal in the diner, for example, or when you are waiting for a train. It is a good plan to have a pencil handy and paper for you to draw on to amuse your youngster, or for him to scribble on if he is old enough. Another good thing to have with you is a small cloth picture book that can be rolled up into a compact cylinder.

Fellow travelers—Most people like children, so don't get too upset if Jimmy talks with his fellow passengers. Many grown-ups find an alert, friendly child a delightful diversion on a long and tiresome trip.

Almost always when you tell the person to whom the child is talking, "Send Jimmy back if he annoys you," you get the assurance, "He's perfectly all right. I enjoy talking to him." Accept such statements at their face value. Don't cramp Jimmy's style "in winning friends and influencing people."

There are times, although they will be rare, when you may need to curb Jimmy's friendliness—when he shows too much interest in an obviously undesirable or uninterested person. Bring him back to your seat to hear a story or to eat an apple, and then keep him busy until he forgets about the stranger.

You will need to keep your eyes glued on overfriendly grown-ups who in a burst of enthusiasm may give your youngster candy or other undesirable food. Many adults are thoughtless about food for children, and if you are unfortunate enough to meet one of these individuals, you will need to be tactful but firm. You can't afford to run the risk of having a sick child.

Many times people will offer to carry your suitcase, to watch one child while you attend to another, to carry your toddler into the dining car, or to keep an eye on your sleeping baby while you go to the rest room.

Use good judgment about accepting such offers to help you. They are usually made in good faith and with the best intentions in the world. And you'll certainly need some help if you're traveling with a youngster in these days of overworked train crews and few redcaps [porters]. But don't ever leave your baby with a stranger in a railroad station, and do hesitate to leave him with a total stranger on the train. Don't leave him for very long with anyone; he may be frightened when you go away. Don't trust your baby to anyone who has a cold or any other visible illness that the baby might catch.

Going by Bus

As a rule buses are even more crowded than trains, and there is far less space. And traveling by bus with a baby or young child requires even better planning than travel by train.

There are a few things you will need to know about bus travel before you start out. Buses make 15-minute rest stops every 2 hours and 40-minute to 1-hour stops three times a day for meals. Any child who occupies a child seat is required to have a half-fare ticket even though he is under 5.

By all means plan your trip for the first or the middle of the week, avoiding the weekend travel peak if at all possible. If you are going on a long trip, plan stopovers that will break your journey. Everything that was said about clothes, supplies, and equipment for traveling by train coach will be needed when you travel by bus. If anything, your things will need to be packed even more compactly.

If your baby is breast fed, traveling will be easier than if he is not. You will need to plan with your doctor about putting your baby on an evaporated-milk formula if he is bottle fed. Remember, too, that you will have to count on preparing his feedings during rest and meal stops.

Emergency supplies of food for yourself and your young child will be necessary even though you hope to buy your meals on the way. Restaurants in bus depots are overcrowded, and you may not be able to get food in the time you have.

For a short trip you had better plan on carrying food for yourself and your youngster.

Going by Car

Families going to strange cities to establish new homes are still able to obtain gasoline with which to travel by car. A few tips on automobile travel may therefore be of value.

Proper care of your baby when traveling by car can be summed up in this way: clean milk, clean water, clean food, and as little change as possible from the regular schedule to which he is accustomed.

Most young children enjoy riding in an automobile although they do get tired and bored on long trips. There are many things that you can do to make traveling by car easier.

When your baby is small, take him in his carrying basket, if you have one, and put him on the back seat in a coach or sedan or on the back ledge of a coupe, if it is wide enough. Small canvas hammocks that fasten onto the back of the front seat may still be available and are a real boon to the baby who must travel. If your baby's crib fits into the back of the car, you will have it ready for him to sleep in when he reaches his new home.

When your baby can sit up, there are canvas seats available that hook over the top of the car seat. These will keep the child comfortable and erect and allow him to look out the window without stretching his neck.

The young child can take his afternoon nap stretched out on the back seat and covered with a light robe or coat. Plan your packing of luggage with this in mind.

The baby's food must loom large in your plans if he is not breast fed. You will either have to find a place each night where you can prepare his feedings and devise a way for keeping them on ice and heating them while you travel, or you will have to put the baby on the evaporated-milk formula [previously] described. . . . If you plan to prepare his usual feeding you must take along all the equipment to do it.

Small portable stoves using canned heat can be used to heat the feeding, or you can stop in restaurants and ask a waitress to have the bottle heated for you. The important thing is to have a feasible plan worked out for doing it. Cereal, canned food, and oranges may be obtained along the way.

When stopping for meals, be sure to select good places where well-cooked food can be obtained for young children. Be certain that the milk served the youngsters is pasteurized. And insist that the milk be served directly from the bottle (opened at the table).

Order sensibly for the children, getting them the same type of meal you would supply them at home.

By all means carry your own water, and for the baby or young child it should be boiled. Give the youngsters a drink from your own supply before stopping for food. Don't let them drink water from drinking fountains, hotels, or tourist homes. This does not mean that the water may not be all right; it is merely a precautionary measure against digestive upsets.

If you are traveling by car, you will be able to take along the baby's own toilet equipment, and remember to carry it with you into rest rooms, hotels, or tourist homes.

Don't attempt to drive too many miles in one day when a baby is a passenger. Babies require many stops, and rest periods for a toddler should be frequent.

Plan to stop each night by 5:30 or 6 o'clock. This will give you time to select a hotel or tourist room and get the baby or toddler comfortably to sleep by his usual bedtime.

If toddlers are part of your carload, you will have amusement problems. Gather together a number of small toys and place them in a box of their own. If yours is a two-seated automobile, allow the youngster to change his seat often. Sometimes he will enjoy riding in the front seat; at other times he will want to play with his toys or take a nap in the back seat. It will help to keep him amused if you can think up stories to tell him about the things he sees along the way—the children, the cattle, the trains, and the factories. Songs you know by heart will be used many times over, too.

A job, this traveling with babies in wartime! Certainly not something to attempt lightly. But if you must travel with your baby, you'll be doing a real war service if you make it as painless as you can to the transportation system, your baby, and yourself.

16   So Your Husband's Gone to War!

Ethel Gorham

Ethel Gorham's So Your Husband's Gone to War! *is one of several practical handbooks published for servicemen's wives confronting a "husbandless world." Gorham, a fashion writer, war wife, and mother, offers sound advice on budgets, volunteer work, loneliness, "wolves in friends' clothing," rationing, shortages, diet, and exercise. Recognizing the vital role that mail played in building morale, Gorham devotes an entire chapter to letter writing during wartime, in which she decries "the lost art of letter writing" and includes helpful suggestions on how to compose a good letter to an absent husband.*

From Ethel Gorham, *So Your Husband's Gone to War!* (Garden City, NY: Doubleday, Doran and Co., 1942), 185–99. Reprinted by permission of Doubleday, a division of Bantam Doubleday Dell Publishing Group.

THIS IS THE AGE OF SPEED and service. Why compose a sonnet to your lady's birth date when Western Union can get it for you wholesale? Why write a song to Sylvia when a Postal Telegraph boy will sing #224 all ready made? The telephone rings and brings the news. And all the letters you get are day letters, night letters with a minimum rate for fifty words.

The era of the epistle is past. There exist, of course, some notable exceptions. Lovers still write letters. Remember all the little notes written in the first fine rapture: "Darling, when I left you at noon I thought my heart would break, can hardly wait to see you after class tonight"? You probably have a whole cache of them tucked away somewhere, wrapped in slightly soiled blue ribbons and never reread without a twinge, part sentimental, part sheepish.

Adolescents write letters to each other. "Just discovered Baudelaire," they write; "no one around can understand me, dear friend; it is good to know that in all this bleak world you and I know the meaning of existence." These letters you have probably destroyed years ago in a flush of embarrassment.

Or you write home and say, "All goes as usual; hope everything is fine; everything is fine here; will write more fully next week." Next week you write, "All goes as usual; very busy; am getting along fine; hope everything is fine with you; will write next week, love."

Yes, these are letters. They are letters, that is, in that they are written on paper and go through the mails. But they are as far removed from the old-fashioned, three-dimensional, thoughtful gossip-of-the-court letter as Sylvia's song from Postal #224.

How long since you have written a real letter, a letter that told what you were doing, what you were thinking, what the world around you was like? Probably not in years, if ever at all.

But now it is one more thing you must learn to do. It is one more thing you want to do. For it is the only way you can keep in touch with your husband and let him know in turn what you are doing and thinking. It is for most of you your only constant means of communication these days, and it has to be cherished and nourished like another sense that needs developing when the senses of sight and smell have gone.

If you don't write to your husband and he doesn't write to you, you have only memory and furloughs to fall back on. The fuller and stronger you make this new written bond between you, the closer your relationship will grow. So ripe and healthy can this sense become that soon you begin to think of your husband in terms of it. It was the most curious sensation after three weeks of steady letter writing to have my husband suddenly telephone one afternoon. I had been thinking of him in terms of letters. I knew his mood on this page and his humor on that page and the maneuvers they were going through in the letter [of the] day before yesterday. His written word had become as familiar as the touch of his hand in other days.

Now, unexpectedly, the operator said, "Toronto calling," and I said, "Hello," and I had no sense of continuity at all. His voice was on another level of familiarity. It belonged to a long time ago. It wasn't up to date. It was part of him three weeks before, but we were three weeks further in our lives.

Other senses get jarred as this new written sense develops. For instance, the whole feeling for time differs. You are answering today a letter written perhaps one day or one week or one month before, and what you say about yourself and your child and the people around you won't reach your husband for that length of time again.

So accustomed are you to the immediacy of reaction over a telephone or across telegraph wires that it takes adjustment to get used to the delayed reaction time of letter writing. It feels rather like being on a conveyor-belt system of thought that remains forever slightly out of joint. When your mood is such, it will not be such when he gets your letter about it, and what he said to you in the letter that arrived today has nothing to do with what he actually thinks and feels now. Perhaps there is a mystic philosophy of time planes involved in it somewhere, but for a simple soul it means compromising with temporary facts and emotions so as to avoid the air of congealed permanence.

One of the best rules to remember, if you want to spare yourself the unhappiness of wishing you hadn't sent yesterday's letter, is to leave out all personal upheavals. Did you run into a bit of in-law trouble? You have before, you know, and will again. Why mention it? Are you feeling lonely and upset and vaguely suicidal? Don't put it into written words unless you're prepared to jump out of the window and this is your last message on it all.

You've felt that way before. This hasn't been an easy time, and some days are worse than others. But on paper it has a permanence that lasts until your next letter arrives, and even though your "blue" mood has long since passed, you're inflicting it on someone as if it were a thing of the present, filled with present concerns.

It is so easy to sit down after a long day of conflict and penny-pinching and lonesomeness and pour out all of it on paper. You feel you want someone you love to share your trouble. After all, he writes all the details about his military life, doesn't he, and he makes no bones about the food, the routine, the constant complaining. Ah, but that's different!

Your letters arrive as the only link he has with his outside life. In your letters he feels the pulse of normalcy. From your letters he draws the small details that go into building a continuity between his past and his future.

If you get a gloomy, depressed letter from him, you say, "Poor darling, I wish I could help." Then you fold it away and get back to all the million and one things you have to do that are part of his life, too. But if he gets a dejected letter from you, he can't slide back into the details of your common life to refresh his memory that not all is as black as you paint it. The routine of what he is doing is so different from his civilian past that the dark picture you draw can't easily be erased by the cool analysis of reality. If you pout, if you sulk, if you complain, it will sadden him for days and yield you no profit. . . .

Don't take the attitude of here I am in my steaming hot kitchen while there you are in your nice cool barracks. Nothing is funnier and more unfair.

Leave out all reference, if you can, to the high cost of living. He probably feels troubled enough about your financial state, and it is better to settle your problems in silence than to use valuable letter space to do it in. Besides, what can he do about it five hundred miles or a thousand miles or perhaps three thousand miles from home?

Presumably both of you knew that war made a mess of the facts of life. If you didn't, you should have consulted Sherman. And one of the minor messes is the need for women to stay home and wait and work and keep things going. There is no use fidgeting in a letter about it.

Letters should be as much like your best moments as possible. They should be about everything that concerns you both. Most men like newsy letters, with lots of detail. If you are the whimsy type and he likes whimsy, you can give him the news the whimsical way. Straight Winnie-the-Pooh grows tiresome even if he is a fan

"THE GIRL HE LEFT BEHIND"
IS STILL BEHIND HIM
She's a WOW
WOMAN ORDNANCE WORKER

Courtesy Library of Congress

of the technique, but thread it through with detail and gossip and
he will live for your letters.

If you are both interested in headlines and editorials and what
people are saying, he'll be delighted with letters that discuss the
reactions of people to the latest war stories. He will appreciate your

inclusion of clippings from the papers. He will look for your comment on current affairs.

If you both are avid book readers, write and tell him about the new books. Or about new recordings if you are record collectors. Or about what your friends are doing and why, if you've always been a sociable pair with a host of friends.

Letters should be as warm and intimate as you yourself have been with the man to whom you are writing.

Incidentally, if he is not your husband, you know what he is. Friend, companion, the boy next door. Treat him as such in your letters, and don't be afraid of the effect. This is no time for coy girlish reticence. If everybody misses him, say so. If you miss him, say so, too. You may never have another chance.

After a while, as you concentrate on this business of letter writing, you will find yourself developing a personality that is completely dependent on the written word.

One wartime wife I know has made a habit of getting out and seeing people only because she had to find something to write to her husband about.

"I was becoming," she told me, "an old fogy. I'd go to the office all day, then directly home to putter around and so to bed. I found I didn't have a blooming thing to write Bob about, except I loved him. But you can't keep that up all the time without getting dull. So now I collect material."

And has herself a lot of fun in the meantime, too. For collecting material means going to a movie or a theater or a U.S.O. dance or to the air-raid post. Instead of languishing at home, crying her eyes out, she now makes friends and influences her letters. The result—better person herself, better letters, happier husband.

One wife, who is now working here in one of the British information bureaus while her husband is fighting somewhere in Africa, says she and her husband have established an entirely new unity between them through their letters.

"I have come so much closer to my husband," she told me. "I'm an American, you know, and I met Tom, who is English, while I was over there on some job or other. We were engaged for two years, then married for almost eight; and in all that time, although we had a great deal of companionship, I put down a certain coldness, a certain lack of verbal affection, to his English temperament. Now everything is changed. His letters carry a warmth he was never able to give me before. And, in return, I find myself writing things

I never dreamed I could say or get Tom to understand. We are so much more sympathetic to each other. Like different people, really—more tender, more unashamed, more revealing, you might almost say."

Keeping your letters varied means keeping yourself that way. It means following the newspapers more closely than you ever have before. It means listening to the war news on the radio. It means knowing what you are writing about to a man who is in the thick of it.

Don't forget, too, that being in the thick of it, he sometimes doesn't know what is going on around the fringe. He'll be grateful for what you can tell him. Tell him, over and over again, what they are doing in your town or city or district about the war. The most important thing to a soldier is knowing that the home front is at war with him.

Tell him about the new people that have joined the forces. Tell him who is going where and how long they expect to be stationed there. A man in uniform wants to know which of his friends and former coworkers are in uniform with him. It's a kind of men-together attitude. They feel better if they know they are not the only ones of the crowd away from home.

What part of yourself you can put in your letters, that part he will have. Make it the most charming, most informative, most truly feminine part. It is hard to practice seduction a thousand miles away, but that's what your letters should do. A kind of mental, spiritual, companionable seduction. Thus you will get him to depend on your reactions, your news, your understanding. If you give him this kind of letter, filled with the life you live, he will feel, each time he answers you, that he has never gone away. . . .

Consistency is one of the most important things you have to follow in your letter writing. If you are going to write every day, you must write every day. If your routine calls for two letters a week, never, never vary it.

What a blow to come to expect a letter every Monday and Wednesday and then find there is none there for you on the day expected. No matter if it finally arrived on Friday. You had conditioned him to look for it on Wednesday, and two days are a long time to wait.

My husband tells me that when he goes to the post-office wicket [grated window] at eleven-thirty in the morning and finds no letter from me, the whole day seems much longer and further removed from home. "Everybody," he tells me, "waits at the window as if they were handing out reprieves. And the lads who don't get a letter turn away as if lost."

"It's the best hold the girls have on us," a young man in the Army air corps told me. "You want to be as nice as you can to them when you're out on leave so you can get them to write to you."

You may not get the same consistency in return, but never forget you have other things to fall back on.

Incidentally, you may find that the longhand in which you were such a star pupil back in the days when you wrote out with beautiful patience, "Time and Tide Wait for No Man," over and over again, is now one of your lesser accomplishments. It can be so bad that if you have used a typewriter for years, you find you can't think without one. Faced with white paper and blue ink, you find yourself completely tongue-tied (or would it be pen-tied?). Fortunately, you will probably have more opportunity at home to continue to use the typewriter. But don't be chagrined if your husband's first letters are halting, stumbling, and brief because of his new means of expression.

A friend of mine with a husband on a first-rank battleship writes him twice each week, on the hour, although she hears from him about once every month or two. She realizes that he probably gets all her letters in one batch, but just on the off chance that his ship might be in Maine instead of Murmansk she gets the letters out consistently so he will receive them that way if he can.

More difficult and heroic is the correspondence of another wartime wife who hasn't heard from her husband since the last days of the fall of Corregidor. She carries on her life on two levels: haunting official offices for casualty lists, and attempting to spin out a series of friendly, chatty letters that may sometime be delivered to him all in one lot if ever he turns up in Australia. She has been given the hope that he was one of those rescued. The months go on, and no word arrives to confirm or deny. Still she writes.

"I have to keep the letters brief," she admits, "or else I couldn't stand to finish them at all. You don't know, you can't imagine how horrible it is to write into a void, like writing to outcheat disaster. Sometimes it seems more than I can bear, but I do it because when he shows up I want him to feel that time didn't lapse with me; that I was there from letter to letter, on schedule Mondays and Fridays."

Do avoid at all times the statement that you are having such a riotous good time back home that of course you can't find time to write. It brands you as callous, shallow. If true, you probably don't care. If not true, it shows you haven't been writing often or consistently enough. And can you blame him if, brave soldier though he may be, he breaks his heart about it? . . .

The best way to get into the writing habit is just to write. Handling the written word comes more easily to some than others, but it comes with greatest comparative ease after constant doing. Set yourself a time and place. Buy enough paper so you don't have to wander about looking for a scrap each time you need one. The paper shortage may affect the quality of paper you can buy; it may even affect the quantity. But until it does, have enough simple paper on hand to write when you want. Also buy stamps and keep them with you. Nothing will delay a letter so much as the missing stamp. You hold on to sealed envelopes long after you have addressed them because the corner shop hasn't a stamp or you haven't three cents at the moment. If you can, buy one or two dollars' worth of postage at one time. Then your letter will stand a likelier chance of going out shortly after it is written.

Set yourself the habit of writing at length. Nothing is more off-the-shoulder than the nibbly little letter. It's a kind of pretext and shows disinterest and dutifulness. And heaven forfend that this letter writing should turn into a matter of duty! If it can't be the warm continuation of your life together, you had better go in for mental telepathy.

If you haven't enough to say twice a week or once a week to make up a solid chunky letter with reams of pages, write only once a month. The only exception is the daily letter. Here, because contact is reestablished every twenty-four hours, you can put it off some days with a brief, "Busy, darling, write more fully tomorrow." The whole attitude is different. It presupposes an abundance of communication between you. However, one short will-write-later note has to be balanced with three or four unmistakably long letters. And you can never skip a day. So if you are not an enthusiastic, dyed-in-the-ink letter writer, the daily-letter system is not for you.

But however often or seldom you write, remember your letters must be rich, full of information, and that the more frequently you write, the less painful will be the separation. You will find that the worst part of the hiatus in your emotional life can be bridged over. You cannot be separated truly if you find yourself held together by a constant stream of words.

There is "love interest" aplenty in the correspondence of Abelard and Heloise and it fairly drips pathos, but more than that, you'll find wit and opinion and comment that make the letters a picture of the times. The letters of Madame de Sévigné are full of news, chit-chat, mischievous gossip. The great Victorians wrote of love, but they wrote also of the new books, that monster Disraeli, the wickedness of the life in Paris, the beauty of England in spring.

You are certainly not interested in your letters as literature, but it wouldn't be out of the way to follow the technique of the great masters in the art. They knew one trick—how to keep emotions fluid through long, unmoving months. "I love you, I miss you, I need you," was only part of what they had to say. The rest was devoted to keeping interest whetted through personal peepholes at the world.

So carry your heart in your letters but your mind, too. And if your words are filled with both sweetness and light, they will reap greater fellow feeling between you and your husband than you ever thought possible.

17   The Negro Woman Serves America

Aframerican Woman's Journal

Although racism and prejudice permeated American life in the 1940s, African Americans demonstrated strong support for the ideals for which World War II was fought. The "Double V" campaign, adopted by the black press in March 1942, called for victory over both totalitarianism abroad and racism at home. It was in this context that significant numbers of black women volunteered for war work.

The following material focuses specifically on the volunteer war work of African-American women, although the vast majority of American women, regardless of their race or ethnicity, devoted millions of hours to volunteer activities. This text

From "Negro Volunteers of the American Women's Volunteer Services," "The Women's Army for National Defense," "Negro Women in the U.S.O.," and "Negro Women in Civilian Defense," *Aframerican Woman's Journal* (Summer 1943): 11–15; Series 13, Box 2, Folder 11, Records of the National Council of Negro Women. Reprinted by permission of the Bethune Museum and Archives, Washington, DC.

originally appeared in "The Negro Woman Serves America" issue of the Aframerican Woman's Journal *in the summer of 1943. Examined here are the contributions of African-American volunteers to the American Women's Volunteer Services (AWVS), the Women's Army for National Defense (WAND), the USO, and civilian defense.*

Negro Volunteers of the American Women's Volunteer Services

WHEN THE AMERICAN WOMEN'S VOLUNTEER SERVICES was organized by Mrs. Alice Throckmorton McLean in 1940, the words "regardless of race, color, or creed" attracted the attention of hundreds of Negro women anxious to serve their country but timid of applying to agencies whose usual answer was a negative one.

Negro women in New York were the first to seek membership in the A.W.V.S., and their lead was soon followed by groups in Corona, N.Y., Beacon, N.Y., Beaumont, Texas, Galveston, Texas, Hollywood, Cal., Chicago, Ill., Omaha, Neb., Durham, N.C., Gary, Ind., Ashland, Ky., Atlanta, Ga., New Orleans, La., Tucson, Ariz., and Pittsburgh, Pa.

In the city of New York, units are established geographically, according to the battalions of the Fire Department. In Harlem there are three such units. Another large and active group headed by a Negro woman but interracial in composition is found in Corona, L.I., a suburb of N.Y. City. From a small beginning in July, 1941, these units have grown to a membership of more than 3,000.

These divisions conduct classes in First Aid, Air Raid Precautions, and Motor Mechanics in their local areas, while many of their members are taking other courses at the Greater New York Headquarters and other A.W.V.S. units, in International Morse Code, Map Reading, Nutrition, War Photography, Public Speaking, Child Care, Consumers Education, etc. Each unit has its Volunteer Workshop, where members who knit and sew make such useful articles as sweaters, helmets, socks, gloves, blankets, and children's clothing. These articles are distributed to local charities, principally to day nurseries serving underprivileged of the community. Each unit has a Junior Auxiliary, of girls from 14 to 18, who take training courses, work at crafts, and conduct a messenger service. All these units have cooperated with the Red Cross Drive for Nurses' Aides, and several members volunteered at the Harlem Hospital for training.

These divisions have been serving as volunteers in aiding local draft boards with the registration of men for the Selective Service and by assisting in the various rationing registrations. Members of these units have also manned booths in banks, theaters, and department stores from which they have sold thousands of dollars' worth of [war] bonds and stamps. Those who completed the course in Communications and Map Reading serve in that division of the Interceptor Command which plots information on the movement of planes as relayed by the plane spotters. They have done a splendid job in the Government's scrap collection campaign; their Victory Pastime Committees collect radios, magazines, books, athletic equipment, games, and other articles for the soldiers in camps and in hospitals; and they have furnished day-recreation rooms for servicemen stationed in the local area.

Two of the New York divisions (12th and 16th) devoted their energy to providing an emergency ambulance for Harlem. A benefit entertainment and dance made possible the purchase of this ambulance, and women from these divisions who completed the required training are now manning the ambulance and performing other duties with the Motor Transport Service of the A.W.V.S.

In other parts of the country, A.W.V.S. divisions with Negro membership are making noticeable headway. The unit in Beaumont, Texas, since receiving its membership certificate in 1942, has set up courses with both white and Negro instructors, in First Aid, Civilian Protection, Nutrition, Home Gardening, Fingerprinting, Child Care, and one in Law for Everyday Use. This unit carried on a month's concentrated war bond and stamp drive, and in collaboration with the white unit, fingerprinted 1,635 schoolchildren. It also, without assistance, raised funds and equipped four defense nursery schools.

The A.W.V.S. Negro unit of Galveston, Texas, is furnishing training in Child Care, has built two air-raid shelters in church basements for children, and has stocked them with fruit juices, sterile water, medicines, and practically everything that might be needed in an emergency. In this same unit, several women who have completed A.W.V.S. training are serving as auxiliary nurses in the John Sealy Hospital where doctors and nurses have praised the untiring and efficient work these colored nurses are doing.

Omaha, Nebraska, has also recognized the need for additional child care due to large numbers of mothers engaged in defense work, and with the cooperation of the Urban League of that city, they have established a day nursery for both white and Negro children, staffed by workers of both races.

In Durham, N.C., the A.W.V.S. Negro unit, besides their general program of training, selling war bonds and stamps, and the usual other activities, have, through their Home Nursing classes, made an incubator for prematurely born babies which has been presented to the city's Department of Health. Members of this unit also serve at a casualty station, have received instruction in the making of Red Cross dressings, and are opening a production room where this work will be carried on.

In Pittsburgh, Pa., the chairman of the A.W.V.S. Negro unit was inspired to form her unit after reading Pearl Buck's "Letter to Colored Americans" published in *Opportunity* Magazine. Full cooperation exists here between the white and Negro A.W.V.S. members, and this group has workers [who have] enrolled in several A.W.V.S. classes, have served in stamp booths, nurseries, and recreation centers, and have cooperated with the Red Cross, the Y.W.C.A., and other community agencies.

Negro women in Gary, Ind., sold $500 worth of tickets for the Paul Robeson [noted black actor and singer] concert which netted $1,000 for the Gary War Chest, and several of them were awarded certificates and pins by the local O.C.D. [Office of Civilian Defense] for their services. Their Speakers' Bureau supplied A.W.V.S. speakers to clubs to discuss timely war subjects and to give morale-building talks. Many of these women did from two to ten hours' work daily on the government's point-rationing programs helping and advising housewives. This unit is now sponsoring nutrition programs in the public schools, in cooperation with the Board of Education. Neither age nor physical handicaps deter these women from expressing in some tangible way their desire to be of service. One invalid Negro woman, who spends her entire life in a wheelchair, volunteered last Christmas to address 1,000 cards which the Gary unit sent to the colored boys in the service. She is at present taking care of a stocking salvage box.

A new Negro unit formed in Grand Cuyahoga county, Ohio, has a membership of 249. This unit, in cooperation with a Sorority, has made plans to set up a child-care center by June 1st, 1943. They have fingerprinted 125 persons, have worked on salvage, have sold over $10,000 worth of bonds and stamps, and have helped U.S.O. hostesses hand out cigarettes, etc., to draftees as they leave for camp. They have set up two Junior units in public schools and made plans for a benefit concert to finance the equipment for a child-care center. This concert, which took place on May 9th, 1943, presented a brilliant young Negro pianist named Natalie Henderson, with the Cleveland Women's Orchestra. This talented artist has appeared with the Lorain Philharmonic Orchestra as well as the Cleveland Women's Orchestra, and has broadcast over a coast-to-coast network, giving 15-minute programs from the Cleveland Radio Station, WHK.

It was a member of one of the Negro A.W.V.S. units in New York City, Mercedes Jordan Welcker, who composed a song that was accepted by the national A.W.V.S. as the organization's marching song. Mrs. Welcker is now a member of the WACs as are many other former A.W.V.S. members, both white and Negro. Divisions are being used as recruiting centers for WAC enlistments, while other A.W.V.S. members are assisting this work at stations throughout the city.

This is only a partial recounting of the conscientious and excellent work done by the Negro units in many parts of the United States, and they should be an inspiration to women of all races. Their spirit and aims are best expressed in a speech made by one of their A.W.V.S. members in Gary, Ind. "We want our Negro soldiers to realize that American Negro womanhood is willing to give its all-out in building up and sustaining the morale of young Negro America. We had and still have many odds against us, the morale among many of our groups has been very low—and not without justification. But Negro soldiers are our boys, and if they are willing to die for a country which denies them full participation in the freedom accorded other groups, they must know that Negro American womanhood glories in their loyalty."

The Women's Army for National Defense

The Women's Army for National Defense [WAND] is a voluntary war service organization, whose membership encourages all American women to prepare for war emergencies, as a patriotic obligation to the country.

A few months ago, Mrs. Lovonia H. Brown, prominent in the fraternal and civic life of Chicago, called a small group of women together to discuss plans for organizing a war service group. The idea was received enthusiastically by those assembled, and thus the Women's Army for National Defense came into being.

Dr. Mary McLeod Bethune, President of the National Council of Negro Women, is First Officer in Command, and has the title, General of the WANDs. Mrs. Lovonia H. Brown is Lieutenant General, and Mrs. Lola M. Parker, National President of the Iota Phi Lambda Sorority, is Major General.

The main purpose of the organization is to mobilize women for civilian defense. The members believe that women have grave, personal responsibilities at this time, and that success in the present conflict depends greatly upon the womanpower of the nation. Women are necessary in the armed forces, in industry, and on the wide home front. Because of this conviction the WANDs have united to sponsor a coordinated program which will give strength and significance to the national effort for victory.

The Women's Army for National Defense, being national in its scope, seeks to organize every home on a wartime basis, by supplying information regarding war services available through Government and War Agencies, under the direction of the Commander-in-Chief of the United States of America. It is the duty of each member to become trained in some phase of war work. Educational programs, victory forums, and classes in defense courses, including War Photography, Radio Operations, Map and Blueprint Reading, and the like are arranged for this purpose.

One of the most important objectives of the WANDs is to compile records of Negroes in war services, with the contributions they make toward the winning of the war. This is very important, the WANDs believe, for when peace comes the record of services rendered in various fields, by members of the Negro race, should be accurate, complete, and easily available. Another objective is the planning of programs and activities benefiting women who are serving with the armed forces. No other civilian war service organization has given its attention to this group. WAND members encourage the sale of war bonds and stamps, work with United Service Organizations, and boast the only Negro Red Cross Canteen Corps in America.

In addition to the usual war services ordinarily rendered by such groups, the Chicago chapters sponsor a Housing Project, located in the Parkway Community House. Named for one of the first Negro women of Chicago to join the Women's Army Corps, it is called the Irma Cayton Barracks, and serves as a residence hall for women in war work, who move to Chicago when the Government Bureaus to which they are attached are transferred to that city. Rooms are also available to WACs who are passing through Chicago from time to time. Another project of the WANDs, sponsored cooperatively with the Parkway Community House, is a child-care clinic, where children of women who work in war industries are cared for during the hours their mothers are employed.

The Women's Army for National Defense desires to honor and keep alive in the minds of the public, those women who have given distinguished service to their race and country, especially those in key positions during this period. For this reason many local chapters of the WANDs stretching across the country, have been named in honor of Mary McLeod Bethune, Harriet Tubman, Maudelle Bousfield, Marian Anderson, Crystal Bird Fauset, Jane Bolin, Hallie Q. Brown, Henrine Ward, and other outstanding women leaders of today.

On May 8th, the Columbia Broadcasting System invited the Women's Army for National Defense and the Parkway Community House to participate in its "Mid-West Mobilizes" program. WAND officers told of the work of the organization, and residents of the Barracks described the comforts to be found there, and expressed their gratitude to the WANDs for providing for them such home-like quarters.

There are many women who are most anxious to render voluntary service in the war effort. The Women's Army for National Defense offers them full opportunity to give assistance of this kind to their Government. The only requirement for membership is a desire and determination to serve.

It is the hope of the officers that women all over the country will soon become WANDs, and help in this service to maintain the freedoms of our nation, the security of American principles, and the future happiness and well-being of every citizen in the commonwealth.

Negro Women in the U.S.O.

"Sew mine next, please, ma'am," said the tall bronze lad clad in the olive-drab uniform of the United States Army, as he proudly handed his chevrons and jacket across the table at a U.S.O. club.

"All right, and there you are, sir," answered the smiling woman at the table. She watched for a moment as he put on the coat that would be prized more than ever now. Then she turned to a new-comer, "I'll have you fixed just like that in no time at all!"

This gracious woman is but one of the countless women across the country who are helping make the U.S.O. a "home away from home." In every city, town, and hamlet, wherever the men of the armed forces are gathered, the Negro woman has rallied to the call for service as a volunteer in the U.S.O. The men have learned to look for the cheery smile and friendly greeting from those host-esses who welcome them in the lobbies of most of the clubs. A question answered here, a word of encouragement there, all go into making the hostess one of the greatest assets to the U.S.O. They may fill the cookie jars, or help write that letter home, or just talk.

Some women serve as librarians, game room hostesses, or lead-ers of various group activities such as music, crafts, and dramatics. Others provide the clubs with flowers regularly. Still others take on such unspectacular tasks as mending and the preparing and serving of food. Many women are kept busy in a rooms registry service—finding rooms for the relatives and friends who are visit-ing servicemen. Others give time each week to hospital visitation. In many U.S.O. clubs, volunteers are available for a shipping ser-vice for the men who want to send just the right gift to the loved one back home or make a purchase for some special occasion. Through the U.S.O. many women serve in home and church hospi-tality groups, providing opportunities for home-cooked meals to small groups and a welcome to the community churches of their choice.

Perhaps the largest group of volunteers is that of young women for hostesses, dance partners, and regular assistants at social af-fairs. These young women are between the ages of eighteen and thirty and must meet the U.S.O. standards in personal conduct and sincerity of purpose.

Each person serving as a Junior Hostess attends a Hostess Train-ing Course where she learns the meaning and function of U.S.O. and her own responsibilities in its program. She is trained in atti-tudes and judgment as well as in charm and poise. She finds that her special interests and skills may be called upon to assist in ac-tivities other than dancing—games, out-of-door activities, crafts, music, other forms of creative programs. Junior Hostesses partici-pate in all coed activities which also include such things as discus-sion groups, forums, and hobbies.

The U.S.O. is not only served by women, but it also serves women—that large group who are directly a part of the war effort. These women include wives and families who follow servicemen into camp areas—wives, sisters, and sweethearts visiting camps, naval stations, and airfields—the women workers on campgrounds, war workers in crowded industrial areas, and the WACs. Some centers serve them exclusively by providing help in finding homes, lounge rooms, parking places for children, stoves for quick meals, as well as advice about jobs, marriage, and family relationships. Others conduct classes for them in First Aid and Budgeting. Clubs are formed to foster congenial group life.

In addition to these ways in which women have become a part of the U.S.O., many are serving creditably on U.S.O. Committees of Management, Advisory Committees, and Councils, helping in the planning of U.S.O. services in the various communities.

The Negro woman through the U.S.O. is functioning as a part of the large national organization, which is composed of six member agencies—Young Men's Christian Association [Y.M.C.A.], Young Women's Christian Association [Y.W.C.A.], [National] Jewish Welfare Board, National Catholic Community Service [N.C.C.S.], Salvation Army, and National Travelers Aid Association [N.T.A.A.]. These agencies are helping in the work of providing activities and giving services to Negroes in U.S.O. centers. There are now 179 Negro clubs operated by the various agencies. These agencies work in close cooperation with National U.S.O. Headquarters at the Empire State Building, New York City.

Special Consultants or Regional Supervisors for the Negro units of the U.S.O. are employed as follows: two by the Y.W.C.A., three by the Y.M.C.A., one by the N.T.A.A., one by the N.C.C.S.

The participation of Negro women in every phase of the work of such an extensive national organization has great significance. It means that Americans move forward with a genuinely democratic spirit, to the participation by all in the life of our country. Negro women are taking their part in the interracial groups which determine policy for the U.S.O. in given communities, policies which, when wisely made and well administered, do much to improve community attitudes. Resourcefulness, cheer, courage—these are the qualities that women of America are exhibiting in this time of national and world crises, and these qualities the Negro woman has in abundance. It is most fortunate that there is so excellent an opportunity for her to contribute them to the needs of her country.

Negro Women in Civilian Defense

One of the greatest opportunities for war service on the home front is provided by the volunteer participation in Civilian Defense. Beginning with the urgent mobilization for protection against air raids, Civilian Defense has broadened to include many other war-created activities.

The impact of war on the community has accentuated existing problems and created many new ones. With the development of war industries, communities have expanded rapidly, and dislocations of serious proportions have resulted. Adequate transportation, housing, health, education, and recreation facilities must be provided. Since individual agencies cannot do the job alone, there must be community-wide planning with the most economical use of volunteer aid. Those programs which depend for their success upon volunteers are the responsibility of the local Defense Council, the coordinating agency for both the protection and civilian war service activities in the community.

Negro women are active in all phases of Civilian Defense. They serve as members of Defense Councils and on the various committees of the Councils. They act as air-raid wardens, nurses' aides, hostesses to servicemen, volunteer in child-care and recreation projects, to mention but a few of their activities. As block leaders, Negro women carry to their neighbors an explanation of many of these civilian war service programs.

Numerous examples may be cited of participation by Negro women in this important war work. For example, a Negro woman is a member of the Recreation Committee of the Brooklyn Defense Council which initiated the Fulton Sumner Canteen where Negro women serve as Senior and Junior Hostesses. The Negro beauticians of New York City sell war bonds, recruit block leaders, and hold discussion meetings on consumer problems. In Baltimore, 195 Negro women are air-raid wardens, 35 are fire watchers, 86 are messengers, and 160 are workers in block organization. New York has a Women's Motor Corps of 80 women, Baltimore a Motor Transport Corps of 19 women, and Roanoke, Virginia, an Ambulance Corps of 30 women.

In Civilian Defense there is a real opportunity for Negro women to contribute to the welfare of their community and in so doing to help the war effort. No Civilian Defense job, however insignificant it may seem in itself, is unimportant. How quickly this war is won depends on how well each of us does his particular job. The many Negro women who have already enrolled in Civilian Defense set a fine example for the rest of the country. Those who have not yet volunteered are urged to register with their local Defense Councils.

V War Jobs

Winning the war against fascism depended on the active participation of all Americans. With some 16.3 million men in the military services, employment opportunities for women expanded at unparalleled rates, allowing them to take on a variety of new and challenging jobs. They learned how to operate welding machines and rivet guns, read blueprints, maneuver heavy machinery, drive and maintain railroad engines, and even become lead "men" on assembly lines. In sharp contrast to the Depression years of the 1930s when working women were often sharply criticized for taking jobs away from men, the woman war worker was highly lauded, and Rosie the Riveter became a national heroine.

In response to the unprecedented demand for new employees, some 6.5 million women entered the work force. The proportion of women who held jobs rose from 25 percent at the beginning of the war to 36 percent at the war's end—an increase greater than in the previous four decades. Just as important, growing numbers of older women and married women with children were employed. Funds from the Lanham Act were used to create 3,100 federally funded child-care centers, but the child-care needs of working women remained woefully unsatisfied. In addition, working women continued to shoulder the brunt of the responsibility for domestic chores; the dual demands of housewife and war worker placed enormous burdens on many women.

Women also came to the rescue of the nation's crops as the percentage of women employed in agriculture rose from 8 percent in 1940 to 22.4 percent in 1945. These workers included farm wives driving tractors, college women milking cows, housewives picking fruit, and secretaries harvesting vegetables during their summer vacations. Of special importance were the efforts of the Women's Land Army, established as part of the U.S. Crop Corps of the Department of Agriculture in April 1943. In effect, the energy and ingenuity of women workers enabled the United States to become both "the arsenal and the bread basket of democracy."

18   Arms and the Girl

Gulielma Fell Alsop and Mary F. McBride

In Arms and the Girl, *Gulielma Fell Alsop, a physician at Barnard College, and Mary F. McBride, director of adult education at the New York YWCA, look at the impact of the war on the lives of young American women. They emphasize that "womanpower is part of this war . . . it is [a] woman's war as no war has ever been." The following excerpts from* Arms and the Girl *provide a compendium of the many new job opportunities available to women.*

NOT ONLY CLAIRE TURNER AND Nancy Felton and the girl from Nebraska who have left home and come to Washington searching for a place in the war effort, not only the thousands of other girls in the offices of Washington, but the thousands of girls in the offices of all our big cities, in the new emergency jobs, doing office war work, are part of the great army of womanpower that is being mobilized in this war. Women have made office work their own, as they have made telephone work their own, by the qualities that are peculiarly women's: their quickness, their capacity for detail, their deftness, their alertness. Even in the Army and Navy the new women of the war are finding their secretarial positions. They are handling all the intricate mass of writing that holds the war offices together, just as the telephone girls handle the intricate web of spoken words that make the affairs of the war run. . . .

But the great war industries, the defense factories, have called for more women even than have gone into offices. In the past, women have not been urged to go into dangerous industries; they have been limited to comparatively safe industries and to the best hours of work, and they have been protected from hazard. They have been given the best jobs, the daytime jobs, in well-organized and safe industries. Now the great need for war workers has swept women and even girls into all kinds of wartime factories. Women who can take and hold a job are considered as fitted for it as a man. They compete, or at present they do not compete at all, for there are more jobs than workers to fill these jobs.

From Gulielma Fell Alsop and Mary F. McBride, *Arms and the Girl: A Guide to Personal Adjustment in War Work and War Marriage* (New York: Vanguard Press, 1943), 41–51.

Infinite precision and the endurance that will permit the performance of the same act with the same precision after eight hours as in the first hour are required of these war workers. They must keep the machines whirring all twenty-four hours of the day. The machines never stop, only the human creatures that run the machines change. Women work in the daytime shift, from seven to four, and to five in some plants. They work in the evening shift from five, or from four, until midnight, and they work in the morning shift from midnight till eight or nine. The hours are long, the speed is stepped up, and behind the rhythm of the factory the urge for output lies in the heart of every worker, man and woman both.

In their blue overalls, in their sneakers, with their hair hidden in caps and kerchiefs, the girls of the war step lightly about the great scaffoldings, drilling, forging, welding, sewing, stitching, filling, packing, making explosives, piling cartridges, arranging bombs, taking part, with their nimble fingers and quick, sure eyes, in every kind of preparation for fighting. These blue-overall girls are everywhere. Lift up one of the masks in the welding department, and an intent but smiling face looks up from the work with a startled humanity. They are almost superhuman. And though, wherever she goes, a woman's nature goes too, though she notices personalities as usual and has her favorites and her enemies, still she is now the new woman. She is different from her mother. She parcels out her emotions, she packs them away out of sight during her work hours with the inanimate tools of the factory and only takes the lid off in the after-hours life. This ability to sink her emotional life out of sight for the time being is something she is learning just as a man has learned it, by necessity. If he must be a tool and without emotion, so, too, must she. If he could learn, so, too, can she. She can be an inanimate precision worker, too.

She is well paid for this work. She is probably better paid than she has ever been. She also works overtime and is paid for that. She has money in her pocket, she has more money to spend than she has had in all her life that has covered the Great Depression period, the period of deflation. She buys War Bonds and War Stamps. Not only does she make the matériel of war, but she spends her money to enable the government to buy other matériel that other girls make. She is right at the heart of the war effort.

She is the womanpower of the war.

The girl in the office, the girl in the factory, is visible and obvious to all of us. We honor her and depend on her. And not only do

Drill press operator in a machine shop, 1943(?). *Courtesy Library of Congress*

we depend on her, but on all the other women in the less spectacular war jobs. The great effort for civilian defense, with its network
of air-raid wardens, of plane spotters, absorbs the time, effort, and
determined skill of another great army of women workers. In civilian defense a different group of women can take their part, women
who are older, who are not able to take full-time war jobs but who
can fill their former leisure time with wartime activities. In these

civilian defense organizations women work at night. They patrol their districts. They help in the planning of the elaborate organizations. They watch at their posts. Their ears are attuned to the first far-distant hum of the machine in the sky. Their quick ears can separate the hum of one plane from another. Their eyes, with powerful telescopes, can pick up the flying planes half shrouded above by the clouds. Each day a woman who is running a house, looking after her children, teaching school, can find free hours for the duties of civilian defense.

These duties involve late hours. They mean getting up at night and patrolling the street, often going on duty at midnight. They upset the habits of a lifetime and tear the pleasant fabric of social life to shreds. They take away the comfort and assurance of ordered living and uproot all the woman's habits. All life has to be made over. All habits are to be tested, even such simple and taken-for-granted habits as sleeping at night, sleeping eight hours a day, walking home from work, or taking the children out to the park in the afternoon for the sun and air and exercise. Such habits as meeting a group of friends every Wednesday or Friday night for a game of bridge, or an evening set apart for exercise—bowling, or ice skating, badminton on an indoor court—all such pleasures of ordinary living are swept into the discard. The war work comes first.

Some of the huge wartime organizations depend almost entirely upon women. The immense network of the Red Cross activities is largely staffed by women. The numberless first-aid classes, the beginners' classes, the two advanced classes, the bedside nursing classes, the canteen classes, the nutrition classes, call for an infinite number of trained women who can in their turn become teachers and train others. The entire nation has taken its nutrition course during this past year. Not a village is so remote from the railroad but that the station wagon of the nearest Red Cross Unit has not come across the hills to teach its nutrition course. Not a farmer's wife but has heard of the value of vitamins and minerals and the needed number of calories in the diet of every person. And the need of women's work in the home garden, in canning and putting up the summer's surplus for the winter, has carried the sense of participation into the life of every woman.

And the land army of the summer, its girls and its boys, took women right out of the kitchen into the kitchen garden, into the great crop-producing lands of the East and West. It has never been America's tradition to have its women work on the farms; it was part of the man's idea of protection that women should be spared hard farm toil. In the old countries women had always worked on the farms. [Jean-François] Millet painted his famous pictures of women stooping at their farm work, folding their hands in a prayer of thanks when it was over, listening to the bells of the Angelus at the end of the back-breaking day. Yes, women have always been part of the land army in the old countries. They crawled across the strawberry fields, they climbed in the apple trees, they tossed hay, they dug potatoes, they hoed carrots. And now they do all that in America, too. Much of the work is lightened by the use of the clever motor-driven modern machines that are everywhere in American life, like creatures of peaceful penetration slipping in between man and his drudgery. They make the women's work on the farm less laborious. But still there are hundreds of occupations, things that must be done by fingers and eyes, beautifully coordinated, that women do. Nothing can be more basic than the woman's part in the land army.

Farm work brings her a great and immediate satisfaction. She knows that food is the life of the nation, not only of the fighting forces, but of all the men and factories behind the fighting forces. She knows something about how the food she raises out in the sunshine beneath the floating white clouds of summer, with the call of the blue jays and the crows overhead, is put up and compressed and dehydrated for carrying in a small pocket box by the soldiers. While she picks her vegetables, she wonders whether this precise lot she is harvesting today will be in the ration kit of a parachutist.

And besides the emotional satisfaction there is the sure satisfaction of life in the open. The sun beats down on her head and face, and the air blows over her cool and sweet. She sees the wayside flowers of the summer come into their fragile beauty. She calls out to the other girls hoeing their rows. She eats with the appetite of the day laborer. Her muscles grow strong. She dances on her toes with the power that runs through her. After the first terrible back-aching days, when she felt she could not move her arm one other time, she reaps the guerdon of work. She grows stronger. She sleeps the sun around each night. She has no such thing as nerves. The indoor sedentary creature that she was she leaves behind her like a useless cocoon. She partakes of the life of the sunny fields and is strong and happy. She calls her farm a part of Our America. She has a new feeling of the land, of its sureness, of the dependence of human creatures upon its bounty. She learns the infinite disaster of mistakes. The machine exacts its penalty for a mistake with a swift cruelty, and so does nature. A human mistake created the dust bowl. Human mistakes have denuded the hills of the life-giving forest. A human mistake starts a forest fire. She learns the qualities that nature demands, the sureness, the endurance, the understanding.

For as the girl in the factory learns the laws of the machine, the physics of its continual whirring, the power of one metal pressed upon another, so the girl working on the land learns the laws of nature, their absolute inexorableness.

Man is dependent. The earth is dependent on the clouds. The clouds are recreated by the excess moisture of the earth. And between this rising and falling of water between the surface of the earth and the empty vacuum of the heavens above it, man stands and waits and learns the art of submission, the clever art of cooperation with nature.

Now, women are willful. If they want a thing to be true, first they pretend it is already true, and then they contrive to make it true. They are willful, but out on the fields, under the summer sun, willfulness is mere foolishness. It is useless. It is laughable. And the woman working on the land will learn the same lesson as the man on the land, will submit herself to the inexorability of the laws of nature, and will reap the same full reward.

The woman of the land army then has two rewards: the immediate personal reward of a great understanding and a great endurance, and the social reward of filling the mouths of the hungry.

A few professions remain almost exclusively woman's, and one of the most enduring of these is the profession of nursing. Nursing springs directly from the mothering quality of women, the quality that sets them in their hearts against war. They do not think war is the best way to decide quarrels. But whenever quarrels exist, they come in to bind up the wounded. For the need of the Army and Navy for nurses is one of the most immediate needs of the war. Wherever there is a wounded fighter there should be a nurse to tend him. And in this profession no hardship keeps the nurse at home in a safety zone. On the high seas, in the hospital ships, she wears her life jacket constantly while on duty, so immediate is the danger. She goes with the man to the edge of the conflict. She sees the sights of horror he sees. She handles broken bones and crushed skulls and maimed bodies. The horrors of war are brought to her. Women have ever been thought to be delicate, fragile creatures, yet they have always bound up the wounds of humanity. Within the outer shell of glamour and of seductiveness in every woman is the deep instinctive core of mothering. But even mothering can be trained; the woman can learn to be more deft, more skillful.

In the operating rooms improvised on the edge of the conflict she can carry out the same principles of surgical asepsis that have been embodied in the great glass-enclosed, sunlamp-lighted operating rooms of cities. She can improvise a hospital from a cracker box or orange box. She stands at the surgeon's side with the instrument he will next use ready in her hand. She anticipates his every move. She knows the steps in operating technique as well as he does, for she operates with him.

Nothing upsets her calm and her poise. She is bred upon danger. Whereas in modern life danger, sickness, despair, and death may have gone out of the everyday life of the average woman, they are the life of the hospital nurse. That is what she works with every day. She knows how despair looks. She has seen it over and over in the gray dawn in the hospital wards, in the waiting room outside of the operating room. She knows it well, and she knows what combats it. She feels within herself that profound courage that can fight against even despair and conquer it.

Every woman is a potential nurse.

And when more nurses are needed, there are more women to be nurses. They spring up overnight. But the trained nurse, the perfection of motherhood, is for the troops. For the civilian population at home, still in the radius of telephone calls, of ambulances, of hospitals equipped with every modern convenience, must come another corps of attendants, quickly trained, less experienced, but endowed with the same willing hands and kind hearts: the Nurses' Aides, the practical nurses, the bedside nurses. This new home-base army of nurses calls on thousands of other women, women who have neither the time nor the opportunity to be regular trained nurses.

For the health of the nation must be first created by food and then tended by care.

From the services of direct care, like the nursing profession, spring the contributory organizations that help in the process of taking care of people who cannot take care of themselves. The day nurseries, now necessary for the children of married women working, need women to take care of the babies. These women may have been trained in welfare work, in nursery work, in kindergarten work, or they may not have been technically trained. A capable, competent older woman can quickly learn how to look after babies and young children and can free their mothers for defense work. Other forms of social service or welfare work, or playground work, must all be carried on to keep the great civilian base in health and strength. Women can find their places everywhere in these new positions.

If a woman wants to do war work, the war work awaits her. She needs only to go to a Federal Employment Bureau in her hometown to find the list of jobs and opportunities that are open to her. She should get a health examination and find out the kind of health and endurance she has, the visual acuity she possesses. If she can give her whole time, the military organizations of the WAVES and the WAACs may absorb her at once into the war effort. If she cannot yield up her complete twenty-four hours to military obedience, but yet can give an eight-hour day, she can go into a defense industry. If she can only give part of her time and must preserve the rest of it to keep her home going, she can fit into one of the civilian defense posts.

No woman should think she is not needed. In some capacity or other her skill and energy, her industry and her goodwill, are needed.

The manpower of the war cannot prevail without the womanpower of the war behind it. The men may be the shock troops, but the women are the base line.

19   Negro Women War Workers

Kathryn Blood

The Women's Bureau of the U.S. Department of Labor was created in 1920 in response to increasing numbers of women in the work force. Since its establishment, the Bureau has sponsored conferences, monitored and published numerous reports on women's working conditions, and lobbied for legislation on behalf of female wage earners.

Mary Anderson, the first director of the Bureau, remained in that position until June 1944. Under Anderson's leadership,

From Kathryn Blood, *Negro Women War Workers* (Washington, DC: U.S. Department of Labor, Women's Bureau, Bulletin No. 205, 1945), iii–iv, 1–12.

> the Bureau published many valuable studies about women
> workers during World War II. Negro Women War Workers, *by*
> *Kathryn Blood, a researcher at the Women's Bureau, was sub-*
> *mitted to Anderson's successor, Frieda S. Miller, in April 1945.*
> *It contains extensive statistics about the contributions of*
> *African-American women to the war effort. Although this re-*
> *port emphasizes the important ways in which "Negro women*
> *. . . helped to bridge the manpower gap," it fails to describe*
> *how employers, even in the face of growing wartime labor short-*
> *ages, were reluctant to hire African-American women. Indeed,*
> *the axiom "last hired, first fired" aptly characterizes the posi-*
> *tion of black women in the work force during World War II.*

"NEGRO WOMEN WAR WORKERS" ATTEMPTS to assemble material currently available to show what contribution Negro women are bringing to the war work of the United States.

While no recent Women's Bureau survey has been made spe-cifically to study Negro women's employment, general occupational surveys made by the Bureau in the last two-and-a-half years show some of the new jobs that have opened for the Negro woman worker which may be considered typical. Such examples, together with a number from other sources, are presented in this bulletin as a series of vignettes of Negro women's work in munitions plants; in steel mills, foundries, shipyards, aircraft plants; on the railroads and in the canneries; in laundries and restaurants; as well as in many other jobs.

What this report tells is a story of ways in which Negro women have helped to bridge the manpower gap. Working together with men and women of every other national origin, their contribution is one which this Nation would be unwise to forget or to evaluate falsely. They are an integral part of America's prospect. Not only have they helped to produce the weapons of war, but their labor has been a large factor in preventing a major breakdown of essential consumer services.

Larger proportions of Negro than of white women, both in 1940 and in 1944, were in paid employment. Nearly 1 in 3 Negro women were employed in 1940, in contrast to 1 in 5 white women. By 1944 the proportion of employed Negro women increased to 2 in 5, while the employed white women increased to almost 1 in 3.

"I have a job to do in this great scheme of production."

These are the proud words of a Negro woman—a welder in a shipyard.

A job? What does a job mean?

It means security—individual, national, world. Security—the best weapon against poverty and disease, against defeat at home and on the battlefront.

Negro women need jobs—with no bars erected because of color, creed, or sex—jobs not only today but in the postwar world.

Behind the noise—the hammer, the thunder, the drive—that typifies America at war is a group of women, Negro women, who have pooled their strength with that of all other Americans in an effort to achieve a common goal—Victory. Carrying their full share of the Nation's wartime load, they are at work in every section of the country. In the steel mills and the foundries, in the aircraft plants and the shipyards, Negro women are helping to make the weapons of war. Not only are they working in war plants but their services in laundries and restaurants, on railroads and farms, and in countless other essential civilian industries have helped to make it possible for America to become the arsenal of the United Nations. Negro women's wartime performance has proved that, given the training, they can succeed in any type of work that women can do.

Trailblazers for Uncle Sam on the Production Front

Shipyards

More than one precedent was broken when in 1942 women mechanics were hired at the Brooklyn Navy Yard for the first time in 141 years. It was a red-letter day for women when the doors of the navy yard swung open. For Negro women especially it was a triumphant day, for a Negro girl received a grade of 99, the highest rating of any of the 6,000 women who took the civil service examination for navy yard jobs. She and another Negro girl who also showed special aptitude for work with precision instruments were assigned to the instrument division, where binoculars, telescopes, and range finders are reconditioned. Of the first 125 women hired at the Brooklyn Navy Yard about 12 were Negro. At a second Eastern navy yard, highly qualified Negro girls were among the first women hired in 1942. Since the work is skilled and strenuous, every new employee is required to pass rigid aptitude and physical tests.

In the Washington (D.C.) Navy Yard, Negro women are employed in the cartridge-case shop as well as in other shops. Some several hundred Negro women—most of whom are married and are mothers—are working there. They are operating punch and blanking presses as well as lathes and tapping machines in the manufacture of cartridge cases.

In the summer of 1943 about 2,000 women were employed in the Washington Navy Yard. Women were hired for naval ordnance jobs only if they had had 100 hours of training in machine-shop practice. In paying tribute to the splendid contribution of Negro women, an official of the navy yard said: "Negro women have played an important role in the production of ordnance materials during the present war. In the production of cartridge cases they are responsible for keeping production at a high peak. Both the output and morale in the shop reflect the cooperative spirit in which women have been accepted. Negro women have demonstrated their ability to adapt themselves to a field of endeavor that was foreign to them as well as to other women in the yard."

Negro women also were working on fuse-loading at the Bellevue (Md.) Naval Magazine. Behind steel barricades they measured and loaded pom-pom mix [ammunition for automatic guns mounted on shipboard], lead azide, TNT, tetryl, and fulminate of mercury. The various loading operations are strung along differently grouped assembly lines. On one line, for example, women loaded tetryl lead-ins for bomb fuses, or delay elements containing small cells of black powder, or mercury fulminate and lead azide for detonators. In small steel booths others received an element through a hole in the wall, put in the measured milligrams of powder, and passed it cautiously through an opposite hole to the next booth for another twist, tap, or turn.

Aircraft

In aircraft plants also there are many Negro women pioneers. More than 2 years ago Negro women were working on production, including machine operation, assembly, and inspection, in at least 15 major aircraft plants on the West Coast, the East Coast, and in the Middle West. Many of them had received their job training from N.Y.A. [National Youth Administration] or other free Government training classes. One of the first aircraft plants to hire Negro girls in mechanical jobs was the airplane-engine division of the Philadelphia Navy Yard.

Electrical equipment and machinery

Another of the large woman-employing industries in which Negro women have been at work for several years is the manufacture of electrical machinery and equipment. From the personnel director of one of the leading electrical manufacturing companies this report came to the Women's Bureau early in the war: "We have on our rolls at the present time approximately 2,000 Negro women, the majority of whom have been added in the last 6 to 9 months. They are engaged in 45 separate and distinct occupational classifications covering a rather wide range of skills. Included among their assignments are bench hands on various kinds of partial and final assemblies, cable formers, clerks, inspectors, many kinds of machine operators, solderers, stock selectors, electrical testers, and wiremen."

"One of the best men in the shop," according to the foreman, was a Negro girl in the electrical-repair department of the overhaul and repair shops of a large Eastern airline field.

Ordnance

In little more than a year after Pearl Harbor, Negro women were assigned to many of the more difficult technical laboratory jobs at the Army Proving Ground at Aberdeen, Md., where all types of guns, tanks, and other fighting equipment are tested. The girls employed in the ballistics laboratory were college graduates, and all had a thorough background of higher mathematics. Only 2 years of college were required, however, in the star-gauging section, where they tested bores and curvatures of guns. According to a War Department personnel specialist, the Negro girls in the Aberdeen laboratories "proved very satisfactory."

Early in the present armament program, Negroes comprised at least 350 of the women employed at an Ohio ordnance plant. One of the Negro women who came in as a warehouse worker was put in charge of a crew of women packers, both white and Negro, and later was made a counselor.

Another Midwestern ordnance plant employed 700 Negro women soon after the war began. They worked in a variety of jobs, and included supervisors, stenographers, machine operators, nurses, photograph technicians, draftsmen, machine adjusters, movemen, janitors, and matrons.

In a survey made by the National Metal Trades Association in 1943, 62 plants were found that employed women. Of these plants 19 employed Negro women, most of whom were in janitor service. However, one plant reported a total of 1,200 Negro women distributed among all the departments where women were at work. Other plants reported successful employment of Negro women in such occupations as work in a foundry, operation of machine tools including turret lathes, all types of winding operations, inspection, a variety of bench work, assembly, painting, electrical work, riveting, flame cutting, and welding.

Steel mills, foundries

Negro women were employed in most of the 41 steel mills surveyed by the Women's Bureau in 1943. Areas visited by Women's Bureau agents included Pittsburgh-Youngstown, Buffalo, Chicago-Gary, and West Virginia, and one mill each in Colorado, Sparrows Point (Md.), and Bethlehem (Pa.). While women were working in most divisions of the steel industry, their proportion was small, about 8 percent, covering all races. In some of the mills, however, women were found in almost every department. There were women working at the ore docks, in the storage yards for raw materials, on the coal and ore trestles, in the coke plants, the blast furnaces, the steel furnaces, the rolling mills, and the finishing mills that were doing fabricating on shells, guns, and regular products such as nails, spikes, and bolts.

The majority of the Negro women, like the white women, worked at labor jobs. The proportion of Negro women in the masonry and outside-labor gangs was large. Where women were employed in the sintering plants they were chiefly Negroes, and were reported as moving as much dirt and material as men. Jobs around a sintering plant are all dirty and chiefly of a labor grade; everything around such a plant is covered with iron dust. The sintering plant salvages ore dust and blast-furnace flue dust by mixing it with water and spreading it on moving conveyors that carry it under gas flames for baking into clinkery masses known as sinters, which are charged back to the furnace. Considerable numbers of women in these plants worked on dumping the cars of ore and dust, inspecting along the sides of the conveyor to remove lumps of slag and foreign matter, shoveling up spills along the conveyor lines, screening coal and dust, carrying tests to the laboratory, etc.

Plants on the Great Lakes receive most of their ore supply by boat. At one of these plants women were working at the ore docks. Though the boats are unloaded by electric ore bridge cranes that scoop up 15 to 20 tons in each bucketload and empty a boat in a few hours, it is necessary for labor gangs to go down into the bottoms of the boats and sweep and shovel up the leavings of ore into piles for removal by special hoists, as the grab-buckets cannot clean up around the sides and edges. To do this work a crew of women, chiefly Negro, and with a woman gang leader, went from boat to boat as needed. When there were no boats ready for cleaning, they worked around the docks and stockyards as a part of the general clean-up labor gang. The ore, coal, and limestone are heavy to handle even when a small shovel is used.

In 2 of the steel mills visited by the Bureau, a Negro woman was employed as panman. The job of the panman is to mix the fire clay, shoveling the materials into a mixing mill, for sealing the casting hole of the blast furnace. The work is carried on in a blast-furnace shed. Mud mixing is not a full-time job and is incidental to other labor.

Another unusual job held by a Negro woman was that of operating a steel-burning machine. This intricate machine, 25 feet long and 6 feet high, cuts parts for 6 different kinds of antiaircraft guns from huge plates of steel. The acetylene torches cut two parts at a time and must be set and guided with precision. The operator must have a dozen or more controls set exactly right.

In the Buffalo area Negro women were breaking into many jobs traditionally closed to women in the steel industry. In one large plant in this area Negro women made up about one-third of the total number of women employed.

Review of the situation in the steel mills, however, indicates quite general acceptance of the position that women's employment in steel is only for the duration of the war, and that men returning from the armed services will take over the jobs on the basis of seniority and priority rights in the industry.

Negro women were employed in 8 of the 13 foundries visited by Women's Bureau representatives in the latter half of 1943. A few of the foundries produced small as well as large castings. In the foundry itself, excluding other departments, the 13 establishments surveyed reported the proportion of women (race not stated) as 16 percent (93,631) of the workers. In one midwestern foundry 50 percent of the women were Negro, and in one steel-casting corporation such percent was 67.

Women were found in occupations ranging from the shoveling and mixing of sand and other unskilled types of labor to fairly skilled work in the fine finishing of molds. A few foundries indicated that they might keep women after the war in some of these jobs, individual foundries stating that women may be retained in jobs at which they excelled. Included in the list of jobs mentioned were clerical work, drafting, laboratory work, sand testing, operation of the heat-treat furnaces, and the making of small cores. Many foundries were convinced that women were better than men at the making of small cores. No large numbers of women, however, seemed likely to remain in foundry work after the war, even if they wished to do so. In a predominantly male industry they would have little opportunity to acquire the higher skills or advance up the job-progression ladder. The heavy nature of much of the work in itself would prevent that.

Arsenal of the United Nations—Detroit

The Bureau of the Census reports that the number of nonwhite women employed in the Detroit-Willow Run area rose from 14,451 in March 1940 to 46,750 in June 1944. Fewer than 30 Negro women were employed in war plants in this area in July 1942, but by November 1943 about 14,000 were so employed. Early in 1944, 7 to 8 percent of the workers in the entire state of Michigan were Negroes, and it was estimated that almost 6 percent of them were women.

Negro women in the Detroit area early in 1944 were working as machine operators, assemblers, inspectors, stenographers, interviewers, sweepers, material handlers, and at various other jobs in all types of work where women can be used. The first woman hired as a detailer by a small engineering company was a Negro woman trained in engineering. A company that for some time resisted taking Negro women employed 2 as inspectors in the middle of December 1943; a few months later it had 47 Negro women inspectors and machine operators.

In one Detroit company Negro women made up 10 to 12 percent of the 1,000 women employed. Another that used a large number of women had about 25 to 30 percent Negro women; they were in every department and worked at almost every skill. In this company, management and the union backed the rights of its Negro workers—men and women—for advancement on the basis of seniority and skill.

A foundry that employed some 250 women had about 12 percent Negro women. Women applicants were interviewed and hired on a basis of qualifications and ability to adjust to other workers without regard to creed or color.

Though a company had been violating War Manpower Commission regulations on discriminatory newspaper advertising, it was persuaded to withdraw the advertisement and cooperate with the W.M.C. and the union in introducing Negro women workers. As a result, in 1944 the proportions of Negro women in this company's two plants were 29 percent and 35 percent.

A company that had hired about 1,500 Negro women reported that they made up from 8 to approximately 25 percent of the women in its various plants. Another company opened certain departments to women in one of its plants. At the beginning it hired 1 Negro in every 2 women employed. In 1944, of approximately 8,000 women in this plant, around 75 percent were Negro, and the company was pleased with their production performance.

Essential Civilian Industries

Service jobs

The foregoing pages report a few of the recorded instances typical of great numbers of Negro women who with loyalty and skill have forwarded the massive war-production program of their country. Even at its maximum, however, that record would register but a small share of the support coming to the war economy through the labor of Negro women workers. Customary work positions and previous experience easily account for their presence in great numbers in essential civilian jobs in laundry, food, and restaurant establishments, in hotels and lodging houses, and in other service industries. Doubtless many of the women so employed do not even realize that they are doing war work, work which affects directly the country's war production.

Said the president of a large West Coast aircraft corporation late in 1943: "We think every worker we can place in a laundry is worth three new workers in our own plants." A company survey had revealed that in these plants most absenteeism was caused not by hangovers but by a lack of such community services as laundries and restaurants. Bomber production was being affected because workers in these plants could not get their washing done, nor buy their meals in restaurants. "The result was," said the president, "that we had to start an advertising campaign to urge unemployed people to take jobs in laundries and restaurants so our own people could stay on their jobs."

Canneries

Large numbers of Negro women were working in New Jersey and New York canneries visited by Women's Bureau representatives in the summer and fall of 1943. Much work in the fields also was being done by them. Products handled by the canneries ranged from soup to coffee and from baby food to army rations.

Cannery labor was secured from many sources—housewives, students, soldiers, sailors, migratory workers taken north in trucks from Florida, Kentucky, Tennessee, West Virginia, and other southern states in numbers far exceeding those of previous years, Jamaicans, and Bahamians. Women were used in a wide range of jobs in the preparation of fruits and vegetables. Their jobs included the more usual ones of sorting, peeling, trimming, feeding machines on the can line as well as jobs new to women in those particular plants: jobs involving the control of retorts and of pulping, extracting, evaporating, and scalding equipment. Some women were doing heavy labor such as unloading [freight] cars, handling cases weighing from 15 to 42 pounds, and handling bushel baskets filled with produce. Others were employed as general laborers feeding cans, salvaging cans, shaking sacks, and as conveyor and belt attendants. As maintenance and miscellaneous workers women were employed as janitors, elevator operators, truckers, directors of shed and yard traffic, and to clean and grease machines.

Housing provided for migratory workers ranged from tent colonies to a trailer camp and a converted summer hotel. In three of the camps in which Negro families were living in tents it was stated that new housing had been planned for them and was to be built by the Federal Public Housing Authority. Nearly 150 Negro women were living in the barracks built originally for a C.C.C. [Civilian Conservation Corps] camp. At a Farm Security Administration camp, 100 Negro families were living in tents but gradually were being provided with other accommodations. At another camp occupied by Negro families, the housing consisted of a combination of frame houses built during World War I, of new prefabricated houses, and of tents. One company built a one-story dormitory on cannery property for 250 women, both white and Negro.

Transportation

Filling jobs from "baggage smasher" to trackworker, Negro women railroad employees have done their share to keep the Nation's war wheels turning. The work of these women is invaluable, since the railroads are one of the country's major war arteries, transporting the armed forces and carrying to them food, clothing, and weapons, and at the same time supplying civilians with the essentials of everyday living. Negro women have filled a variety of jobs, ranging from the unskilled, such as cleaning and janitor work, to the semiskilled. A few have held highly skilled jobs. Neither Negro nor white women, however, have found their way as yet into many skilled jobs in transportation, which long has been considered a man's industry.

A railroad survey made by Women's Bureau representatives revealed that one large railroad system employed over 4,500 Negro women in 1943; in fact, Negroes made up 21 percent of all women employed by this road. The largest groups worked as section and extra gang men (1,138); laborers (1,019); coach cleaners (967); and callers, leaders, and truckers (546). This railroad was also employing Negro women as dining-car waitresses and as coach-lunch waitresses. A Negro woman was head waitress on one of the diners. Other Negro women worked in the railroad's commissary kitchen and as station elevator operators. A Negro woman was forewoman of a gang of 38 coach cleaners at one of the yards.

The Bureau found 400 Negro women working for one western railroad system, making up over 13 percent of the total of their sex employed. The largest groups of these women were general laborers (148), section and extra gang men (114), and coach cleaners (83). Another western railroad had 48 Negro women as coach cleaners in one of its yards.

One of the most unusual railroad jobs for a woman was held by a Negro woman in Georgia. Probably the first woman train announcer in the United States, she started her railroad career 25 years ago by doing odd jobs, icing and watering the trains, and cleaning up the station's carpenter shop. Her job as caller started accidentally when the stationmaster asked her not to let anyone miss a train. She got copies of all the schedules and began to memorize them. Today her voice is a station essential.

Track women, B & O Railroad, 1943. *Courtesy National Archives*

Various street-transportation companies have hired Negro women as car and bus cleaners and as helpers in shops. In several large municipalities, they have acted as car or bus operators and conductors. For example, New York City's first woman streetcar operator was a Negro woman.

The intercity bus industry has employed Negro women in various sections of the country, chiefly as cleaners and maids. One company employed Negro women at filling stations, servicing trucks.

This company not only states that their work has been satisfactory, but stresses their stability and says they have presented no special problem in absenteeism or labor turnover.

The inland waterways, including the Great Lakes, have employed Negro women as cooks, waitresses, maids, and stewardesses. A few women have done overhaul and repair work for the airlines.

In the Line of Duty

In the performance of their work many Negro women achieve unusual individual distinction. An outstanding example of such a woman is an Arkansas arsenal worker. A munitions laborer in the production division, she twice rescued fellow workers from burning to death when fire broke out in the plant's incendiary section. For this heroism she became the first woman to receive the War Department's highest civilian award for exceptional service. The Award of Emblem for Exceptional Civilian Service, the civilian equivalent of the Distinguished Service Medal, was presented to her. The citation accompanying the award praised her for "exceptional conduct in performance of outstanding service beyond the call of duty."

Among the Negro women who have shown exceptional skill in their war-plant jobs is a worker who became champion arc welder and one of two winners in the Negro Freedom Rally's competition for "Miss Negro Victory Worker of 1944." One of 7 Negro girls in a New York war plant, she admits it was no easy task to surpass her fellow workers and thereby win the national merit award that was given her and the cowinner, a Negro girl from Detroit. After the presentation of the award in Madison Square Garden, both girls were taken to New York City Hall to receive Mayor [Fiorello] LaGuardia's congratulations.

In speaking of her award, the champion arc welder said: "When you work in a war plant—and maybe this is my own personal feeling—you talk very little while you work but you do a lot of thinking. And with the roar of machinery you sort of get a message which seems to say to you that this job must be well done, because the stake in getting it out is perhaps the life of some boy fighting on the beachheads. That's what I keep thinking."

Also in the "champ" class are two Negro women riveters, who set a record of 104 rivets in 120 seconds. Workers in a West Coast aircraft plant, these women were giving more than full measure of their strength and skill. They worked as a team on bomb-bay doors for the PV-1 Ventura bomber, among the first American planes consistently to bomb the Japanese homeland of Paramoshiri, northernmost bastion of the Nippon home defenses.

Among the Negro women workers serving in leadership positions in their unions was an Illinois gun-plant employee who was elected shop steward early in the war by a department composed of 5 Negro women and 90 white women. In a New York plant making cloth and leather war goods, 6 of the 14 union shop chairladies were Negro. They were elected by the 1,000 men and women members, half of whom were white and half Negro. Another Negro woman early in 1945 was the only woman on the general executive board of a union of transport and service workers, and president of the local to which she belonged. A Negro woman, educational director of the local union of garment workers, was 1 of the 4 representatives of American women workers to visit Great Britain early in 1945 in an exchange designed to bring about a better understanding between the two countries. The 4 women were selected by their respective unions, and arrangements for their trip were made by the Office of Labor Production of the War Production Board and the Office of War Information.

Recognition came to another Negro woman war worker when she entered a national magazine contest on "What My Job Means to Me" and won first place plus a $50 war bond. In her essay she said in part:

> I am an inspector in a war plant. For 8 hours a day, 6 days a week, I stand in line with 5 other girls performing a routine operation that is part of our production schedule. We inspect wooden boxes that are to hold various kinds of munitions, and that range in size from 8 inches to 6 feet. When we approve them they are ready to be packed with shells, bombs, fuses, parachutes, and other headaches for Hitler and Hirohito. Did I say my job isn't exciting or complicated? I take that back. It may be a simple matter to inspect one box or a dozen, but it's different when you are handling them by the hundreds. The 6 of us in my crew sometimes inspect as many as 1,400 or 1,500 boxes during one shift. That means 250 apiece—an average of one every 2 minutes, regardless of size.

Of course the work is hard and sometimes dangerous, but Victory in this war isn't going to come the easy way.

20   Shipyard Diary of a Woman Welder

Augusta H. Clawson

The American public was fascinated by the fact that many women performed "men's jobs" during World War II. Newspapers and popular magazines regularly published firsthand accounts of the tribulations and triumphs of women on the assembly line. Boston Globe journalist Nell Giles, for example, worked in a factory on assignment. Her stories appeared in the newspaper and were later published in a book entitled Punch In, Susie! A Woman's War Factory Diary *(1944). Other works with titles such as* I Took a War Job *(1943) and* Mothers in Overalls *(1943) celebrated the virtues of Rosie the Riveter.*

In 1943 home economist Augusta H. Clawson was hired by the federal government to investigate the training and working conditions of welders in shipyards. In this selection, drawn from her Shipyard Diary of a Woman Welder, *Clawson describes her life as a welder on a Liberty ship (mass produced to carry cargo) in a West Coast shipyard and how proud she felt when "her first welds slid into the water."*

Sunday

I AM BACK FROM MY first day on the Ways [staging on which ships are built], and I feel as if I had seen some giant phenomenon. It's incredible! It's inhuman! It's horrible! And it's marvelous! I don't believe a blitz could be noisier—I didn't dream that there could be so much noise, anywhere. My ears are still ringing like high-tension wires, and my head buzzes. When you first see it, when you look down Way after Way, when you see the thousands each going about his own business and seeming to know what to do, you're so bewildered you can't see anything or make sense out of it.

From Augusta H. Clawson, *Shipyard Diary of a Woman Welder*, illus. Boris Givotovsky (New York: Penguin Books, 1944), 54–71. © 1944 by Penguin Books. Reprinted by permission of Viking Penguin, a division of Penguin Books USA.

First came the bus ride to the Yard. Crowded as usual. I was intrigued by knowing that this time I was going to Mart's Marsh. The name has always fascinated me. I gather that it refers to bottom or marshy land once owned by a family named Mart. From the [welding] school our road led along the water where I could see several of the ships already launched and now lying at the outfitting dock to receive the finishing touches. It was easy to spot the various stages of completion; each ship gets moved up one when a new ship arrives for outfitting.

When the bus came to a stop, I followed the crowd across a pontoon bridge between rails at which stood guards checking for badges. The far side of the bridge brought us to the part of the Yard where the prefabricated parts are stored, right in the open, pile upon pile. I saw a huge building marked "Assembly Shop," another "Marine Shop," and still another "Pipe Assembly." There were lots of little houses marked with numbers. Most of them seemed to be in the sixties. And I was looking for check-in station No. 1.

I hunted and hunted without success, and finally asked someone where "new hires" check in. He immediately directed me. I showed my badge, told my number, and was given another badge to be picked up and turned in daily as we did at school. It was marked "New Hire." About then who should come along but Redheaded Marie and the Big Swede! We went together to the Welders' Office where our off days were assigned to us. I was given "C" day and told that it was the only day available. This means that I get Tuesday off this week, Wednesday next, and so on. The Big Swede said she had to have "D" day to get a ride to work and to have the same day as her husband. Although "C" day was "the only one available," strangely enough she was given "D" day. One has to learn to insist on what one wants even when told it is impossible.

The Big Swede is a real pal. She had not forgotten the patch for my overall trouser leg. She had cut a piece from an old pair of her husband's, scrubbed it to get the oil out, and brought it to me with a needle stuck in the center and a coil of black thread ready for action. "Here," she said, "I knew you wouldn't have things handy in a hotel room. Now you mend that hole before you catch your foot in it and fall."

We were turned over to Marie because she knew her way around—was familiar with the Yard and acquainted with lots of the people already. She was "riding high" and "fresh as paint." She took us first to get our rod boxes. Just for deviltry, I'm sure, she said we'd have to go "this way"—which was through the skids; a space so small that even the average-sized person would have to lie flat and roll through. And neither the Big Swede nor I could claim to be average sized. She started to balk. "I'm not going that way. Marie's just trying to show off." "I know it," I answered, "that's why she's not going to get a rise here." The Big Swede shrugged agreement and we crawled through.

We went to some subterranean shop which I know I couldn't find again and sat while a man stenciled our numbers on gray "rod boxes." A thick rope furnishes a loop which goes over the shoulder to carry this box. A pretty brunette whose speech seems to be limited to "Hell, no" and "Hell, yes" waited with us. Next stop was at a tool crib where we signed for stinger [welding rod] and brush. From there to a rod shop to get rod and glass for our hoods. And finally to a lunchroom where we left our lunchboxes.

At last I was ready to go up on deck and meet my lead man. It was some time before I could find him. He seemed a pleasant, straightforward sort of chap, and very businesslike. I had a feeling that when he looked at me he thought, "Ye gods, another woman!" But all he said was, "Wait here and I'll find you a job."

I waited about three-quarters of an hour. I stood at the rail and stared out over the Yard. It all looked like chaos and confusion to me. I counted a number of people who were idle and wondered why. Presently a shipfitter's helper came to take me to my first job. "What's it like out here in a shipyard?" I asked; "I've never worked in one before." She shrugged her shoulders. "You'll earn your pay just by dodging being killed. There are so many green workers it's a wonder something doesn't happen to you every day." Lugubrious thought.

Today my book on welding came from the Washington office. I read that a welder's qualifications are "physical fitness which insures a reasonable degree of endurance during a full day of work; steady nerves and considerable muscular strength." For a shipyard welder I'd amend that to read: "An unreasonable degree of endurance during a full day of strain, plus muscular strength, plus no nerves." If you haven't the muscular strength before you start, you will have it afterward. If you haven't the nerves before, you may have them afterward, though I doubt it. By tomorrow I shall be "reasonably" acclimated, but tonight I quite frankly "ain't."

I, who hate heights, climbed stair after stair after stair till I thought I must be close to the sun. I stopped on the top deck. I, who hate confined spaces, went through narrow corridors, stumbling my way over rubber-coated leads—dozens of them, scores of them, even hundreds of them. I went into a room about four feet by ten where two shipfitters, a shipfitter's helper, a chipper, and I all worked. I welded in the poop deck lying on the floor while another welder spattered sparks from the ceiling and chippers like giant woodpeckers shattered our eardrums. I, who've taken welding, and have sat at a bench welding flat and vertical plates, was told to weld braces along a baseboard below a door opening. On these a heavy steel door was braced while it was hung to a fine degree of accuracy. I welded more braces along the side, and along the top. I did overhead welding, horizontal, flat, vertical. I welded around curved hinges which were placed so close to the side wall that I had to bend my rod in a curve to get it in. I made some good welds and some frightful ones. But now a door in the poop deck of an oil tanker is hanging, four feet by six of solid steel, by my welds. Pretty exciting!

The men in the poop deck were nice to me. The shipfitter was toothless. The grinder had palsy, I guess, for his hands shook pitifully and yet he managed to handle that thirty-pound grinder. The welder was doing "pick-up" work, which meant touching up spots that had been missed. An inspector came through and marked places to chip, and the ship's superintendent stopped and woke the shipfitter's helper.

Then I went down more stairs, and still more, and finally crawled through a square hole in the floor and down a narrow ladder held by the shipfitter below and emerged into a little two-by-twice room. I felt as if we were a thousand leagues under the sea. In the "dark, dank dungeon" two decks above, there had been a hole in the ceiling through which the air lines came, and around the lines one could just make out sky and sunlight. I realize now what Oscar Wilde meant when he wrote of "that little tent of blue which prisoners call the sky."

I do know one thing from just today. There is nothing in the training to prepare you for the excruciating noise you get down in the ship. Any who were not heart and soul determined to stick it out would fade out right away. Any whose nerves were too sensitive couldn't take it, and I really mean couldn't. There are times when those chippers get going and two shipfitters on opposite sides of a metal wall swing tremendous metal sledgehammers simultaneously and you wonder if your ears can stand it. Sometimes the din will seem to swell and engulf you like a treacherous wave in surf-bathing and you feel as if you were going under. Once I thought to myself, "If this keeps on, I wonder—" It makes you want to scream wildly. And then it struck me funny to realize that a scream couldn't even be heard! So I screamed, loud and lustily, and couldn't even hear myself. It was weird. So then I proceeded to sing at the top of my lungs (I'm discreet usually, for my pitch is none too good), and I couldn't hear the smallest peep. It's an ill wind that blows nobody good, and I decided to make the most of it, so I hauled out my entire seafaring repertoire and sang "Rocked in the Cradle of the Deep," "Anchors Aweigh, My Boys," and "The Landlubbers Lie Down Below." You could almost doubt your sanity sitting there making an unholy din and not even hearing it.

At the school I'd considered chipping slag slightly noisy. But when I chipped slag today, I couldn't hear my hammer hit. It does to your hearing what an arc flash does to your vision. After a flash you can't see a thing for a few seconds. And after all this racket stops, you can't hear anything for a short space of time. Then your hearing flows slowly back, and you find you're still sane and normal. And people wonder whether it involves "adjustment" when a housewife takes up ship welding. It does—and I am sure we can prepare her better for it. She can take it, but I think she'd do better if she were ready for what's coming.

I wonder, too, whether in our training we couldn't be taught to weld from unusual angles and positions. Today I had to stand on a stool to do one of mine, and curve my bent rod around so that I was welding an angle between two sheets of metal—and I couldn't see the angle.

Actually I doubt if I welded a solid hour altogether today. One does see a good many standing idle, waiting for a shipfitter or a chipper or a pipefitter to get the work to the point where a weld is immediately necessary; then they start welding. Some of my pals welded on deck in the sunlight all day. When I was assigned, one said to me, "Oh, you're getting double bottom." My heart sank to triple bottom, after all I had heard of double. But I don't seem to have reached double bottom yet. Anyway, I'm after experience, so I'll take it if it comes.

It is 7:30 P.M. I am signing off and going to bed. I'm already getting my second wind; if I stay up much longer I'll be tempted to do some work, and I'm not going to tonight. Much to my surprise, though, I could if I had to. Guess that's why so many women do.

I have the most difficult time finding my way around. When I left my lunchbox after lunch, I noted the sign over the door with care. It read "Room 11, Women Welders, Day." When I went back after the whistle to get the lunchbox and leave my rod box, hood, and other tackle, Room 11 had completely changed appearance. I found I had landed in one on Ways 3, and it should have been Ways 2. When I got to Ways 2, the door was padlocked and the matron in charge had gone. I waved goodbye to my lunchbox through the window, and trudged off to Mart's Marsh to get a bus. I saw five ships (already launched) along the water's edge being outfitted. I gave my number to the guard who let me through, and I asked him where to catch the bus. But the last bus had gone—greenhorns aren't supposed to lose their way and be late from shift. A good-natured young engineer gave me a ride. You've no idea what luxury it seemed to ride sitting down instead of hanging from a metal bar. I could even see where we were going.

Monday

Do you know what day tomorrow is? It's my day off—and the first one since a week ago Sunday. I've worked eight straight days. Already I've relaxed so much in anticipation that I feel like a slow-motion movie. And tomorrow is going to be a very full day. I shall arm myself with my ration card and get food so I can fix my own lunches. I'm sick of paying 25 cents each for sandwiches that aren't nearly as good as one can make oneself. I'm going to get some fruit, too. I hope to get a haircut. And I might even see a movie. (I doubt the latter, though. I hate to waste precious hours of a day off on a movie.) I have much mending to do, some laundry. And I do have to write and tell my family that I'm still alive.

Did I hope that I would bump up against a lot of tough adjustments here so that I would get a real picture of shipyard life? Well, I have done it. I caught an early bus this morning before 6 A.M. just to get to work and get my equipment out of the Men Welders' lunchroom before anything could happen to it. Too late. When I arrived I found my hood, rod box, pliers, chipping hammer, and steel brush—but nary a sign of gloves or stinger. The stinger will probably cost me $6 or $7, and the gloves must be at least $3. That makes yesterday's pay "ain't." I suppose it was my fault, since I got lost and put things in the wrong room; but it does seem a bit tough. I saw several other stingers when I was looking for mine, and it was all I could do to keep from taking one. For once I would have been glad to park my conscience and even things up.

I reported to my lead man and told him what had happened. He told me where I could go to get somebody's cast-off gloves to use for the day. I resented those old gloves every time I thought of my nice new ones. I went back to Ways 3 with my borrowed gloves to report for work and began the "climbingest" day I have ever known. There were 93 steps to climb before I reached the top deck of Ways 3. No sooner had I reported there than I was sent to Ways 8. So down the 93 steps I went again, walked a couple of blocks, and started up Ways 8. Only 53 steps this time, since the hull on Ways 8 has not yet been built up so high. There I reported to Mr. Norman and was told that they needed a welder on Ways 7, so I reversed those 53 steps and climbed 60 up to Ways 7. I was to work for a black-haired, blue-eyed Irishman called Pat, a shipwright.

When Pat and I reached the top step of the Ways—where ordinarily I would have stepped off onto the deck—there was no deck. I was all ready to turn around and go down again, when I realized that Pat had different ideas. That top step was sort of a landing with a guardrail running around it. Leaning over the guardrail, I looked down into sheer space some forty feet. I backed away from it quickly because I do not like heights. But not Pat. He swung under the guardrail, grabbed hold of a post, pulled himself around that, edged along the side around another post, and walked off on the deck which began farther back. And don't think for a minute that he offered to help me, or even asked whether I thought I could make it. For about thirty seconds I saw red. I wasn't going to swing out over that space for anybody. I knew that if I lost my footing my arms would not hold me. My arms are not strong enough yet. Then I looked at Pat striding across the deck. I guess I don't have red hair for nothing, because I made up my mind not to give him a chance to say women can't take it. I swung under the guardrail and around the post, finally made the deck, and strode manfully after him. But my knees felt shaky under my leathers.

Twice during the morning he sent me down below for rod. So four times more I skirted that forty-foot drop. I could have choked him. The last time I came up he was standing there grinning. He shook his head and said, "That's pretty bad, isn't it?" I pretended for a few seconds not to know what he meant; then I looked back at the drop and conceded, "Well, it's not too good." A few minutes later the safety man arrived to inspect and immediately ordered a catwalk with rails to bridge that space. Whew, but I was relieved!

The crane had deposited the heavy metal floorings of the main deck in their approximate positions. Clips (or braces) are welded in pairs (one on one section of deck, one on another) immediately opposite. Then a screw jack, placed between, exerts a pressure of 25 tons to force the plates apart into their proper positions. And those welds have to stand 25 tons' pressure. I was the only welder on the deck. I'd be in the middle of tacking one clip when Pat would yell, "Welder, come here and tack this clip," and up I'd get and go where I was needed and then return to the point I'd left. Once another said, "I need a tack"—so then I had to climb down through a hole on a narrow ladder, into a tiny room. There the ceiling was so low that I had to almost crawl to get to the far corner and weld a brace which would hold a plate in place when they released some other fastening. Pat was nice but very businesslike and kept me busy every instant. I welded certainly four out of the four and one-half hours. I don't know what "Housemaid's Knee" is, but I have "Green Welder's Knee." I knelt on one knee or both most of the day. Sometimes I'd stand to weld and bend double, since all my welding was on the deck floor. Once in a while I'd sit flat on the deck, but it is harder to control your rod that way. My knee is bright red even now, and I find I have lots more muscles in back and thighs than I knew were there. In fact, I'm more generally stiff than at any time so far. But I don't care, for I welded in the sun (and in the rain, too) all day. Only one weld was below decks.

It was a funny sensation to be bent over with hood down welding with the rain trickling down the back of my neck. When we went to lunch, it poured. Back we came to sopping decks. I mopped up part of the deck by sitting in the puddles while I welded and soaking them up in my clothes. The sun came out and dried the rest. And tonight I have an honest-to-goodness sunburn, most of it on the back of my neck.

After lunch I continued to weld every single minute. Though I got pretty tired after a while, there was nothing to do but keep on. They had another welder by then, but the men needed tacks all the time. So I kept going until suddenly Pat came up to me and said, "How about me doing it for a bit? Give you a rest." He did several welds, then pulled out his watch and poked at it. Two of the men had just signaled something to him and pointed down. I don't know whether that's what they meant or not, but he grinned at me and

said, "It's time for you to go home. You've done enough." It was
3:15—and I went.

In spite of that climb, I like Pat. He probably thought women
can't take it, besides resenting the fact that I earn the same $1.20
an hour that he does.

Today was much easier than yesterday in spite of the fact that I
worked more. When you are outdoors, the chippers on the deck
aren't so bad; you can hear people when they yell at you. A chipper
uses a power-driven tool that looks like a chisel to chip away extra-
neous metal. This tool vibrates at a terrific speed, and the noise is
almost beyond imagining. Chippers in a tiny room below decks
make an unbelievable din. I'm afraid that's where I'll be Wednesday, for the men I worked with there had more to do and I bet I'll
be sent to them. Oh, well, it makes for variety, anyway! Today I
talked with a middle-aged woman expediter who said that her work
was not hard at all, and was quite interesting. I guess there are some
jobs here that aren't too hard. But give me the middle-aged worker
any day. On the whole, from what I have seen, she is both steadier
and harder working than many of the young things.

Wednesday

There's one thing about this job: every day is different. Today
even started differently, with a full moon in the sky when I arrived
at the Yard. We tried to report to our lead man on Ways 3 as usual,
but he wasn't there. No one of us wanted to climb the 93 steps on a
wild-goose chase. Just then along came a welder's helper. We sent
her to the checking station to find out where he was. It was fun—
first time I've felt as if anyone were more of an underling than I
am. The four of us who were welders basked in our superiority
until she returned to tell us to report to Ways 5.

There I was assigned to work for Dave Williams, a young and
very inexperienced shipfitter. Since my work with shipwrights on
Monday, I could notice that Dave was not using his wedges to the
best advantage. He was never quite sure where he wanted me to
tack my butterflies, or clips, or beams. All these strangely titled
articles are pieces of metal of various shapes. Butterflies are trian-
gular. Dogs are like rectangles with a strip about an inch and a half
in width cut off of the bottom of the rectangle for half its distance.
A similar strip is cut off the top of the rectangle on the opposite
side. This cutting away provides space under which wedges can be
driven. Clips are rectangular pieces bent at right angles: short angle

Chippers, Marinship Corp., 1942. *Courtesy National Archives*

bars. All these various pieces are welded wherever needed to give strength or leverage against which to exert pressure on placing decks or bulkheads or other parts.

The morning went rather quickly. I worked intermittently, part of the time in such a pouring rain that my welds boiled the water around them, and the glass in my helmet was so wet I could scarcely see. I wore my helmet to lunch so that it wouldn't get stolen, and it made a very practical umbrella. Two of the girls from school and I decided we'd gulp our lunch on the run and go to see No. 3 launched.

Lots didn't go because of the rain; they stayed behind to talk and eat. The lunchroom group seems less friendly than the school crowd was. It breaks into cliques: one group of young things who discuss their babies and wise-crack about the men; the other (the older) group discusses the work, or their lead men, or the war and their relatives who are in the armed forces.

I climbed up on Ways 4 and heard the speeches and heard (but did not see) the wife of the welding superintendent christen the ship the S.S. *Fallen Timbers*, and my first welds slid into the water. She was pretty, for the sun had suddenly come out and played with the colored banner floating from her mast.

I stopped in the washroom on my way back from lunch. It was crowded, but people seemed to be moving in and out rapidly. I've seen no loitering there, but probably because I never come down except at lunch. Facilities are adequate and very well kept. One of the circular industrial washing fountains is there, with a very gritty soap spouted out by containers. The containers for paper towels and paper cups always seem well filled. A matron is usually around.

As the crowd was dispersing after the launching, I stood munching an apple and watching them. A pretty young brunette came out, got into her car, and promptly backed up into the crowd—more specifically, into me. The bumper struck my leg with an awful wallop. It is still as lame as can be: not tender to the touch, but sore deep in the muscle. I'll not be so good on the ladders tomorrow. For about sixty seconds I did not like the "idle rich" at all.

Perhaps the most interesting part of the launching was to see the first large section, the keel plate, of a new ship swung down into place as No. 3 hit the water. A "whirly" swung it into position. The other day I was directed to my station by someone who told me, "Just past that whirly there." I didn't know then what a "whirly" was. But now I do—it's a crane.

This afternoon was devilish. Dave Williams sent me down into a hole, up onto a scaffolding, and into a corner where I was to overhead-tack the ceiling in about six places. A beam just in front prevented a straight view of the spot I was to tack. I was too tall to stand, and when I knelt the place was so high that I could only reach it with a long rod and my arms extended full length. I had no control of the rod whatever. I've run only about five beads in an overhead weld (at school after passing my test), and that was standing full height, welding on a plate within easy reach. But this job today was as hard an overhead as one would get. I made a mess of it. Finally, Dave looked at it and agreed. The water was pouring off my face and my glasses kept fogging so I couldn't see. He said, "Here, I'll try it." He tried, and (praise be!) he couldn't do it either. So we called a girl who had been welding some weeks, and she did it fairly well.

I thought my machine was too cool, so I kept trying to heat the metal before starting. Then it would stick like sin. My next job was to crawl down another ladder, balance with one foot on the ladder and one on a beam, and do some vertical tacking. Again I did a very poor job.

In the midst of all this, my lead man came and asked how I was getting along. I replied, "Terrible—worse than when I started!" He came down, did a few tacks, and then said: "Your rod's much too hot. Your machine must be too high. You can't do anything with a rod like that but put it down and let it cool." And I had been doing just the opposite! I had told Dave several times that I didn't think my machine was right. I felt chagrined to have Pete see all the worst work I had done, because I had done fairly decent work my other two days.

As a result of all this, I feel very strongly that we'd go to the Yard better prepared if in the school we did more welding in varied positions. Even a fillet weld of two plates could be placed on the floor, and one could get down and do it there and so learn something of what will later be required in the Yard. I don't see why, too, the butterflies, the clips, and even the bolts couldn't be welded at various angles in school. We could practice some one-handed welding instead of always using two hands while sitting at a bench with plates conveniently placed. There are times when you have to use one hand to cling to a ladder or a beam while you weld with the other. I notice that the most experienced welders I have watched seldom use two hands. One large, fine-looking woman (Norwegian, I think) who has been there three months told me: "They don't teach us enough at school. Why don't they let us weld there the same things we'll do here?" I countered with, "Oh, they do teach a lot or we'd be no good here at all; but what you say would certainly help." I think she "has something," however. We do need more experience in setting our machines and recognizing when they are too hot or too cold. Struggling with an inaccurate setting and the wrong amount of heat makes a harder day than doing a lot of actual work. Yet it's hardly the fault of the training that we lack adequate experience. More and more I marvel at training that in eight days can give enough to make us worth anything on the job. And we are worth something. We're building ships.

21 Women and Farm Work

More than 1.5 million women joined the ranks of the Women's Land Army, an agency of the U.S. Department of Agriculture, during World War II. As the largely forgotten rural counterpart of Rosie the Riveter, these women performed crucial agricultural work that had not been available to them in times of peace. The first excerpt in this selection, written by Mrs. Leslie Tresham of Hornick, Iowa, was the winning essay in a General Federation of Women's Clubs 1944 contest on the topic, "My Experience Doing Emergency Wartime Farm Work." The second, The Women's Land Army of the U.S. Crop Corps 1944, is a reprinting of a recruitment pamphlet produced by the U.S. Department of Agriculture.

My Experience as an Emergency Farm Worker

Leslie Tresham

IT WAS WITH A FEELING of pride and uncertainty that I started my day as a farm helper. I had promised a farmer, whose only son had enlisted in the Marines, to haul corn from a picker to the [grain] elevator. Before daylight, I prepared the tractor for the day's work . . . this meant filling it with gas, water, and oil.

Carefully, I hooked an empty wagon to the tractor. As I released the clutch the tractor gave a lurch, almost throwing me from the seat. As I neared the picker, standing on the field, I decided I was too close and turned the wheels sharply to the left. When I finally stopped, I was several feet from where I should have been. The farmer was considerate, and helped me push the tug on the wagon until we could fasten it to the picker.

I hooked a full load of corn to the tractor and started for the elevator. As I neared the hoist I became frightened. I knew there was only 3 or 4 inches clearance on either side of the wheels. If I made a mistake I might upset the hoist, breaking chains and glass, and possibly injure myself.

I managed to pull through without mishap. Next came the really hard part. I had to unhook from the wagon, turn the tractor around in a limited space, and line up the pulley on the tractor with the elevator pulley. I had never done anything like that before. After twisting and turning, backing and going forward, I finally decided I was in line. I put on the belt, but hadn't thought of the frost on the pulleys. The belt refused to stay on the pulleys! Tears came to my eyes! After what seemed hours of more maneuvering, I finally pulled it tight enough. This time when I threw the tractor in gear the elevator commenced to shriek and moan as only an elevator can, but it sounded like music to me.

In a few seconds I had the front wheels of the wagon hoisted into the air . . . the yellow ears tumbled into the elevator and up and out of sight. Thinking to hasten things along, I climbed into the wagon, but I hadn't reckoned with the steep incline, slippery floor . . . my feet slipped out from under me and I went sliding with the corn.

When the last ear had tumbled out of the wagon I was so relieved. I didn't know whether to laugh or cry! I was soon hooked back on the wagon and starting for the field. As I swung the empty wagon alongside of the picker, this time in the right place . . . the farmer shouted, "Have any trouble?" "Not a bit," I lied, "it was easy." And so it went load after load, day after day, until I have now hauled over 10,000 bushels of corn. Tired? Of course I get tired, but so does that boy in the foxhole. That boy, whose place I'm trying so hard to fill.

From Mrs. Leslie Tresham, "My Experience as an Emergency Farm Worker," in U.S. Department of Agriculture, Extension Service, *Women's Land Army, Extension Farm Labor Program, 1943, 1944, 1945* (Washington, DC: U.S. Department of Agriculture, [1945]), 12.

~

The Women's Land Army of the U.S. Crop Corps 1944

U.S. Department of Agriculture

How to Get a Farm Job

SHAPED BY NEEDS AND DEMANDS, the Women's Land Army is largely an army of seasonal workers. The need for women farm workers can best be determined locally, since weather plays an important part in the amount of yield and in the time of harvest. The responsibility for assisting farmers to meet their labor needs has been placed upon the county agricultural agents, approximately 3,000 in number. Many of these agents have a farm-labor assistant. There are several thousand farm-labor offices. County agents' offices are located at the county seat, usually in the county courthouse or the Federal building.

The woman wishing to do farm work near home for short periods of time should wait for the local call. It will come over the radio and through the press just before help is needed. Directions will be given at that time as to when and where to go.

The woman wishing to plan for a working vacation on a farm or in a labor-supply camp, or to do farm work the year round, should first consult her county agricultural agent. Further information can be obtained from the assistant State farm-labor supervisor in charge of the Women's Land Army. She usually is located at the State agricultural college, or her name will be furnished by the Women's Land Army Division, Extension Service Farm Labor Program, War Food Administration. . . .

What It Is

The Women's Land Army is vital to the Farm Labor Program of the War Food Administration, authorized by Congress April 29, 1943. The purpose of the program is to supplement the efforts of farmers to provide themselves with "an adequate supply of workers for the production [and] harvesting of agricultural commodities essential to the prosecution of the war."

Any woman, 18 years of age or over, physically fit to do farm work, who assists in the wartime production of food, feed, or fiber on a farm is eligible for the Women's Land Army. Both nonfarm and farm women performing agricultural tasks are included, as well as those women who by performing household duties release farm women for agricultural work.

The Women's Land Army in each State is under the direction of a supervisor with headquarters at the State's agricultural college. She recruits workers and helps to place them on the farms where they are most needed and where they will fit in best.

Why It Is Needed

In 1944 the American farmer is expected to produce more food than he has ever produced before. He broke all previous records in

1943, with an output 32 percent above the 1935–39 average, 5 percent above the previous all-time record of 1942, and 50 percent above any year's production during the First World War. This production victory was achieved despite the fact that between 1940 and 1943, about 1 million young farm men had joined the armed forces and another 3 million potential farm workers had gone into war plants and other industries. Women, youth, and older men must replace them!

How Many Are Needed?

The farm manpower problem in 1944 is to obtain 4 million workers in addition to the regular farm-labor force of approximately 8 million. The goal for women is about 800,000. This is 200,000 more women than worked last year, and the Women's Land Army expects to recruit and place about half of this number.

Who They Are

Who are the women who helped the farmer to reach his production goals in 1943, and who in greater numbers will help him in 1944?

First of all, they are farm wives and daughters. Studies in 1942 showed twice as many farm women doing farm work as in 1941, and this trend continues. In some areas, from 50 to 75 percent of the farm women are doing agricultural tasks, many for the first time. Farm women are eligible for the Women's Land Army, and many enrolled in 1943.

Some of the women workers placed by the Extension Service do seasonal farm work regularly, but many—and nationally the number is difficult to estimate—are brand new to farm work of any kind. California's findings are revealing. In that State, approximately 35,000 women worked on farms in 1943. Ten thousand of these were farm women (6,000 of whom had not formerly done farm work); 10,000 were part of the prewar, normal local and migrant seasonal labor supply; and 15,000 were nonfarm volunteer women who helped out primarily because of the war emergency.

The nonfarm women working in agriculture include college girls and teachers, many of whom work from 3 to 5 months; business and professional women such as nurses, librarians, technicians, salesgirls, clerks, and stenographers, who spend vacation periods of 1 or 2 weeks in harvest work; industrial workers who use their "off time" in emergencies; homemakers, including wives of servicemen, who work parts of days at the time of greatest need.

What They Do

Variety of tasks characterizes the farm activities of women. Possibly the greatest contribution these women make is in the harvesting of vegetables and fruits, where their dexterity, carefulness, and persistence are great assets. But to name any farm job that will not be done by some woman somewhere in 1944 would be difficult.

A leader in one of the Southern States describes women's farm work as follows: "Women are managing the farming operations; marketing the produce; driving tractors, combines, and trucks; plowing; raking hay; shaking and stacking peanuts; picking cotton; harvesting and curing tobacco; and riding the range."

At work on a farm near Detroit, Michigan, July 1943. *Courtesy Library of Congress*

Peak-load jobs in which women help to save the day in the Midwest include picking up potatoes, bean hoeing, corn detasseling, corn husking, small-grain harvesting, and fruit and truck gardening. Placements of women are made in the far West for general farm work, irrigating, driving tractors, pruning fruit trees, working with dairy herds and poultry, and haying. Women help in almost every kind of harvest—prune, peach, apricot, grape, rice, walnut, berry, pear, tomato, and cherry.

In year-round jobs, women excel in dairy work, where gentleness and high standards of cleanliness are important. There are women cow testers; and many women are on poultry farms.

Where They Live

The great majority of seasonal women workers live at home and go out to help as the daily needs are announced. Some are housed in camps or other group-living units. Camps furnish a farm-labor supply center for farmers of the immediate neighborhood, allowing the worker to give a short or long period of time to farm work and the farmer to order a daily quota of workers. Experience in California, Connecticut, Maine, Maryland, Massachusetts, Michigan, Minnesota, New Hampshire, New Jersey, New York, Ohio, Pennsylvania, Vermont, and Virginia shows that women like the opportunity to make new friends and combine simple recreation with hard work. Where camps are practical, they meet one of the problems in employing women for farm work—adequate living arrangements. The "unit," or group-living, plan will probably be used more extensively for women farm workers in 1944.

Some general statements, based on 1943 experiences, may be made concerning the kind of woman who makes good as a farm worker and as to the kind of employer who employs women workers to the best advantage.

Most women who volunteer for service on a farm are motivated by a sincere patriotic desire to help produce food for the armed services and for our allies in the war. This kind of motive is helpful in tiding the green worker over the first hardships.

Good physical condition is important, since farm work is primarily physical labor involving bending, stooping, reaching, pulling, hauling, and lifting. Women who like outdoor life and growing things and know from experience in sports or work that they have good muscular coordination, are adaptable to farm work. All women who plan to live with farm families or in labor-supply camps, or wish to work the year round, should have a physical examination to show their fitness for farm work. Those who plan to work for short periods should satisfy themselves that they are in condition to do the work planned. Preliminary "toughening-up" exercises are helpful.

Adaptability is a second important attribute of the good woman farm worker. The sun is hot, soil is dirty, plants prickle and stain; each unaccustomed chore requires the exercise of muscles seldom used. Country living conditions often do not include some of the conveniences found in towns and cities.

Dependability is a quality greatly prized by farmers in their workers. This is not peculiar to farm work, but is a particular blessing to the farmer-supervisor who has a dozen tasks besides watching his workers.

Patience is probably the prime requisite for the farmer who is hiring inexperienced women. He will need to instruct his workers carefully and thoroughly at the start and encourage them to ask questions. Women learn quickly if there is full explanation and demonstration of the job to be done.

The farmer who recognizes that he and the women who work on his farm are striving together toward the common goal of record food production and who shows them that he recognizes this, will be rewarded by the loyalty of his workers. Assignment of workers to jobs for which they are best suited will result in better work. An occasional word of merited praise will do wonders. Consideration for the health, safety, and comfort of women workers also pays dividends in good performance.

Many farmers expressed satisfaction with women's work in 1943, and the women, themselves, expressed pleasure in doing their farm job well. One farmer said, "Women are conscientious, do a thorough piece of work, and are dependable." A woman farm worker said, "[It was] one of the best summers in health gained, new friends made, and, perhaps most important of all, the consciousness of doing some useful work."

Training

Most women farm workers are trained on the job. However, many States arrange brief, specific training courses for such special tasks as driving and servicing tractors, pruning fruit trees, and picking and packing apples. In certain States where the need for year-round dairy and poultry workers is acute, short courses in these two fields were given in 1943 and will be available again in 1944. Women receive subsistence during training. Instruction is largely practical, and the trainee learns by doing.

Wages

Women farm workers are paid the prevailing wage in the area in which they work, for the amount and type of work they do. The wage is a matter of agreement between the worker and the farmer. Year-round wages range from $25 to $50 a month, with room and board furnished. In a few places a higher wage is paid.

Most seasonal workers are paid by the hour or by the measure. Hourly rates range from 25 to 50 cents; in some places, more. Rates per measure vary with the crop and the area. An inexperienced worker who is paid piecework rates often finds it difficult to earn the cost of her board and room unless she works long enough to gain proficiency. In a few camps in 1943, a guaranteed wage of $30 to $40 a month, with room and board, was paid.

Except in a few areas or for a few crops, farm wages do not provide the strongest incentive for doing farm work in wartime. Women are motivated by a desire to perform patriotic service. They also take into account the educational values to be gained, as well as the advantages of improved health, camp life and companionship, new friends, out-of-door life, and contact with farm people.

Clothes

The Women's Land Army work outfit is designed especially for women farm workers. It consists of dark-blue overalls; a choice of long-sleeved or short-sleeved light-blue shirt; a short, dark-blue jacket; and a hat of the two shades of blue, with a visor to shade the face from the sun. The W.L.A. insignia in red, white, and blue are on the overalls and hat. The work outfit may be purchased at a nominal cost by any woman helping to produce food, feed, or fiber on a farm. Order blanks are furnished by the county agent.

Other suitable clothing includes overalls or slacks, cotton shirts, wide-brimmed straw hats, and low-heeled shoes with thick soles. Open-toed shoes are not practical. Clothing should be comfortable and easily washable.

Accident Insurance

A personal-accident policy is available to women farm workers. It covers medical expenses up to $250 and includes a death benefit, as well as benefits for loss of feet, hands, or sight. The policy costs $4 for 3 months or $1.50 for 1 month. Application blanks may be obtained from the county agent.

Record for 1943

250,000 women workers were placed on farms by the local placement offices of the Extension Service Farm Labor Program between April 29 and December 31, 1943. 5,500 were reported as placed in year-round work.

29,000 farm women doing agricultural work enrolled in the Women's Land Army.

11 States had assistant supervisors spending full time on the Women's Land Army program. Some of them were assisted by State or district representatives.

31 States had assistant supervisors spending part time on the Women's Land Army program.

8 States gave special agricultural short courses to train women for year-round farm work.

13,500 women were given some training for farm work in 35 States.

From U.S. Department of Agriculture, Extension Service, *The Women's Land Army of the U.S. Crop Corps 1944* (Washington, DC: U.S. Department of Agriculture, 1944), 1–18.

VI Preparing for the
   Postwar World

Shortly after the German invasion of Poland in 1939, Vera Micheles Dean, research director of the Foreign Policy Association, stated that American women were presented with "an extraordinary opportunity . . . to plan for the kind of peace that they would like to emerge from this war." Perceiving the war against fascism to be an opportunity to press for major reforms that would guarantee the human rights of each and every individual, women throughout the United States lobbied assiduously for full participation in national policymaking councils and international conferences concerned with preparing for the coming peace.

By the latter months of 1942 a coordinated campaign to assure the fair representation of women at postwar councils had materialized with the founding of an interracial umbrella organization, the Committee on the Participation of Women in Post War Planning. In fact, a wide array of women's organizations, including such diverse groups as the American Legion Auxiliary, the National Council of Negro Women, the National Federation of Business and Professional Women's Clubs, the American Association of University Women, the National Council of Jewish Women, the Young Women's Christian Association, and the League of Women Voters, worked tirelessly for the inclusion of women at the peace table.

Women organized special conferences, formulated rosters of women qualified to serve on postwar councils, sponsored national essay contests, wrote articles for the press, and coordinated letter-writing campaigns to high-ranking government officials. Led by important public figures—Eleanor Roosevelt, Mary McLeod Bethune, Margaret Hickey, Mary Anderson, Emily Hickman, Lucy Somerville Howorth, and Virginia Gildersleeve—women compellingly asserted their belief that they had the right and the responsibility to participate fully in postwar planning. Despite the energy and hard work exhibited by America's wartime women, the nation's political leaders, consumed with military, strategic, and geopolitical concerns, demonstrated only lukewarm support for the inclusion of women on postwar councils. They were excluded from the influential Dumbarton Oaks conversations, which drew up the blueprint for the United Nations organization, and they were woefully underrepresented at other postwar conferences and councils. As marginalized members of the peacemaking deliberations, women were denied an effective voice in the postwar discourse. Without question, the postwar agenda constructed at national and international councils was impoverished by the underutilization and omission of American women from peacemaking deliberations.

22   Out of the Kitchen—Into the War

Susan B. Anthony II

Even as the war raged, women began to contemplate the post-war world. Susan B. Anthony II, niece of the nineteenth-century woman's rights champion, included a powerful chapter on women in the postwar world in her 1943 book Out of the Kitchen—Into the War. *Anthony describes American women as the "great reservoir of anti-fascist fighters" and emphasizes that "the kind of war we wage now will directly determine the kind of peace we will enjoy for generations to come."*

RIVETING THE WING OF A plane in the great roar of the Michigan bomber plant, standing watch on the long voyage to Murmansk, or running a tractor over the broad fields of Kansas, the minds of American women and men meet on the two major conditions of their lives.

They are thinking, first, that they must keep them flying, keep them sailing, and keep producing to crush the fascists in overwhelming and decisive defeat.

They are thinking, second, of what is going to happen to *them*, to their families, and to their lives, when war ends.

The woman riveter, the seaman, the farm laborer are wondering, "Are we living only on borrowed time?"

They have jobs today, with good pay, and a war to win that calls for every atom of their energy. The remembrance of things past, however, of days before the war, when they or theirs were on breadlines, or when they were wandering migrants, or on relief, haunts them. Perhaps it holds them back from producing all they can; for they are wondering, "What's the use of working beyond my strength, or trying to get ahead? After this war—the way it was after the last war—it will be the same old story of no job, no dough, no hope."

The woman who remembers or whose mother tells her of the mass expulsion of women from industry that followed World War I is apt to say, "Why should I leave home today, take training

From Susan B. Anthony II, *Out of the Kitchen—Into the War: Woman's Winning Role in the Nation's Drama* (New York: Stephen Daye, 1943), 232–46.

for a job, when they'll just kick me out tomorrow when the war is over?"

This lowered morale and lowered energy output for winning the war is the reason why I am talking now about postwar America.

The kind of war we wage now will directly determine the kind of peace we will enjoy for generations to come. The only possible excuse for thinking now of postwar problems is to release the maximum energy, build the highest morale for the one and the only task that confronts us—that of defeating the fascists.

Any plans for the postwar world which do not contribute directly to our defeat of Hitler are in themselves a serious hindrance to the war effort, a diversion of the thought and strength of the peoples both of this nation and of the United Nations. Talk of occupation of the world, speeches on division of the world's air lanes, sea lanes, and territory breed premonitory disunity among the United Nations. But these United Nations must grow much closer in thought and in formal alliance if we are to win the war.

Plans for the postwar world which contribute to winning the war are, therefore, the only actions germane to the United States in this year of 1943.

What are these plans? What assurance have the women of America that maximum exertion of their energies now will give them not only a place in the war today but a place in the world tomorrow?

The premedical student, the young college science major, the women who require training for their careers are anxious to know whether the long and expensive years of preparation will be wasted in long expensive years of unemployment. The housewife who has wrenched herself out of her accustomed home grooves, the girl who left a good job to join the WAVES as an apprentice seaman, the woman who pulled up stakes from teaching and went to the bomber plant—all these *deserve* an answer to their question. . . .

If we are to win the war it is clear that nursery schools, public cafeterias, housing projects, medical services, recreation facilities, and special services for maternity cases are vital necessities. But they are more than that—they are the key to the postwar position of women and a promise to men and women of a standard of living that will enable *three-thirds of a nation* to be well housed, well fed, and well cared for.

If we do not obtain nursery schools, if we do not obtain adequate health programs, school lunch, and milk for our children

now, when they are desperately needed as wartime measures, you
can be sure of a reversion in the postwar world to substandards of
living. . . .

Victory can no longer be regarded as separate from the assurance to our people of a future that will hold a place for them. To
arouse the spirit of victory the people must be given a demonstration of what democracy means, what full employment means, what
public services mean.

We are in a death struggle against fascism—a system whose
ideology and practice reduces men and women to slaves, living on
starvation levels. What better proof could we offer the American
people of our absolute irreconcilability with Hitler's methods than
to start *now* to provide employment and security for all?

The war today is giving employment to a part of the largest
body of nonemployed persons in the nation—women. The peace
tomorrow must also give them employment. Ralph E. Flanders,
president of the Jones and Lamson Machine Company of Vermont,
has put it this way:

> The world we are working toward is one of greater production,
> but with a satisfactory amount of leisure. While this greater pro-
> duction will be obtained in part by improved machinery processes
> and organization, we would also plan that it be obtained by hav-
> ing a much higher percentage of the total population engaged in
> productive work. . . . This in itself means that opportunities for
> women would be better than they have been in the past, even in
> those lines of work in which women are used as a second choice
> and principally in emergencies. This is perhaps the fundamental
> consideration leading to a hope for better peacetime employment
> opportunities for women.

One of the Four Freedoms* for which we are fighting is freedom from want. Freedom from want applies to all those millions of
American women who, in peacetime, eke out a miserable existence
on their own wages or on those made by their husbands. A single
earner has had to provide for a wife and often many children.

Women have been discriminated against in work on the utterly
fallacious assumption that their menfolks—their fathers or husbands—could support them. As a result men in many instances have

*See pp. 220–21.

had to work doubly hard to support adults who were perfectly capable of supporting themselves. They have had to place the support of their wives and children before their personal choice of occupation, or before their other obligations to society. In effect they have been shackled in the cause of supporting women—not only when they were legally wedded to them, but also when they were legally divorced from them. There are men in prison today because they could not pay alimony to a former wife. . . . And how many men are supporting not one woman but two and three women? . . .

Women become crippled veterans of the single-earner system when, due to long years of nonproductive existence, they become petty, frustrated, and useless "old hags" at a time when their menfolks are at the peak of their powers.

America has limped along for too many centuries utilizing half the productive forces of the nation. Only in wartime does our vast industrial and agricultural machine become nearly fully used. Only in wartime does the vast energy and talent of the American woman begin to be unleashed. It has been said that women are the margin for victory in this war. I would add that women are the margin for the economic life of the peace. The kind of war we wage determines the kind of peace. The kind of peace we have will be determined largely by the kind of use we make of our labor potential.

If we plan a nation producing enough food, housing, clothing, for all of our people, then we will need the labor of all of the adult men and women to staff the factories, farms, and offices. Energies going into the weapons of war today should be used for the essentials and for the luxuries of life tomorrow. Unless we envisage a return to the economy of scarcity of prewar America, we are going to need our women as well as our men in production. Unless we envisage losing the war, we need community services *now* to release women for the big wartime tasks of production.

With them America will be on the road to victory, both in war and peace. Without them America cannot mobilize its labor forces either for war or peace. If we provide these services now, they will be a means to victory. They can then be utilized as a means of raising the peacetime standards of living of *all our people*.

Yet women need more than the mere extension of community services to give them a full stake in the war. They need the assurance that *never again will they be deprived of the right to work, and the right to hold top positions*. Temporary orders permitting equal pay for equal work, transitory demands of employers for their services, are not enough. . . .

When women formed only one-quarter of the productive forces of the nation, it was easy to push aside their claims to equal participation in governing the nation. The right to vote has been relied upon as the complete answer to our demands for a voice in the highest councils of the Government. In almost doubling the number of women workers this war doubles the justice of our demands for an equal place in the legislatures, on the court benches, and in law enforcement.

No longer can women be satisfied with a backseat in Congress, with one seat in the President's circle of advisers and administrators, *with no seat on the Supreme Court Bench.* Wherever people are governed, representatives of those people should be amongst the governors. That is part of the fundamental democratic principle for which we are now fighting. Women, being governed, must logically be among the governors. We would be but a poor pretender to democracy if, after having worked our women to the utmost to win the war, we barred them from a meaningful role in the peace. How can we claim to be purified of fascist tendencies in our own nation if we permit a fascist concept of women to prevail?

As we know, the fascist concept of woman is that her life's work is to breed and feed. She breeds a dozen years and feeds for a lifetime. After breeding—after having fulfilled her biological function—she is then, according to the fascists, only useful to brood over the kitchen stove. The boundary for woman, under fascism, is the home; and beyond that boundary she must not go. Democracy's task is to elevate woman so that the world is her home—not the home her world.

Fascism is determined to make women servants of the house. Democracy must encourage women to be servants of the world. The conditions of war are definitely pulling women out of the house into the world. The peace must not push them back into the house, unless they wish to go there.

We must recognize that woman's place is in the world as much as man's is. Woman's place is in the factory, in the office, in the professions, in the fields, and at the council table—wherever human labor, human effort, is needed to produce and create. In the postwar world there must be an abolition of the false distinctions between men and women—between "men's jobs" and "women's jobs." Personal ability and choice, not sex, must determine the job-holder. Present discriminations must be done away with, for they work against men as well as women.

The greatest distinction between men's and women's work is that jobs at the top are tacitly regarded as being "For Men Only." The menial and the semiskilled jobs are thought to be ideal for women. Wartime necessity will to some degree wipe out this distinction; but extreme vigilance will be needed in the postwar period if we are to maintain any of the higher positions we reach now as an expedient because the men are fighting.

The hopeful thing is that each major American war has resulted in the extension of democracy to a group that was formerly under-privileged. The American Revolution extended to white men the right to vote, the right to elect the world's first republican form of Government. The Civil War extended to black men the right to vote. The First World War extended to white and black women the right to vote.

This extension of democracy in past wars has not come easily. It has not been handed down generously from above. It has been wrenched from the hands and against the prejudices of those in power; it has been reluctantly granted, after great pressures and bloody battles.

In these wars of American history, the Government has had to extend democracy to new sections of the population for a specific reason of winning the war. Each war in our history has demanded the lives and the sweat of larger and larger sections of the population.

Today, we are engaged in the greatest war of our history. More men, more machines, more material are being used against the enemy. Today, for the first time, whole populations, men and women, are involved as active belligerents.

And out of the necessities of our struggle against fascism, this nation is being forced to mobilize that great reservoir of anti-fascist fighters—the American women. As in the Civil War when the Union freed the Negroes to fight to win the war, so today our Government is being forced to free women to win this war. America must unlock millions of doors that have imprisoned millions of women. Women must be let out—liberated from the homes, so that they can take their place in the war of the world today—and in the work of the world tomorrow.

23 Women Workers in Transition from War to Peace

Mary Elizabeth Pidgeon

Toward the end of the war, the Women's Bureau began to focus attention on how the wartime gains of working women could be safeguarded in times of peace. In a January 1944 address to the annual meeting of the American Economic Association, Bureau director Mary Anderson emphasized that "full employment means women as well as men" and called for the appointment of qualified women to postwar planning committees. To this end, the Women's Bureau sponsored six conferences on postwar employment during 1944 and 1945.

A Preview as to Women Workers in Transition from War to Peace *was written by Mary Elizabeth Pidgeon, chief of the research division of the Bureau and author of several important wartime studies on women workers. It links the "broad objective of the great struggle in which the United States is engaged" to the establishment of the Four Freedoms in the "American economy at home, as well as in the world at large."*

Unfortunately, the Bureau wielded little power in shaping postwar labor policies that protected and advanced the interests of female wage earners. In the transition from war to peace, as millions of veterans returned to civilian life, many women lost their jobs. From a wartime high of 36 percent, their proportion in the work force declined to 27.9 percent in 1947. Nonetheless, the working experiences of these women strengthened their sense of self and ultimately paved the way for new opportunities for female wage earners.

WHAT WILL BE THE SITUATION of the woman worker after the war? This is a question of vital importance to the Nation. It is being asked with increasing insistence by all groups and agencies concerned with the postwar world, and most of all by women workers themselves.

From Mary Elizabeth Pidgeon, *A Preview as to Women Workers in Transition from War to Peace* (Washington, DC: U.S. Department of Labor, Women's Bureau, Special Bulletin No. 18, 1944), 1–5, 21.

Employment and satisfactory conditions of work for women are part and parcel of sound economic conditions for the welfare of the whole people, and hence not to be overlooked or neglected in a time when every effort is to be devoted toward creating a better society. In regard to women workers, as well as to other elements in American life, what is done now, decided now, and planned now will determine to a large extent what can be expected tomorrow.

Close of the war will bring to an end, perhaps in many cases quite suddenly, much of the activity in which women have engaged in some of the major war industries, such as making ammunition, guns, ships, aircraft, and parts, which will not be needed in the quantities now required. In fact, considerable numbers already were being laid off from various ordnance plants in the late months of 1943, and this continues in 1944.

Every effort must be made to find jobs for the men and women returning from the armed services and for displaced industrial workers as well. Returning servicemen have veterans' preference, and those who formerly had permanent employment are legally guaranteed their old jobs (or equivalent ones). Others formerly had only temporary work, and very many never before had a job. By the end of 1943 more than a million men had been mustered out of the armed forces, and 1944 is expected to add another million to these. Carefully worked-out organizations are being developed to aid these men to find jobs and resume a normal life. Similar attention should be given to the needs of displaced workers, including women. The economic and family situation of women workers, the extent to which they have constituted a usual part of the prewar labor force, and the nature of their own plans for their postwar life are subjects of field investigations the Women's Bureau now has in progress.

One of the important aids in finding postwar jobs for the women who expect to remain in the labor market lies in the fact that many articles curtailed during the war will be produced again to meet a large consumer demand, and some of these are industries in which in the past women have represented a considerable part of the labor force.

Goals for Mankind

The broad objective of the great struggle in which the United States is engaged should be kept continually in the forefront. It has been defined [by President Roosevelt] as the establishment for mankind of Four Freedoms: Of Speech; Of Religion; From Want; From Fear. As the war continues, it becomes increasingly clear that action toward these ends in the economy of this country actually is an integral part of the struggle, and cannot await the close of hostilities —that an essential part of conducting and winning the war is to establish the Four Freedoms firmly in the economic life of America itself.

One of the most important goals for this country may be stated in very general terms as the organization of efforts to satisfy the almost universal desire for a high level of employment and a better standard of living. Freedom from want and freedom from fear both require that jobs must be available for persons who need them. It is encouraging that many agencies are working toward these ends. Both the A.F.L. [American Federation of Labor] and C.I.O. [Congress of Industrial Organizations] have special postwar planning committees devoting much work to determining the most advantageous lines of movement toward these goals. Adequate social insurance is an important subject that is currently to the fore because of anticipated needs in the period of transition to peacetime production. Business interests are making vigorous plans for full employment through the Committee for Economic Development and other agencies. The National Planning Association has been formed to promote the cooperation of business, labor, agriculture, and Government. Its representatives consider that no group is self-sufficient, all are interdependent. Together they recognize collective bargaining and the need for security, participation of all in productive enterprise, [and] organization and development of technical and commercial research.

Picturing the Postwar Period

The general picture after the war will be one of large numbers of men returning from the services and needing jobs, large numbers of workers leaving war industries and transferring to other work, much shifting of population from war-industry areas to home States or elsewhere. This period of transition already has begun, and bids fair to continue on an accelerated scale. Employment cannot be expected to remain very long at the war peak. However, it is most encouraging that business, management, labor, and Government have efforts afoot to attain a permanent employment level considerably higher than that before the war.

Women after the War

The situation of women will depend to a large extent on many economic factors. Foremost of these, of course, are the extent to which the entire economy can develop a high level of employment and the extent to which the industries expand that require the particular types of work women do best. Of great importance will be the opportunity for employment of men at wages sufficient to support their families, since many women who now have a real job at home as well as at the factory will leave the labor market if the male earners receive enough pay.

There are many other factors that will share in determining how far women will remain in employment—for example, the extent to which plants have been engineered for women's performance and employers convinced of its effectiveness; the skills women have demonstrated; the demand for work in industries that in past years have employed many women. Operating against women is the fact that as a class they have entered industry more recently than men and have relatively short seniority records. A strong psychological factor that does not favor women is the tradition that they do not support dependents, and that this is in a considerable degree false must be reiterated continually, with new evidences, before the mistaken theory can be overcome.

In summary, the general outline as to the present undeveloped stage of thinking and action on war and postwar policies for women workers is somewhat as follows:

Industry in general has provided no clear-cut policy. Women have been considered in terms of "a minority group," though before the United States entered the war (that is, in 1940) they were over 24 percent of all workers, while the minority group next in size (Negroes of both sexes) constituted only 10 percent, and "children" (under 18) less than 3 percent. Chief discussions as to women's employment have centered around:

• The extent of their entrance into employment
• The types of work they are doing
• Satisfactory conditions surrounding their jobs
• The extent to which they will retire from the labor market.

The Women's Advisory Committee for the War Manpower Commission has stated basic policies for employment and retention of women workers.

Women's organizations have defined policies for the retention of women workers.

In 1940, something over 11 million women were actually employed, and about 2 1/2 million others were seeking work. Even then women were practically one-fourth of all workers, and this proportion has risen through the war period to one-third in the latter part of 1943. After the war, the number of women who will need to remain in the labor force probably will be at least 2 or 3 million higher than the number in 1940. A much larger proportion of these than formerly will be women aged 45 to 64 years. There is evidence that the need for women workers will continue along the following lines:

In producing consumer goods, where women long have been employed, as in the electrical, shoe, textile, food, jewelry, and other industries.

In service industries where shortages will continue acute, as in restaurants, laundries, households, and various selling trades.

In community services, as in health, welfare, social security, child care, and recreation, both in America and in reconstruction elsewhere.

In specialized technical and professional work, as in medicine, nutrition, education, rehabilitation of the handicapped, research, and various scientific services.

In the manufacture of goods to help in the reconstruction of devastated countries, as well as the replenishment of depleted stocks in this country.

In various business and clerical operations, as in secretarial work, statistics, and accounting.

Women's Share in the Support of Families

An important feature of the postwar period will be the extent to which it will be necessary for women to support dependents. This is no new phenomenon, though it has become increasingly marked through the last half-century. In fact, this need has existed since much earlier times, and the way in which it was met by many women in the American colonial days has been described with interesting detail in at least one book on that period.

In recent prewar years, Bureau of Labor Statistics studies of income in some 131,000 families indicated that practically one-fifth of the employed women were the principal wage earners in their families. A Social Security Board analysis of reports on more than 700,000 city households has shown that women were at the head of a tenth of the families of 2 persons or more that constituted single households. A study made in Cleveland by the Women's Bureau showed that women wage earners contributed all the funds for the support of about a third of some 2,000 families with women wage earners reported.

The death of many men in the present war, and the consequent depletion of male population, will require still more women to contribute to their families' support. Even as far back as the date of the 1930 Census there were more females than males in 66 of 93 major cities in the United States. By 1944, this had become the situation in the country as a whole. Support of the families of handicapped men is likely to increase considerably the financial obligations of women workers, in spite of aid tendered them by the Government. Reports in April 1944 give total casualties of the Armed Forces as 189,300—43,800 dead, 70,900 wounded, 41,300 missing, 33,300 prisoners.

The numbers killed and disabled are not distributed evenly over the country, and hence the effects of their loss will be greater in some localities than in others. In the first place, they are concentrated at certain ages, selectees being from the more youthful group of 18 to 38 years. Furthermore, the age distributions in the population differ by locality, and this is an added reason why the severity of the losses will be greater at some points than at others. This will mean that greater proportions of the woman population in some than in other localities must assume a large share of the support of their families. . . .

Planning for Women

Sound policies outlining women's postwar situation and opportunities are the subject of much thought among women themselves. They are being discussed at numerous public conferences and form the basis for active programs of national organizations of women. It is realized strongly that the economic situation as a whole will have the most profound effect on women's opportunities. Besides this, certain basic principles specifically applying to women have been thought out and expressed. Practical methods for putting these into effect, taking account of controlling economic factors, have not been fully developed, though some steps in this direction have been initiated.

The more outstanding facts and principles being stressed by women who are thinking through these problems are along the following lines:

Even before the war, women constituted a very considerable proportion (24 percent) of the labor force. For decades this had been an increasing proportion. A large part of the woman labor force has been responsible for the support of dependents. The extent of this is increased by war conditions. War casualties will contribute to the excess of female over male population, which already had developed in many areas in this country.

Many women who have entered employment for patriotic reasons or because their husbands were in service will wish to leave the labor force after the war. Many other women will be unable to retire from gainful work or will wish to continue to use the skills they have developed.

The skills developed by women in their war work are a national asset that should continue to find effective use.

Opportunity should be afforded to women for education, training, job placement, and advancement in their chosen lines of work.

Efforts to provide jobs for the postwar labor force should fully include women workers. Arbitrary dismissals of women should be forestalled by developing constructive measures to expand the economy and provide full employment for all who want it.

24   Women's Responsibility in World Affairs

Lucy Somerville Howorth

The national dialogue on women's participation in postwar planning reached the highest levels of government when the White House Conference on How Women May Share in Post-War Policy Making was convened on June 14, 1944, in response

From Lucy Somerville Howorth, "Women's Responsibility in World Affairs," *Journal of the American Association of University Women* 37 (Summer 1944): 195–98. Reprinted by permission of the American Association of University Women.

to numerous requests by First Lady Eleanor Roosevelt that "women . . . be represented at the peace table . . . [and] in every international conference." The gathering, described by conference organizer Charl Ormond Williams as "an historic milestone in women's contributions to society," was attended by 213 distinguished women from throughout the United States.

What follows is a reprint of the keynote address, "Women's Responsibility in World Affairs," delivered by Lucy Somerville Howorth, a senior attorney in the Office of the Legislative Council at the Veterans Administration as well as a member of the Committee on the Participation of Women in Post-War Planning. Howorth asserted that if women did not "push and shove themselves into policymaking positions," they would be "ineffective in this hour of destiny." Reflecting an opinion held by many of the conference speakers, Howorth expressed support for gender differences, arguing that "women are the natural planners of the human race." She believed that women and men would each bring distinct qualifications to postwar councils that would substantially enhance the peacemaking process. However, carefully entwined into this argument about gender differences was her belief that qualified women, as citizens of the United States, had the right and responsibility to participate fully in postwar planning.

WE ARE MET IN A ROOM hallowed by great events. We are met in a time of solemn urgency.

We must project ourselves to the time when we shall no longer be united by impending danger, no longer be sobered by the shadow of personal sorrow.

Women of the United States from Revolutionary days have had a high tradition of courage and steadfastness under the shock of war. With tenderness and pride in our hearts, we pay tribute to the wives and mothers of men on the bitter sands of Normandy, the peaks of Italy, the jungles of New Guinea, on and over and under the oceans.

World conditions demand even more of women today. Those new demands have brought us to this Conference. You are the voice of multiplied thousands of women in homes and kitchens, in fields and factories, in cloistered college and public ways. It is for you not only to think and act, but to stir those whom you can reach to thought and action.

Consider these facts:

On June 3, the Census announced that adult women outnumbered adult men in the United States for the first time. Many jokes will result from that announcement, but, seriously, it is most significant. It will highlight the power and failures of American women.

American women are strong and healthy, their life expectancy is greater than that of men.

American women own, it is said, more than 50 percent of the property in this country.

American women work in every profession and nearly every occupation. In the Army alone, members of the Women's Army Corps fill 239 categories of jobs.

American women vote, they hold office, they speak their minds freely on public issues.

High schools and colleges, nearly bereft of boys, are crowded with girls.

An avalanche of problems is moving down upon us and all the world. If planning is done in the United States to meet that avalanche, it must be done by women, older men, and men disqualified for military service. Most of these men are engrossed in war work. Women are the natural planners of the human race. The "little woman" plans and plans, sometimes to the annoyance of all the family. That same quality, if translated into action in world affairs by this group here today, may well save the world blood, sweat, toil, and tears tomorrow.

Look at these facts, thus:

If down the ages, after each war, women had been haled before a judgment bar and asked: "What have you done to make an enduring peace?"—they could have said: "We had no vote, we had no money, we had no strength after the day's work was done, we could only do our daily tasks and hope and pray. There is no guilt upon us."

If after this war that same question were to be asked, would we have to answer: "We can vote, we could hold office, we were rich in money and goods, our bodies were strong, our minds were trained, well informed, we could speak with voices reaching to every land, yet we did nothing to cure this world sickness"?

Surely the richly gifted women of this Conference will not permit such an answer to be the only one that can be made.

Our consciousness is split these days. Our hopes and fears are across the seas. Our job is here, our minds must be centered here.

There is unfolding in the midst of battle, an approach to the problems of the world. It is becoming clear that there are to be a series of general international technical conferences. Senator [Elbert] Thomas of Utah said in the Senate: "The aim of such conferences is to put together the fragments of a broken world. . . . Events seem to suggest that the forthcoming peace settlement will be built on a broad, firm base, with dozens of minor, technical matters talked out and thought out before the great political issues are settled and agreed upon."

The *Washington Star* states: "As matters stand today, sources high in the Administration do not expect a full-dress peace conference on the Versailles model to follow the surrender of Germany."

Four such conferences have been held: the Food Conference at Hot Springs, the Conference on Relief and Rehabilitation at Atlantic City, the Philadelphia meeting of the International Labor Organization, the Conference on Education in London. An International Monetary Conference will convene on July 1, and the press reports a Conference on International Aviation is in contemplation.

The functioning of international conferences should be understood. As in every home and office, there are two kinds of responsibility—responsibility for policy and responsibility for work. In the family, mother and father are responsible for policy; they generally do the work also. In larger institutions these functions are separated. Organizations, such as those represented here, have elective and appointive officers to shape policies and staffs to do the work. Exactly the same division of responsibility for policy and work exists in government and world affairs.

International conferences held to date have had two groups of policymaking representatives: official delegates and official advisers. The technical and general secretariat compose the nonpolicymaking representatives. In government agencies the policymaking positions are the heads of departments, members of boards, and assistant administrators. Officials of lower rank may obstruct policies; they do not make policies. This may seem elementary to you, yet these simple matters of government structure are a puzzle to many otherwise well-informed people. It is part of our duty as leaders to make such matters clear.

So remember, while it is fine for young Mary Jones to take a . . . job in the government, she will not, and the thousands like her will not, shape the destiny of the nation, unless they push and shove themselves into policymaking positions. So it is with women of the United States. Except as they hold policymaking positions, national and international, they will be ineffective in this hour of destiny. We know what women can do, we have before us in recent years the fine records of able women who have held and are holding policymaking positions.

It is well to pause here. This meeting is too important to be misinterpreted. While thousands of our beloved husbands and sons are fighting and dying to free the world, we must not be portrayed as grasping for special favors. This Conference is dedicated to what we may call the "new humanism," to adapt a phrase from [philosopher] Josiah Royce. It is dedicated to humanity, to solving the world's problems in terms of human rights and human needs.

With our philosophy stated, let us spade the ground a bit. How do women, or men, get appointed to policymaking positions? The process is not secret, it is not draped in mystery; it can be outlined in three short steps:

1. Names, names of individuals, not groups or classes of people, must be given to the appointive authority, with a short biographical sketch for each.

2. The appointive authority must be convinced that the person recommended can do the job.

3. The person recommended must not only be qualified for the job, but must not be obnoxious to the public, or that part of the public concerned with the position sought. It is preferred that persons recommended have some assurance of public support.

Organizations and individuals here today can assume a definite responsibility in each of these steps.

First, a roster should be made up of the names of able, intelligent, personable women, qualified to serve in conferences to come, remembering the different requirements for policymaking and staff positions. Organizations represented here today are national, with units in every state; if they will comb their rolls, no capable woman will be overlooked.

Second, organizations and individuals must unite to convince the appointive authority that the women recommended can do the job.

This is where we strike a sharp snag. Organizations, some of them at least, have rules. The purpose of the rules is worthy. But there comes a time when rules must be changed or exceptions allowed. Somehow, some way, the transition from the general to the particular must be made.

Picture this scene: A committee of distinguished women from this Conference confers with a cabinet member about a forthcoming international conference. One of the committee, in her most agreeable manner, says: "Mr. Secretary, we ask that you appoint several women delegates to this conference." Mr. Secretary replies: "I shall be glad to do so, if suitable persons are brought to my attention."

"Oh," say the committee, "we never recommend individuals, but we hope, if you do find a woman to appoint, she will be properly qualified."

I think you did not come here today for any such inanity.

The times demand that we be broad enough, bold enough, generous enough, patriotic enough to rally behind suitable women without fear of disunity, without fear of stirring factional strife within our ranks. I, for one, believe we can do it.

There was the day, not so long ago, when most women's organizations would take no positive stand on legislation. That day is happily gone. And no organizations were wrecked; the sailing might have been rough at times, but they made port.

Third, organized women particularly can rally public support to aid and uphold the arms of women appointed to national and international policymaking positions. This technique is well understood. It does not need discussion here.

If there comes out of this Conference a determination to take these three steps, then this Conference will indeed be history making.

This Conference meets under favorable auspices. The prestige of the great lady who is our hostess supports our endeavors. Our government is friendly to our cause; able women have been appointed as delegates to international conferences, and we feel sure others will be appointed in the future; women leaders in other lands are urging that women have voice and vote in the making of the peace. Surely we will not be paralyzed by timidity, tradition, and taboo. Instead, let us here highly resolve to go bravely forward, using the talents God has given us, in service to our country and humanity.

25   Our Stake in Tomorrow's World

Mary McLeod Bethune

On February 13, 1945, the State Department announced that Virginia Gildersleeve, dean of Barnard College, would be one of the eight U.S. delegates to the conference to form a world organization, the United Nations, to be held in San Francisco the following April. This announcement was heralded by those groups that had arduously worked for women's participation on postwar planning councils.

Accompanying the eight delegates to San Francisco were 246 consultants, associates, advisers, experts, aides, and other assistants, representing forty-two private organizations, which the State Department described as constituting a "fair cross section of citizens' groups." However, African-American women were notably absent from the list. The distinguished educator and political activist, Mary McLeod Bethune, fired off a series of letters to State Department officials protesting this omission. Bethune eventually found her way to San Francisco as a representative, along with W. E. B. Du Bois and Walter White, of the National Association for the Advancement of Colored People. Bethune's summary report, "Our Stake in Tomorrow's World," describes her work at the conference.

T HE SAN FRANCISCO INTERNATIONAL SECURITY CONFERENCE is a great historic occasion for all of us. It marks a new epoch of world democracy—for here we see the world in action—with sincerity and faith as never before, absorbed in perfecting the blueprint for a new world—the world of tomorrow.

Women are interestingly and impressively a definite part of the Conference, performing a variety of services ranging from authority and responsibility at the core of developments—on issues and policies—to the fringe on the outskirts of the Conference where we see the high-school girl gazing with naive fascination at some delegate from the Far East in picturesque garb. But it is not the mere

From Mary McLeod Bethune, "Our Stake in Tomorrow's World," *Aframerican Woman's Journal* (June 1945): 2; Series 13, Box 2, Folder 17, Records of the National Council of Negro Women. Reprinted by permission of the Bethune Museum and Archives, Washington, DC.

presence of the few women delegates, counselors, consultants, special advisers, observers, secretaries, stenographers, teletype operators, messengers, information booth attendants, and canteen workers that is significant. The presence of women here marks their maturing political vision and the gradual recognition of them by men, as well as the growing awareness among women themselves of their contribution as citizens of the world.

The extended horizon that has so rapidly appeared for women during the war has opened new areas which of necessity have brought rich experiences. Women have found themselves in new fields of work and service which have given them an unparalleled opportunity to develop new skills and habits of thought and behavior—a new kind of mental attitude and stamina, essential in tomorrow's world. May we accept the challenge to work together toward a new world of peace and security! It will take great skill in human relations—it will take common sense and an alert consciousness of national and world problems.

May we never think of the National Council of Negro Women as a segregated force in the building of this new world, but as a vastly important grooming ground for citizens who must eventually take their places in tomorrow's world. There are zones of activity which call for equally vital, strong, if not spectacular leadership in which women can give significant service. They are the areas in which women naturally work—areas which require high standards of human relationships.

May I conclude with a quotation from the undelivered [due to his sudden death] Jefferson Day Address, April 1945, of Franklin Delano Roosevelt: "Today we are faced with the preeminent fact that if civilization is to survive, we must cultivate the science of human relationships—the ability of all peoples, of all kinds, to live together and work together in the same world, at peace. . . . The only limit to our realization of tomorrow will be our doubts of today. Let us move forward with strong and active faith."

Suggested Readings

The following contemporary works were written by American women at war and published between 1940 and 1946.

Home Front

Alsop, Gulielma Fell, and Mary F. McBride. *Arms and the Girl: A Guide to Personal Adjustment in War Work and War Marriage*. New York: Vanguard Press, 1943.

Anthony, Susan B., II. *Out of the Kitchen—Into the War: Woman's Winning Role in the Nation's Drama*. New York: Stephen Daye, 1943.

Banning, Margaret Culkin. *Letters from England: Summer 1942*. New York: Harper and Brothers, 1943.

———. *Women for Defense*. New York: Duel, Sloan and Pearce, 1942.

Collins, Clella Reeves. *The Army Woman's Handbook*. New York: Whittlesey House, 1942.

———. *The Navy Woman's Handbook*. New York: Whittlesey House, 1942.

Gorham, Ethel. *So Your Husband's Gone to War!* Garden City, NY: Doubleday, Doran and Co., 1942.

Greenbie, Marjorie Barstow. *The Art of Living in Wartime*. New York: Whittlesey House, 1944.

Gruenberg, Sidonie Matsner, ed. *The Family in a World at War*. New York: Harper and Brothers, 1942.

Klaw, Barbara. *Camp Follower: The Story of a Soldier's Wife*. New York: Random House, 1944.

Shea, Nancy. *The Army Wife*. New York: Harper and Brothers, 1942.

Journalists

Argall, Phyllis. *My Life with the Enemy*. New York: Macmillan Co., 1944.

Bourke-White, Margaret. *Shooting the Russian War*. New York: Simon and Schuster, 1942.

Meyer, Agnes E. *Journey through Chaos.* New York: Harcourt, Brace and Co., 1943.

Moats, Alice Leon. *Blind Date with Mars.* Garden City, NY: Doubleday, Doran and Co., 1943.

Mydans, Shelley Smith. *The Open City.* Garden City, NY: Doubleday, Doran and Co., 1945.

Military

Angel, Joan. *Angel of the Navy: The Story of a WAVE.* New York: Hastings House, 1943.

Archard, Theresa. *G.I. Nightingale: The Story of an American Army Nurse.* New York: W. W. Norton and Co., 1945.

Cooper, Page. *Navy Nurse.* New York: McGraw-Hill Co., 1946.

Flikke, Colonel Julia O. *Nurses in Action: The Story of the Army Nurse Corps.* Philadelphia: J. B. Lippincott Co., 1943.

Flint, Margaret. *Dress Right, Dress: The Autobiography of a WAC.* New York: Dodd, Mead and Co., 1943.

Haskell, Ruth G. *Helmets and Lipstick.* New York: G. P. Putnam's and Sons, 1944.

Harris, Mary Virginia. *Guide Right: A Handbook of Etiquette and Customs for Members of the Women's Reserve of the United States Naval Reserve and the United States Coast Guard Reserve.* New York: Macmillan Co., 1944.

Jacobs, Lieutenant (j.g.) Helen Hull. *"By Your Leave, Sir": The Story of a WAVE.* New York: Dodd, Mead and Co., 1943.

Knapp, Sally Elizabeth. *New Wings for Women.* New York: Thomas Y. Crowell Co., 1946.

Lutz, Alma, ed. *With Love, Jane: Letters from American Women on the War Fronts.* New York: John Day Co., 1945.

Lyne, Mary C., and Kay Arthur. *Three Years Behind the Mast: The Story of the United States Coast Guard SPARs.* [Washington, D.C.]: n.p., [1946].

Myers, Bessy. *Captured: My Experiences as an Ambulance Driver and as a Prisoner of the Nazis.* New York: D. Appleton-Century Co., 1942.

Peckham, Betty. *Women in Aviation.* New York: Thomas Nelson and Sons, 1945.

Pollock, Auxiliary Elizabeth R. *Yes, Ma'am!: The Personal Papers of a WAAC Private.* Philadelphia: J. B. Lippincott Co., 1943.

Redmond, Juanita. *I Served on Bataan.* Philadelphia: J. B. Lippincott Co., 1943.

Ross, Mary Steele. *American Women in Uniform*. Garden City, NY: Doubleday, Doran and Co., 1943.

Ross, Nancy Wilson. *The WAVES: The Story of the Girls in Blue*. New York: Henry Holt and Co., 1943.

Shea, Nancy. *The WAACs*. New York: Harper and Brothers, 1943.

Stansbury, Jean. *Bars on Her Shoulders: A Story of a WAAC*. New York: Dodd, Mead and Co., 1943.

White, First Lieutenant Barbara A. *Lady Leatherneck*. New York: Dodd, Mead and Co., 1945.

Wood, Winifred. *We Were WASPs*. Coral Gables, FL: Glade House, 1945.

Novels

Halsey, Margaret. *Some of My Best Friends Are Soldiers: A Kind of Novel*. New York: Simon and Schuster, 1944.

Shea, Margaret. *The Gals They Left Behind*. New York: Ives Washburn, 1944.

Wilder, Margaret Buell. *Since You Went Away . . . Letters to a Soldier from His Wife*. New York: Whittlesey House, 1943.

Red Cross

Goodell, Jane. *They Sent Me to Iceland*. New York: Ives Washburn, 1943.

Stevenson, Eleanor "Bumpy," and Pete Martin. *I Knew Your Soldier*. Washington, DC, and New York: Infantry Journal, Penguin Books, [1945].

USO

Carson, Julia M. H. *Home Away from Home: The Story of the USO*. New York: Harper and Brothers, 1946.

Landis, Carole. *Four Jills in a Jeep*. New York: Random House, 1944.

War Jobs

Baker, Laura Nelson. *Wanted: Women in War Industry*. New York: E. P. Dutton and Co., 1943.

Bowman, Constance. *Slacks and Calluses*. New York: Longmans, Green and Co., 1944.

Clawson, Augusta H. *Shipyard Diary of a Woman Welder.* New York: Penguin Books, 1944.

Flynn, Elizabeth Gurley. *Women in the War.* New York: Workers Library Publishers, 1942.

Giles, Nell. *Punch In, Susie! A Woman's War Factory Diary.* New York: Harper and Brothers, 1944.

Hawes, Elizabeth. *Why Women Cry: Wenches with Wrenches.* New York: Reynall and Hitchcock, 1943.

Lapin, Eva. *Mothers in Overalls.* New York: Workers Library Publishers, 1943.

Lingenfelter, Mary Rebecca. *Wartime Jobs for Girls.* New York: Harcourt, Brace and Co., 1943.

[National Association of Manufacturers]. *American Women at War.* New York: National Industrial Information Committee, 1942.

Pidgeon, Mary Elizabeth. *Women's Work and the War.* Chicago: Science Research Associates, 1943.

Steele, Evelyn. *Wartime Opportunities for Women.* New York: E. P. Dutton and Co., 1943.

Von Miklos, Josephine. *I Took a War Job.* New York: Simon and Schuster, 1943.

War Refugees

Vail, Margaret. *Yours Is the Earth.* Philadelphia: J. B. Lippincott Co., 1944.

In addition to the previously cited works, the popular press published hundreds of articles by women about their wartime experiences. Of special importance are the articles that appeared in *American Magazine, Better Homes and Gardens, Collier's, Cosmopolitan, Good Housekeeping, House Beautiful, Ladies' Home Journal, Life, Saturday Evening Post,* and *Woman's Home Companion.* Journals published by leading women's organizations also carried many articles by wartime women. See, for example, the wartime issues of the *Aframerican Woman's Journal,* the official publication of the National Council of Negro Women; *Independent Woman,* the journal of the National Federation of Business and Professional Women's Clubs; and the *Journal of the American Association of University Women.* Military magazines, such as *Our Navy,* the *Marine Corps Gazette,* the *U.S. Coast Guard Magazine,* and *Yank,* featured stories by women in the service.

The federal government published a plethora of studies by and about wartime women. Agencies that were primarily staffed by women, such as the Women's Bureau and the Children's Bureau, produced hundreds of useful reports and pamphlets. Mary Elizabeth Pidgeon, chief of the research division of the Women's Bureau, authored a number of important works, including *A Preview as to Women Workers in Transition from War to Peace* (Washington, DC: U.S. Department of Labor, Women's Bureau, Special Bulletin No. 18, 1944). Kathryn Blood, *Negro Women War Workers* (Washington, DC: U.S. Department of Labor, Women's Bureau, Bulletin No. 205, 1945), is another example of the important research conducted by this agency. The Children's Bureau issued numerous pamphlets on raising children in wartime. See, for example, *If Your Baby Must Travel in Wartime* (Washington, DC: U.S. Department of Labor, Children's Bureau, Bureau Publication No. 307, [1944]). The Extension Service of the U.S. Department of Agriculture, which included on its staff many Home Demonstration agents (the female counterpart of County agents, they brought the results of research in food, nutrition, appliances, and other areas to farm women), published many reports on the activities and needs of farm women during World War II. Useful information on the Women's Land Army appears in several Extension Service publications, including U.S. Department of Agriculture, Extension Service, *Women's Land Army, Extension Service Farm Labor Program, 1943, 1944, 1945* (Washington, DC: U.S. Department of Agriculture, [1945]). The Women's Bureau also produced significant reports on the Women's Land Army. Of particular importance are two works by Elizabeth Valentine: *Successful Practices in the Employment of Nonfarm Women on Farms in the Northeastern United States* (Washington, DC: U.S. Department of Labor, Women's Bureau, Bulletin No. 199, 1943); and *Women's Emergency Farm Service on the Pacific Coast in 1943* (Washington, DC: U.S. Department of Labor, Women's Bureau, Bulletin No. 204, 1945).